Mastering Ext JS

Second Edition

Learn how to develop advanced and efficient Internet applications with Ext JS

Loiane Groner

BIRMINGHAM - MUMBAI

Mastering Ext JS
Second Edition

First published: July 2013

Second edition: February 2015

Production reference: 1180215

Published by Packt Publishing Ltd.
Livery Place
35 Livery Street
Birmingham B3 2PB, UK.

ISBN 978-1-78439-045-7

www.packtpub.com

Credits

Author
Loiane Groner

Reviewers
Peter Holcomb
Girish Srivastava
Thorsten Suckow-Homberg

Commissioning Editor
Ashwin Nair

Acquisition Editor
Kevin Colaco

Content Development Editor
Adrian Raposo

Technical Editor
Vijin Boricha

Copy Editor
Sarang Chari

Project Coordinator
Sanchita Mandal

Proofreaders
Simran Bhogal
Maria Gould
Paul Hindle

Indexer
Hemangini Bari

Graphics
Abhinash Sahu

Production Coordinator
Aparna Bhagat

Cover Work
Aparna Bhagat

About the Author

Loiane Groner has over 9 years of experience in software development. While at university, she demonstrated great interest in IT. Loiane worked as a teaching assistant for 2.5 years and taught algorithms, data structures, and computing theory. She represented her university at the ACM International Collegiate Programming Contest—Brazilian Finals (South America Regionals) and also worked as a student delegate of the Brazilian Computing Society (SBC) for 2 years. Loiane won a merit award in her senior year for being one of the top three students with the best GPAs in the computer science department and also graduated with honors.

Loiane has worked at multinational companies, such as IBM. Her areas of expertise include Java SE and Java EE and also Sencha technologies (Ext JS and Sencha Touch). Nowadays, Loiane works as a software development manager at a financial institution, where she manages overseas solutions. She also works as an independent Sencha consultant and coach.

Loiane is also the author of *Ext JS 4 First Look*, *Mastering Ext JS*, *Sencha Architect App Development*, and *Learning JavaScript Data Structure and Algorithms*, all published by Packt Publishing.

She is passionate about Sencha and Java; she is a leader of Campinas Java Users Group (CampinasJUG) and a coordinator of Espirito Santo Java Users Group (ESJUG), both Brazilian JUGs.

Loiane also contributes to the software development community through her blogs, `http://loianegroner.com` (English) and `http://loiane.com` (Portuguese-BR), where she writes about IT careers, Ext JS, Sencha Touch, PhoneGap, Spring Framework, and general development notes, as well as publishing screencasts.

If you want to keep in touch, you can find Loiane on Facebook (`https://www.facebook.com/loianegroner`) and Twitter (`@loiane`).

Loiane's profile is already available on the Packt Publishing website, `https://www.packtpub.com/books/info/authors/loiane-groner`.

Acknowledgments

I would like to thank my parents for giving me education, guidance, and advice all these years and helping me to become a better human being and professional. A very special thanks to my husband for being patient and supportive and giving me encouragement.

I also would like to thank the readers of this book and the other books I have written, for their support and feedback. Your feedback is very valuable to me to improve as an author and as a professional. Thank you very much!

About the Reviewers

Peter Holcomb has been working with Ext JS for several years, right from version 2, and has thoroughly enjoyed being a part of the Sencha community as it has grown. A tinkerer at heart, Peter tries to spend his free time on a variety of projects to keep his skills sharp and stay on top of new frameworks and technologies. He's currently a lead frontend engineer at SailPoint Technologies, Inc., a company that he's been fortunate to be a part of for over 8 years. He lives in Austin with his wife, Courtney, and two children and thoroughly enjoys breakfast tacos.

Girish Srivastava works as a technical associate at Vision Technologies, Bengaluru (formerly, Bangalore). He is a good speaker and an industry expert on data warehousing and web-based solutions and their implementations. He used to facilitate training sessions on different technologies such as Java SE/Java EE, JavaScript, Ext JS, IBM PureData System for Analytics (IBM Netezza), Perl/CGI, SAP BO, Tableau, and so on. Girish has worked as a technical consultant in the IT industry.

I would like to thank the Almighty, my parents, B.M.P. Kiran and Mina Devi, my family, and my loveable friends, who have supported and backed me throughout my life. I would also like to thank Rawal Thakur, the managing director of my company, who gave me brilliant opportunities, ample time, and some extraordinary resources to explore new and emerging technologies. My thanks also goes to Packt Publishing for selecting me as one of the technical reviewers for this wonderful book. It is an honor to be a part of it.

Thorsten Suckow-Homberg is a software developer from Aachen, Germany. He took his first programming steps with AmigaBASIC, peeked into Turbo Pascal, Modula-3, and learned to love the strange yet wonderful abstract world of object-oriented programming (OOP) with Java. Most of the time, he works on PHP/JavaScript-driven web applications, such as `conjoon.com`, of which he is the main developer. If he's not traveling around teaching JavaScript and Ext JS, you'll most likely find him in the woods, riding his mountain bike, or sitting in front of his desk, sipping coffee and engineering code.

www.PacktPub.com

Support files, eBooks, discount offers, and more

For support files and downloads related to your book, please visit www.PacktPub.com.

Did you know that Packt offers eBook versions of every book published, with PDF and ePub files available? You can upgrade to the eBook version at www.PacktPub.com and as a print book customer, you are entitled to a discount on the eBook copy. Get in touch with us at service@packtpub.com for more details.

At www.PacktPub.com, you can also read a collection of free technical articles, sign up for a range of free newsletters and receive exclusive discounts and offers on Packt books and eBooks.

https://www2.packtpub.com/books/subscription/packtlib

Do you need instant solutions to your IT questions? PacktLib is Packt's online digital book library. Here, you can search, access, and read Packt's entire library of books.

Why subscribe?

- Fully searchable across every book published by Packt
- Copy and paste, print, and bookmark content
- On demand and accessible via a web browser

Free access for Packt account holders

If you have an account with Packt at www.PacktPub.com, you can use this to access PacktLib today and view 9 entirely free books. Simply use your login credentials for immediate access.

Table of Contents

Preface

If you are an Ext JS developer, it probably took you a while to learn the framework. We know that the Ext JS learning curve is not short. After we have learned the basics, and we need to use Ext JS in our daily jobs, a lot of questions pop up: how can one component talk to another? What are the best practices? Is it really worth using this approach and not another one? Is there any other way I can implement the same feature? This is normal.

This book was written thinking about these developers.

So this is what this book is about: how do we put everything together and create really nice applications with Ext JS? We are going to create a complete application, from the mockup of the screens all the way to putting it into production. We are going to create the application structure, a splash screen, a login screen, a multilingual capability, an activity monitor, a dynamic menu that depends on user permission, and modules to manage database information (simple and complex information). And then, we will learn how to build the application for production, how to customize the theme, and how to debug it.

We will use real-world examples and see how we can implement them using Ext JS components. And throughout the book, we've also included a lot of tips and best practices to help you boost your Ext JS knowledge and take you to the next level.

What this book covers

Chapter 1, Sencha Ext JS Overview, introduces Sencha Ext JS and its capabilities. This chapter provides references that you can read before diving into the other chapters of this book. This is done taking into consideration the possibility that this is your first contact with the framework.

Chapter 2, *Getting Started*, introduces the application that is implemented throughout the book, its features, and the mockup of each screen and module (each chapter covers a different module), and also demonstrates how to create the structure of the application using Sencha Cmd and how to create a splash screen.

Chapter 3, *The Login Page*, explains how to create a login page with Ext JS and how to handle it on the server side and also shows some extra capabilities, such as adding the Caps Lock warning message and submitting the login page when pressing the *Enter* key.

Chapter 4, *The Logout and Multilingual Capabilities*, covers how to create the logout capability and also the client-side activity monitor timeout, which means if the user does not use the mouse or press any key on the keyboard, the system ends the session automatically and logs out. This chapter also provides an example of multilingual capability and shows how to create a component so that the user can use it to change the system's language and locale settings.

Chapter 5, *Advanced Dynamic Menu*, is about how to create a dynamic menu that depends on user permission. The options of the menu are rendered depending on whether the user has permission or not; if not, the option will not be displayed.

Chapter 6, *User Management*, explains how to create a screen to list all the users that already have access to the system.

Chapter 7, *Static Data Management*, covers how to implement a module where the user is able to edit information as though they were editing information directly from a MySQL table. This chapter also explores capabilities such as live search, filter, and inline editing (using the Cell Editing and Row Editing plugins). Also, we start exploring real-world issues when we develop big applications with Ext JS, such as the reuse of components throughout the application.

Chapter 8, *Content Management*, further explores the complexity of managing information from a table of the database and all its relationships with other tables. So we cover how to manage complex information and how to handle associations within data Grids and FormPanels.

Chapter 9, *Adding Extra Capabilities*, covers how to add features, such as printing and the ability to export to PDF and Excel, that are not supported natively by Ext JS. This chapter also covers charts and how to export them to image and PDF and also how to use third-party plugins.

Chapter 10, Routing, Touch Support, and Debugging, demonstrates how to enable routing in the project; it is also about debugging Ext JS applications, including what we need to be careful about and why it is very important to know how to debug. We also quickly talk about transforming Ext JS projects into mobile apps (responsive design and touch support), a few helpful tools that can help you in your daily work as a developer, and also a few recommendations of where to find extra and open source plugins to use in Ext JS projects.

Chapter 11, Preparing for Production and Themes, covers how to customize a theme and create custom UIs. It also explores the steps required for, and the benefits of, packaging the application to production.

What you need for this book

The following is a list of the software you will need to have installed prior to executing the examples of the book. The following list covers the exact software used to implement and execute the examples of this book, but you can use any similar software that you already have installed that has the same features.

For a browser with a debugger tool, use the following:

- Firefox with Firebug: `https://www.mozilla.org/firefox/` and `http://getfirebug.com/`
- Google Chrome: `http://www.google.com/chrome`

For a web server with PHP support, use the following:

- Xampp: `http://www.apachefriends.org/en/xampp.html`

For the database, use the following:

- MySQL: `http://dev.mysql.com/downloads/mysql/`
- MySQL Workbench: `http://dev.mysql.com/downloads/tools/workbench/`
- MySQL Sakila sample database: `http://dev.mysql.com/doc/index-other.html` and `http://dev.mysql.com/doc/sakila/en/index.html`

For Sencha Cmd and the required tools, use the following:

- Sencha Cmd: `http://www.sencha.com/products/sencha-cmd/download`
- Ruby 1.8 or 1.9: `http://www.ruby-lang.org/en/downloads/`
- Sass: `http://sass-lang.com/`

- Compass: `http://compass-style.org/`
- Java JDK (version 7 or later): `http://www.oracle.com/technetwork/java/javase/downloads/index.html`
- Java environment variables: `http://docs.oracle.com/javase/tutorial/essential/environment/paths.html`
- Apache ANT: `http://ant.apache.org/bindownload.cgi`
- Apache ANT environment variable: `http://ant.apache.org/manual/install.html`
- And of course, Ext JS: `http://www.sencha.com/products/extjs/`

We will use Ext JS 5.0.1 in this book.

Who this book is for

If you are a developer who is familiar with Ext JS and want to augment your skills to create even better web applications, this is the book for you. Basic knowledge of JavaScript/HTML/CSS and any server-side language (PHP, Java, C#, Ruby, or Python) is required.

Conventions

In this book, you will find a number of text styles that distinguish between different kinds of information. Here are some examples of these styles and an explanation of their meaning.

Code words in text, database table names, folder names, filenames, file extensions, pathnames, dummy URLs, user input, and Twitter handles are shown as follows: "If we want to create a class to represent the client details, we could name it `ClientDetails`."

A block of code is set as follows:

```
Ext.define('Packt.model.film.Film', {
    extend: 'Packt.model.staticData.Base', //#1
```

When we wish to draw your attention to a particular part of a code block, the relevant lines or items are set in bold:

```
Ext.application({
    name: 'Packt',

    extend: 'Packt.Application',
```

```
        autoCreateViewport: 'Packt.view.main.Main'
});
```

Any command-line input or output is written as follows:

```
sencha generate app Packt ../masteringextjs
```

New terms and **important words** are shown in bold. Words that you see on the screen, for example, in menus or dialog boxes, appear in the text like this: "Scroll until the end of the page and select **OPEN SOURCE GPL LICENSING.**"

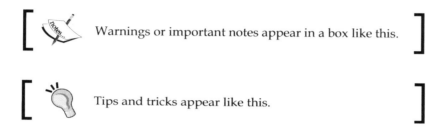

Warnings or important notes appear in a box like this.

Tips and tricks appear like this.

Reader feedback

Feedback from our readers is always welcome. Let us know what you think about this book—what you liked or disliked. Reader feedback is important for us as it helps us develop titles that you will really get the most out of.

To send us general feedback, simply e-mail feedback@packtpub.com, and mention the book's title in the subject of your message.

If there is a topic that you have expertise in and you are interested in either writing or contributing to a book, see our author guide at www.packtpub.com/authors.

Customer support

Now that you are the proud owner of a Packt book, we have a number of things to help you to get the most from your purchase.

Downloading the example code

You can download the example code files from your account at http://www.packtpub.com for all the Packt Publishing books you have purchased. If you purchased this book elsewhere, you can visit http://www.packtpub.com/support and register to have the files e-mailed directly to you.

Errata

Although we have taken every care to ensure the accuracy of our content, mistakes do happen. If you find a mistake in one of our books — maybe a mistake in the text or the code — we would be grateful if you could report this to us. By doing so, you can save other readers from frustration and help us improve subsequent versions of this book. If you find any errata, please report them by visiting http://www.packtpub.com/submit-errata, selecting your book, clicking on the **Errata Submission Form** link, and entering the details of your errata. Once your errata are verified, your submission will be accepted and the errata will be uploaded to our website or added to any list of existing errata under the Errata section of that title.

To view the previously submitted errata, go to https://www.packtpub.com/books/content/support and enter the name of the book in the search field. The required information will appear under the **Errata** section.

Piracy

Piracy of copyrighted material on the Internet is an ongoing problem across all media. At Packt, we take the protection of our copyright and licenses very seriously. If you come across any illegal copies of our works in any form on the Internet, please provide us with the location address or website name immediately so that we can pursue a remedy.

Please contact us at copyright@packtpub.com with a link to the suspected pirated material.

We appreciate your help in protecting our authors and our ability to bring you valuable content.

Questions

If you have a problem with any aspect of this book, you can contact us at questions@packtpub.com, and we will do our best to address the problem.

Sencha Ext JS Overview

Nowadays, there are many flavors for frontend frameworks and libraries in the market. There are frameworks you can use if you only want to manipulate the **Document Object Model (DOM)**, frameworks used only for styling, frameworks for user-friendly components, frameworks used to design your project, and so on. Also there is Ext JS, a framework used to create **Rich Internet Applications (RIA)**, but it has many other features than just pretty components.

In this book, we are going to learn how to develop an application from the beginning to the end with Ext JS 5, also covering some pieces of the backend required to make our application work. We will learn how to use Ext JS with hands-on examples covering some components, how they work, and how to use them in each chapter.

But first, you are going to learn what Ext JS is capable of if this is the first time you have come into contact with the framework.

Understanding Sencha Ext JS

Can we use Ext JS to manipulate DOM? Can we use it if we want pretty and user-friendly components (forms, grids, trees, and so on)? Can we use it if we need some nice charts? Can we use the **Model View Controller (MVC)** architecture to organize the application with Ext JS? What if we want to use a two-way data-binding between the Model and the View? Can we do that using Ext JS? And what if we do not like the colors of Ext JS components' look and feel? Can we easily change it too? And now a difficult one; can we make a build to obfuscate and optimize the CSS and JavaScript files of our application using Ext JS? Is Ext JS responsive? Can we use it in mobile devices?

Amazingly, the answer is positive to all the preceding questions! As we can see, Ext JS is a complete frontend framework. The mastermind company behind Ext JS is Sencha Inc. (http://sencha.com).

Sencha Ext JS also has a cousin called **Sencha Touch**. It also has the amazing features we just mentioned, but focuses on the mobile cross-platform world. We will talk very briefly about Ext JS and Sencha Touch in later chapters of this book.

Architecture of Ext JS applications

Before we get started, let's make sure we understand a few of the core concepts. Ext JS is a frontend framework based on JavaScript and HTML5. This means Ext JS does not connect to the database directly. For storage, we can use one of the types of HTML5 storage, such as Web SQL or local storage, but these types of storage allow us to store only 5 MB of data, which is very little for a common application.

Usually, we want to use MySQL, Oracle, MS Server or any other database. To be able to store information in a database, we need to use a server-side language, such as PHP, Java, C#, Ruby, Python, Node.js, and so on. Ext JS will communicate with the server-side language (or web services), and the server will connect to the database or any other storage (documents repository, for example).

The following diagram exemplifies the architecture of an application developed with Ext JS:

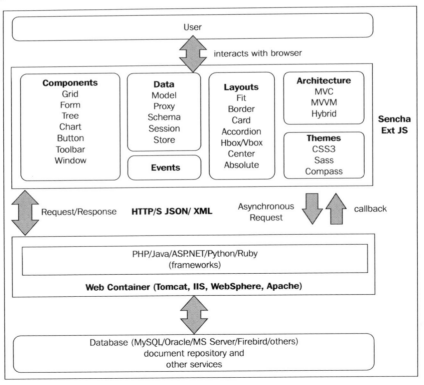

Ext JS overview

We have already mentioned some Ext JS capabilities. Let's take a brief look at each one of them. But first, if you want to take a look at the official Sencha Ext JS webpage, visit `http://www.sencha.com/products/extjs/`.

Basic tutorial

Before diving into this book, it is recommended that you read the contents of the following links. They contain the basic information that any developer needs to learn before starting with Ext JS:

- Basic tutorial and Ext JS overview: `http://www.sencha.com/products/extjs/up-and-running`
- Ext JS guides: `http://docs.sencha.com/extjs/5.0/`
- Ext JS documents: `http://docs.sencha.com/extjs/5.0/apidocs/`
- Ext JS examples: `http://dev.sencha.com/ext/5.0.1/examples/index.html`
- Forum (become part of the community): `http://www.sencha.com/forum/`

Class system

Ext JS uses an **object-oriented** (**OO**) approach. We declare classes with attributes known in Ext JS as configurations and methods (functions in JavaScript).

Ext JS also follows a naming convention. If you are familiar with OO programming, you are probably familiar with the naming conventions of Ext JS as well. For example, class names are alphanumeric, starting with an uppercase character, and and then the rest of the letters are in CamelCase. For example, if we want to create a class to represent the client details, we could name it `ClientDetails`. Method and attribute names start with a lowercase character and then the rest of the letters are in CamelCase. For example, `retrieveClientDetails()` is a good name for a method and `clientName` is a good name for an attribute.

Ext JS is organized in packages as well. Packages are a way of organizing the code that has the same purpose. For example, in Ext JS, there is a package called `data` that handles everything related to data in the framework. There is a packaged named `grid` that contains all the code related to GridPanels.

For more information about the class system, please read `http://docs.sencha.com/extjs/5.0/core_concepts/classes.html`.

Components

The main reason some people consider using Ext JS is probably because of its rich and user-friendly components. Ext JS contains some of the most used components in web applications, such as forms, grids, and trees. We can also use charts that are touch-friendly (meaning they work on touchscreens as well) and the drawing package that uses all the advantages of **Scalable Vector Graphics** (**SVG**) and HTML5.

You can checkout the official Sencha Ext JS examples page at `http://dev.sencha.com/extjs/5.0.0/examples/index.html` to have an idea of what we can do with the examples.

The component hierarchy

You will notice that throughout this book, we will mention terms such as component, container, and widget. The following diagram exemplifies the component hierarchy in Ext JS:

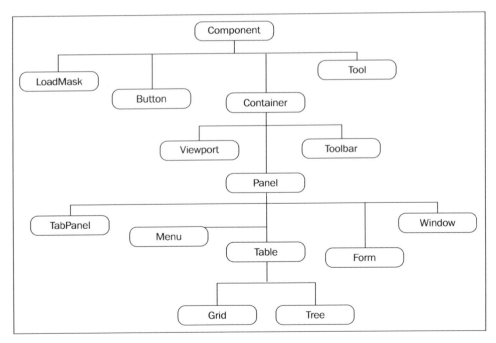

The **Component** class is the parent class for all Ext JS widgets. Below the **Component** class, we have the **Container** class. The **Container** class might contain other components. For example, let's take a look at the following GridPanel:

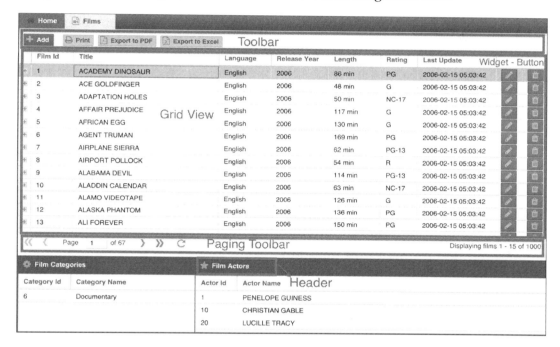

The `Grid Panel` class extends from the `Panel` class, a very popular component in Ext JS. The `Panel` class supports headers, docked items (toolbars), and it contains a body space. Subclasses of the `Panel` class, such as `DataView`, `Tree`, `Grid`, and `Form`, are panels, but instead of the body, they have a specialized `View` class that is responsible for rendering the specific information. For example, the `View` class of a `Grid` panel is specialized in rendering the Grid Column; the `View` class of a `Tree` Panel is specialized in rendering hierarchical information, and the `View` class of a `Form` panel (called BasicForm) is specialized in rendering form fields.

GridPanel

The grid component is one of the most used components in web applications. It is used to display tabular data.

To create a grid, the developer needs to declare at least two configurations: `columns` and `Store`. The `Store` class organizes a collection of data in Ext JS, and it is responsible for feeding the grid with the information to be displayed. We will explore it when we discuss the data package.

The grid component can be used as a plain and simple data grid, with only the information records being displayed. Or, if we have a large amount of data, we can use its paging capabilities, or we can also use a Big Data Grid if we really have a large amount of data. There are also other features such as grouped header grid (also known as Pivot Grid); we can also have a grid with locked columns or even with widgets, such as chats, as demonstrated by the previous screenshot. Among other features, we can also sort and filter the information inside the grid and use some of its plugins to accomplish tasks such as expanding the rows to display more information without popups, using checkboxes to select rows and automatic numbered rows as well. And there is more: the grid component also supports editing by opening a small pop-up row so that you can edit the information directly in the grid. The grid also supports cell editing, which is similar to what we can do in MS Excel — edit the information by double-clicking on a cell.

 For more information, please take a look at `http://docs.sencha.com/extjs/5.0/apidocs/#!/api/Ext.grid.Panel` and `http://docs.sencha.com/extjs/5.0/components/grids/grids.html`.

TreePanel

Trees display hierarchical data, such as a file directory. A tree's data comes from a TreeStore or is predefined in the `root` configuration. The tree also supports sorting and filtering, select a row using checkboxes, and we can also mix a tree with a grid and use the TreeGrid component.

It also supports plugins such as drag and drop between trees.

 For more information, please take a look at `http://docs.sencha.com/extjs/5.0/apidocs/#!/api/Ext.tree.Panel` and `http://docs.sencha.com/extjs/5.0/components/trees.html`.

Forms

Next, we have the form component. We can implement powerful forms using text, area, and number fields. We can also use the date/month picker, checkboxes, radio buttons, comboboxes, and even file upload. All fields have the basic native validation support (with error messages to the user), such as mandatory fields and minimum and maximum value or length, but we can easily customize and create custom validation (IP address for example).

For more information, please take a look at http://docs.sencha.
com/extjs/5.0/apidocs/#!/api/Ext.form.Panel and http://
docs.sencha.com/extjs/5.0/components/forms.html.

Other components

We also have the charts. We can build column, bar, line, area, scatter, pie, radial, gauge, and even financial charts. We can have basic, stacked, multi-axis, and 3D charts as well. The charts are also fed by a Store.

And of course, there are basic components that will help our application look even better, such as menus, tabs, panels, windows, alerts, toolbars, and so on. The components have **Web Accessibility Initiative – Accessible Rich Internet Applications (WAI-ARIA)** support and also support right-to-left languages.

Seems nice, right? We will cover most of the components and its capabilities throughout the examples of this book.

Layouts

Ext JS supports different possibilities. It also has a great layout manager (only when we create an Ext JS application using its base component, the Viewport. For components that are used in a standalone form (rendered in a <div> tag, the layout manager does not work when you decrease the size of the browser window).

Some of the layouts supported are Absolute layout (where we need to use the absolute x and y positions of the component in the screen or within the component); Accordion layout, Border layout, Card layout, Center layout, Column layout, Fit layout, Hbox and VBox layouts, and Table layouts.

The layouts that are most used in applications are Border, Card, Fit, and HBox and VBox. We will cover different layouts through the examples of this book as well.

 For more information, please take a look at http://dev.sencha.com/
ext/5.0.1/examples/kitchensink/#layouts and the layout.
container package at http://docs.sencha.com/extjs/5.0/
apidocs/#!/api/Ext.layout.container.Absolute.

Data package

The data package is one of the most important packages from the Ext JS SDK. Ext JS components such as grid, Tree, and even the Form are data-driven.

Server-side languages usually support data well. In Java, PHP, **C#**, and other languages, we can create entities known as **Plain Old Java Object (POJOs)**, **Persistent Domain Objects (PDOs)**, and **Value Objects (VOs)**, and other names that we usually give to these entities. Ext JS supports data, so we represent entities in the frontend as well.

There are basically three major pieces:

- **Model**: This represents the entity. It can represent a class we have on the server side or a table from the database. Model supports fields, validations, associations (**OneToOne**, **OneToMany**, **ManyToMany**).
- **Store**: This represents a collection of models. It also supports groups, filtering, and sorting.
- **Proxy**: This represents the way we are going to connect to the server (or a local storage). It can be Ajax, REST, JSONP, Memory, or HTML5 LocalStorage. Inside the proxy, we can define Reader and Writer. The Reader attribute is responsible for decoding the data we receive from the server (we can define it if it is JSON or XML, and we can also define its format). The Writer attribute is responsible for encoding the data to be sent to the server; it can be JSON or XML, and we can also define its format. The Proxy can be placed inside a Model or a Store.

 For more information please read http://docs.sencha.com/extjs/5.0/core_concepts/data_package.html.

The MVC and MVVM architectures

While working with Ext JS, we can choose between two architectures for our frontend code: **Model View Controller (MVC)** and **Model View ViewModel (MVVM)**. There is also a third option, which is a **hybrid** between **MVC** and **MVVM**.

Throughout this book, we are going to learn more about MVC, MVVM, and also the hybrid approach.

 For more information please read http://docs.sencha.com/extjs/5.0/application_architecture/application_architecture.html.

Look and feel of Ext JS applications

We can also customize the theme of Ext JS applications. The theming is based on Sass and Compass. We will dive into themes in the last chapter of this book.

 For more information please read `http://docs.sencha.com/extjs/5.0/core_concepts/theming.html`.

Installing Ext JS

Let's take a look at how to install Ext JS locally. This step is required because we will need to have the Ext JS SDK in our computer prior to creating the application with **Sencha Cmd**.

Prerequisites for Ext JS and Sencha Cmd

Before downloading Ext JS and Sencha Cmd, we need to set up our computer to be ready. The following is a list of software needed so that we can create an Ext JS application:

1. **Ruby 1.8 or 1.9**: The current version of Ruby is 2.x at the time of writing this. To be able to create an Ext JS application, we need to have Ruby 1.8 or 1.9 installed. Ruby is required because the theming engine used by Ext JS is based on Sass and Compass, which are Ruby gems. To download and install Ruby, please follow the instructions at `https://www.ruby-lang.org/en/installation/`.

2. **Sass and Compass**: These are not CSS frameworks. Sass is a new way of writing CSS. It is possible to use variables and define functions and mixins. It is an alternative to **Less** (maybe you have worked with Less or heard about it—Sass is very similar). After downloading and installing Ruby, please install Sass as well. The instructions can be found at `http://sass-lang.com/install` (follow the command-line instructions). Compass is a Sass framework and is also required. Please install it as well from `http://compass-style.org/install/`. Sass and Compass are the heart of the Ext JS theming engine. All custom CSS we are going to create for our application will be compiled by Sass/Compass as well.

3. **Java JDK**: If you are a Java developer, you probably have the Java JDK installed already. If not, please download and execute the installer at `http://www.oracle.com/technetwork/articles/javase/index-jsp-138363.html`. After installing the Java JDK, we also need to configure the `JAVA_HOME` environment variable. Instructions can be found at `http://goo.gl/JFtKHF`. The Java JDK is required because of ANT, our next step.

4. **Apache ANT**: The Sencha Cmd engine to create the application and build it is based on ANT, a Java library. We need to download ANT from `http://ant.apache.org/bindownload.cgi`, unzip it to a directory of our choice, and set the `ANT_HOME` environment variable (`http://ant.apache.org/manual/install.html`).

We can check whether we have the correct environment by executing the following commands in a terminal application:

```
● ○ ○                    ⬆ loiane — bash — 81×15
Loiane:~ loiane$ ruby -v
ruby 2.0.0p481 (2014-05-08 revision 45883) [universal.x86_64-darwin13]
Loiane:~ loiane$ sass -v
Sass 3.2.13 (Media Mark)
Loiane:~ loiane$ compass -v
Compass 0.12.2 (Alnilam)
Copyright (c) 2008-2014 Chris Eppstein
Released under the MIT License.
Compass is charityware.
Please make a tax deductable donation for a worthy cause: http://umdf.org/compass
Loiane:~ loiane$ javac -version
javac 1.7.0_45
Loiane:~ loiane$ ant -version
Apache Ant(TM) version 1.9.3 compiled on December 23 2013
Loiane:~ loiane$ ▊
```

Note that the Ruby version installed is 2.x, but as long as you have a 1.8 or 1.9 compatible version in your classpath, you should be OK.

The last step is a web server. The simplest one that we can use to execute the examples of this book is Apache Xampp. Download and follow the installation instructions at `https://www.apachefriends.org`.

 All the software required to set up the environment mentioned in this book is available for Linux, Windows, and Mac OS.

Downloading Ext JS and Sencha Cmd

Now that we have our environment configured, we can download Ext JS. Ext JS has some different license flavors: commercial and open source. For this book, we are going to use the open source one. You can download the open source version at http://www.sencha.com/products/extjs/details. Scroll until the end of the page and select **OPEN SOURCE GPL LICENSING**, as demonstrated in the following screenshot:

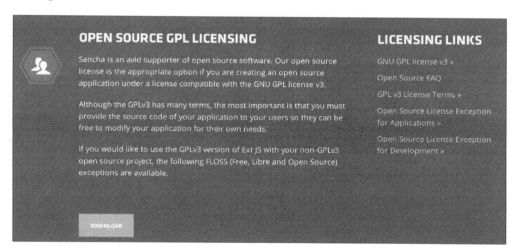

 The latest version of Ext JS at the time of writing this book is 5.1.

We also need to download and install Sencha Cmd from http://www.sencha.com/products/sencha-cmd/download. Sencha Cmd is responsible for creating the application and making, building, and compiling Sass and Compass to generate the application's CSS. After the installation of Sencha Cmd, the sencha command will be available from the terminal application as well.

After downloading the Ext JS SDK, unzip it inside the Apache Xampp `htdocs` folder. Once we start the Apache server, we will be able to execute the Ext JS examples from our local environment:

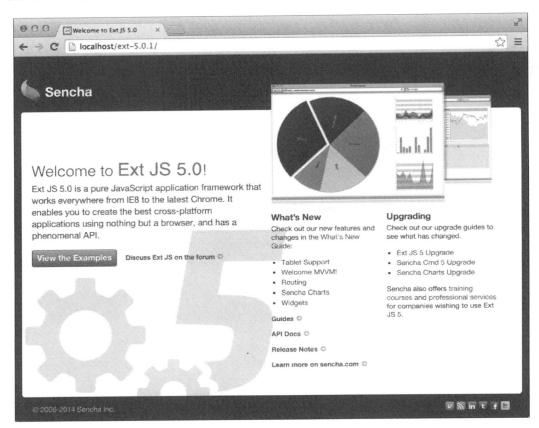

Offline documentation

While developing with Ext JS, we will consult the documentation a lot. Whenever we mention the name of an Ext JS component in this book, it is recommended that you go to the documentation and take a look at it. The Ext JS documentation is available at `http://docs.sencha.com/extjs/5.0/`. It contains guides (it is also highly recommended that you spend some time reading the guides before diving into this book since the guides provide basic knowledge about the framework), and links to blog posts and also to the documentation itself. As we will consult it a lot, we recommend installing the documentation locally as well. To do so, go to `http://docs.sencha.com/`, open the **Sencha Guides** menu, and select the **offline docs** link as demonstrated in the following screenshot:

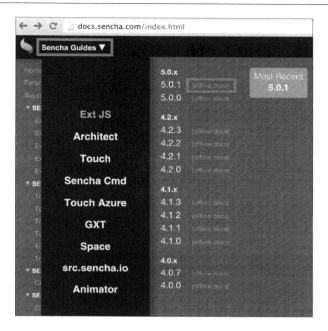

Unzip the docs inside the Xampp `htdocs` folder as well and access your `localhost`, as shown in the following screenshot:

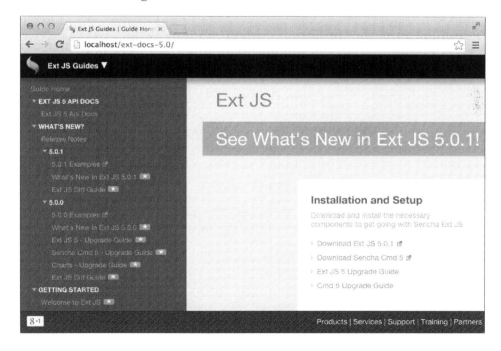

A video tutorial with step-by-step instructions to set up the environment for Ext JS is available at `http://youtu.be/B43bEnFBRRc`.

IDE

You can use any IDE or editor of your preference to develop with Ext JS. There are a few editors that are very popular: Sublime Text, Atom, Eclipse (if you are a Java developer), Netbeans, and Visual Studio (if you are a C# developer), Notepad++, and WebStorm, among others.

If you are looking for the autocompleting feature, you can use the Sencha Eclipse Plugin that is part of Sencha Complete (paid) at `http://www.sencha.com/products/complete/`) or you can use WebStorm (also paid) at `https://www.jetbrains.com/webstorm/`).

There is also Sencha Architect (which also has the autocompleting feature). It is a **what you see is what you get (WYSIWYG)** editor and is a great Sencha tool that can be used with the IDE of your preference (to develop the server-side code of the application).

Feel free to use the editor or IDE you are most comfortable with to develop the source code of this book!

Summary

In this chapter, we quickly overviewed Ext JS and provided some references that are useful to read to gather the basic knowledge required to understand the terms and components we will be using in this book.

In the next chapter, we will present the application we are going to work with throughout this book, and we are also going to create it using Sencha Cmd.

2
Getting Started

In this book, we are going to dive into the Sencha Ext JS 5 world and explore real-world examples. We will also build a complete application from scratch, from the wireframe phase until the deployment in production.

Throughout this book, we are going to develop an application to manage a *DVD rental store*. In this chapter, we will introduce the application and describe its capabilities. You will also learn how to organize the files of the application, which is going to be built throughout the chapters of this book. This chapter will also present the mockup (wireframe) of the application and how to start organizing the screens (which is a very important step and some developers forget to do it). In this chapter, we will cover:

- Preparing the development environment by installing the required software
- Presenting the application and its capabilities
- Creating mockups/wireframes of each screen
- Creating the structure of the app using Sencha Cmd
- Creating the loading page (splash screen)

Preparing the development environment

The application that we are going to develop has a very simple architecture. We are going to use Ext JS 5 on the frontend, which is going to communicate with a server-side module using Ajax/JSON, which will then communicate with a database.

The following diagram encapsulates the preceding paragraph:

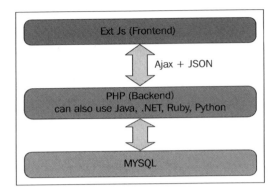

The server-side module will be developed using PHP. You need not worry if you don't know PHP. We are going to use very basic code (no frameworks), and we are going to focus on the programming logic that needs to be implemented on the server side. This way, you can apply the same logic using any other programming language, such as Java, ASP.NET, Ruby, Python, or any other (that supports the exchange of data in JSON or XML format as this is the communication format used by Ext JS). For the database, we will use MySQL. We will also use the Sakila sample schema (http://dev.mysql.com/doc/sakila/en/), a free MySQL sample database, which is perfect to demonstrate how to work with **Create, Read, Update, and Delete/Destroy (CRUD)** operations on a database table and also use more complex operations, such as views and stored procedures (we will learn how to handle all this information with Ext JS).

If you are a Java developer, you can find some sample code on how to integrate Java with Ext JS at http://goo.gl/rv76E2 and http://goo.gl/nNIRuQ.

Also, we will need to have Sencha Cmd installed (we have already installed Sencha Cmd during *Chapter 1, Sencha Ext JS Overview*). However, we still need to execute some extra steps to have it configured. Once configured, we will be able to create the application structure, customize the theme, and also make the production build. Sencha Cmd requires having Ruby compatible with versions 1.8 or 1.9 (version 2.x will not work). We also need to have Apache Ant installed (and because Apache Ant is built with Java, we also need to have Java installed and configured in our computer).

After we have finished implementing the application, we will customize the theme, and because of this, we will need to install Ruby (1.8 or 1.9) and the Sass and Compass gems.

To deploy the application, we need a web server. If you do not have any web server installed on your computer yet, do not worry. In this book, we will use Xampp as the default web server.

We will also need a browser to run our application in. The recommended ones are Firefox (with Firebug) or Google Chrome.

If you do not have any of the software or technologies mentioned previously installed on your computer, don't worry. To summarize all the tools and software we need to have installed prior to starting the fun, here is a list with the links where you can download them and find installation instructions (all items are available for Windows, Linux, and Mac OS):

- A browser with a debugger tool:
    - Firefox with Firebug: `https://www.mozilla.org/firefox/` and `http://getfirebug.com/`
    - Google Chrome: `www.google.com/chrome`

- Web server:
    - Xampp: `http://www.apachefriends.org/en/xampp.html`

- Database:
    - MySQL: `http://dev.mysql.com/downloads/mysql/`
    - MySQL Workbench: `http://dev.mysql.com/downloads/tools/workbench/`
    - MySQL Sakila sample database: `http://dev.mysql.com/doc/index-other.html` and `http://dev.mysql.com/doc/sakila/en/index.html`

- Sencha Command required tools:
    - Ruby: `http://www.ruby-lang.org/en/downloads/`
    - Sass: `http://sass-lang.com/`
    - Compass: `http://compass-style.org/`
    - Java JDK (Java 7 or later): `http://www.oracle.com/technetwork/java/javase/downloads/index.html`
    - Java environment variables: `http://docs.oracle.com/javase/tutorial/essential/environment/paths.html`
    - Apache Ant: `http://ant.apache.org/bindownload.cgi`

Of course, we also need Ext JS SDK and Sencha Cmd, which we downloaded and installed in *Chapter 1, Sencha Ext JS Overview*.

 To help you configure the required development environment in order to be able to create the application from this book, here is a video that demonstrates it step by step (step by step done for Windows environment — the Linux and Mac OS setup is very similar): http://youtu.be/B43bEnFBRRc.

Presenting the application and its capabilities

The application we are going to develop throughout this book is very common to other web systems you are probably used to implementing. We will implement a DVD Rental Store management application (that is why the use of the Sakila sample database). Some of the features of the application are the security management (able to manage users and their permissions within the application), which manage actors, films, inventory, and rental information.

Ext JS will help you to achieve your goal. It provides beautiful components, a complete architecture, the possibility to reuse components (and decreases our work), and a very complete data package (that makes it easier to make connections to the server side and send and retrieve information).

We will divide the application into modules, and each module will be responsible for some features of the application. In each chapter of this book, we will implement one of the modules.

The application is composed of:

- A splash screen (so the user does not need to see a blank screen while the application is still launching)
- A main screen
- A login screen
- User administration screen
- MySQL tables management (for categories, and combobox values — static data)
- Content management control

For each of the modules and screens mentioned in the preceding list, we will create mockups, so we can plan how the application will work. Here, you will learn more about each one of them.

The splash screen

Our application will have a splash screen, so the user does not need to see a blank page while the application is still loading the required files and classes prior to its initialization. Here's a screenshot that illustrates a splash screen aptly:

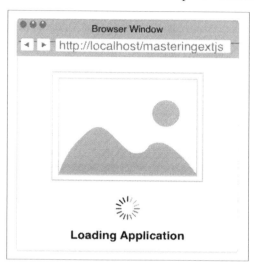

We will cover the implementation of this screen later in this chapter.

The login screen

After the application is fully loaded, the first screen the user will see is the login screen. The user will be able to enter the **User Name** and **Password**. There is also a multilingual combobox, where the user can choose the language of the system (multilingual capability). Then, we have the **Cancel** and **Submit** buttons, as shown in the following screenshot:

The **Cancel** button resets the **Login** form and the **Submit** button will trigger an event that will create an Ajax request and send the user credentials to the server for authentication. If the user is successfully authenticated, then we display the main screen; otherwise, we display an error message.

We will cover the implementation of the login screen in *Chapter 3, The Login Page*.

The main screen

The general idea of the application is to have a main screen that will be organized using border layout. Border Layout is divided into five regions: north, south, east, west, and center, of which all but the east region are demonstrated in the following diagram:

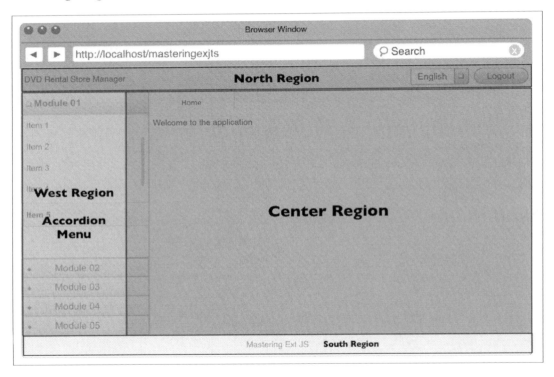

In the **Center Region**, we will have a tab panel, and each tab represents a screen of the application (each screen will have its own layout)—only the first tab can not be closed (**Home**) tab. In the **North Region** we will have a header with the name of the application (**DVD Rental Store Manager**), the multilingual combobox (if the user wants to change the current language of the application) and a **Logout** button. In the **South Region**, we will have the footer with a copyright message (or it can be the name of the company or developer that implemented the project). And in the **West Region**, we will have a dynamic menu (we will implement user control management). The menu will be dynamic and will be rendered based on the permissions that the user has in the application.

The main screen will look somewhat like the following mockup:

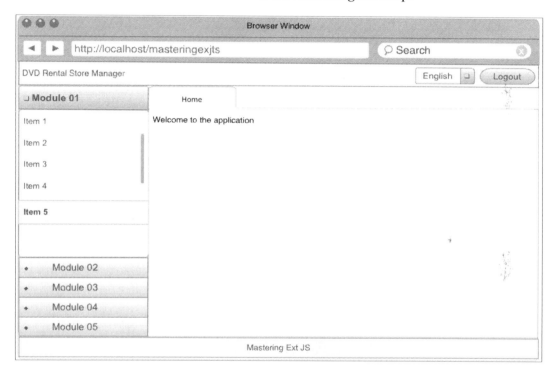

We will cover the implementation of the main screen and the multilingual and logout capabilities in *Chapter 4, The Logout and Multilingual Capabilities*. And in *Chapter 5, Advanced Dynamic Menu*, we will cover how to generate a dynamic menu.

User administration

In the user control management, the user will have access to create new users and new groups and assign new roles to users. The user will be able to control the system permissions (which user can see which modules in the system). This is how the **Create/Edit User** page looks:

We will cover the implementation of user administration in *Chapter 6, User Management*.

MySQL table management

Every system has information that is considered static data, such as film categories, film language, combobox options, and so on. For these tables, we need to provide all CRUD options and also filter options. The screens from this module will be very similar to the **Edit Table Data** option from **MySQL Workbench.**, as shown in the following screenshot:

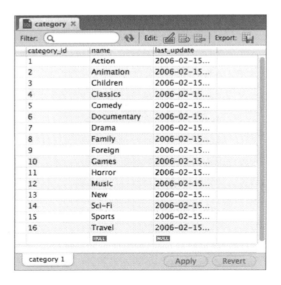

The user will be able to edit the data in the rows of the grid, similar to what can be done in MS Excel. Once the user is done making the changes, they can click on the **Save Changes** button to save all modified data to the server and database. The following is how the **Browser Window** view looks:

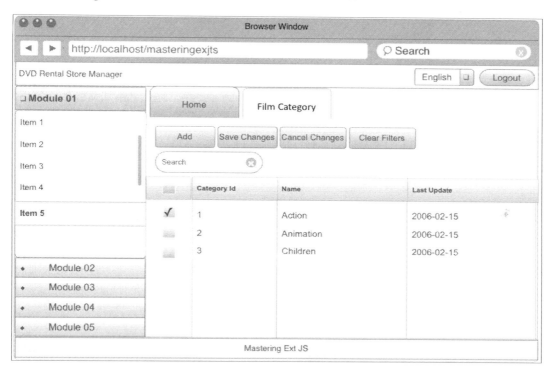

We will cover the implementation of this module in *Chapter 7, Static Data Management*.

Content management control

In this module, the user will be able to see and edit the core information from the system. As most of the database tables we will be handling in this module have a relationship with other tables, the editing of the information will be more complex, involving the master-detail relationship. Usually, we will present the information to the user in a data grid (a list or a table), and the addition of the information will be made in such a form that it will be displayed inside a pop-up window.

It is also very important to remember that most of the screens from a module will have similar capabilities, and since we are going to build an application with a lot of screens, it is important to design the system to be able to reuse as much code as possible, making the system easy to maintain and easy to add new features and capabilities to. The following screen depicts the capabilities we have discussed in this section:

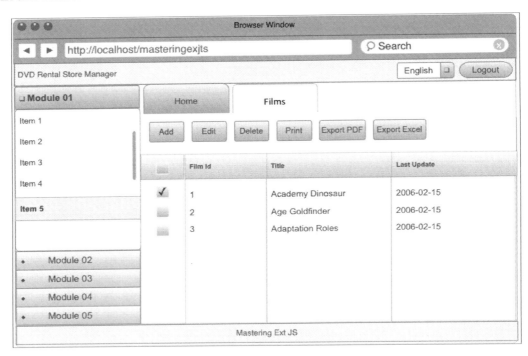

When clicking on **Add** or **Edit**, a new pop-up window will open to edit the information, as follows:

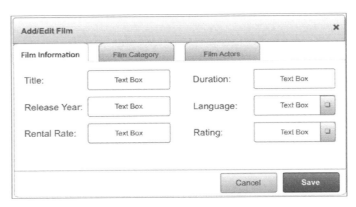

We will cover the implementation of this module in *Chapter 8, Content Management*, and *Chapter 9, Adding Extra Capabilities*.

Charts

In the charts module, we will create a chart in Ext JS. For the same chart information, the user will be able to generate different types of charts. The user will also be able to export the chart to an image, SVG, or PDF, as follows:

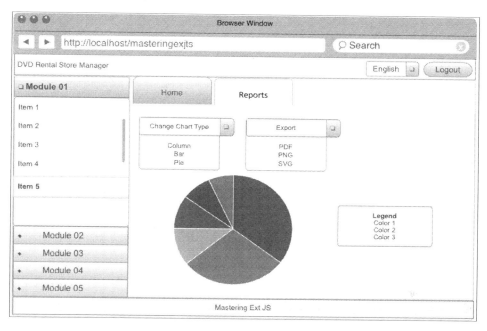

We will cover the implementation of this module in *Chapter 9, Adding Extra Capabilities*.

Creating the application with Sencha Cmd

Let's get started and get our hands on the code. The first thing we are going to do is create the application using the MVC structure. Sencha Command (referred to as Sencha Cmd from now on) provides the capability of creating the application structure automatically for us. Utilizing Sencha Cmd is helpful not only because it creates the structure according to the MVC architecture for our application, but also because it provides all the files we need later on when going live with the software and to customize its theme—we'll learn more about this in a later chapter.

A quick word about MVC

MVC stands for **Model-View-Controller**. It is a software architecture pattern that separates the representation of the information from the user's interaction with it. The Model represents the application data, the View represents the output of the representation of the data (form, grid, chart), and the Controller mediates the input, converting it into commands for the Model or View.

Ext JS supports MVC, which is a Model-View-Controller pattern (as one of the architecture options, it also provides a **Model-View-View-Model** (**MVVM**), which we will discuss later). The Model is a representation of the data we want to manipulate in our application, a representation of a table from the database. The View is all the components and screens we create to manage the information of a Model. As Ext JS is event-driven, all the View instances fire events when the user interacts with them, the Controller can be configured to listen to events raised from the View, and the developer can implement custom handlers to respond to these events. The Controller can also redirect the command to the Model (or Store) or the View. And the Store in Ext JS is very similar to the **Data Access Object** (**DAO**) pattern used on server-side technologies (with more capabilities such as sorting and filtering, introduced in *Chapter 1, Sencha Ext JS Overview*).

For a quick example, let's say we have **WidgetA**, which is a GridPanel that displays all the records from a table. This table is represented by **ModelA**. **StoreA** is responsible for retrieving the information (collection of **ModelA** from the server). When the user clicks on a record from **WidgetA**, a window will be opened (called **WidgetB**) displaying information from a table (represented by **ModelB**). And of course, **StoreB** will be responsible for retrieving the collection of **ModelB** from server. In this case, we will have **ControllerA** to capture the `itemclick` event from **WidgetA**, do all the required logic to display **WidgetB**, and load all the **ModelB** information. If we try to put this into a quick reference diagram, it would be something like this:

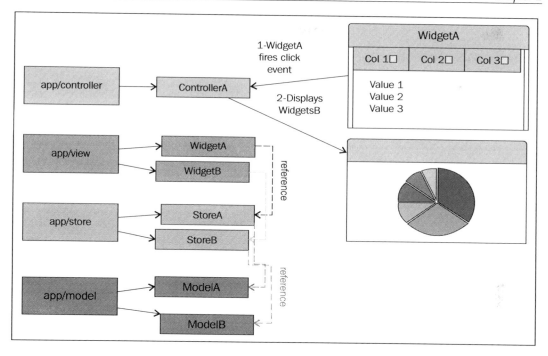

Creating the application

We are going to create the application inside the `htdocs` folder of our Xampp directory. Our application will be named `masteringextjs`.

Before we start, let's take a look how the `htdocs` folder looks:

We still have the original Xampp files in there, and the Ext JS 5 SDK folder, along with the Ext JS 5 documentation folder.

The next step is to use Sencha Cmd to create the application for us. To do so, we need to open the terminal application that comes with the operating system we're using. For Linux and Mac OS users, this would be the terminal application. For Windows users, it's the Command Prompt application.

Here are the steps that we are going to execute:

1. First, we need to change the current directory to the Ext JS directory (`htdocs/ext-5.0.0` in this case).

2. Then, we will use the following command:

   ```
   sencha generate app Packt ../masteringextjs
   ```

The `sencha generate app` command will create the `masteringextjs` directory inside the `htdocs` folder with the necessary file structure required by the MVC architecture as used by ExtJS. `Packt` is the name of the namespace of our application, which means that every class we create is going to start with `Packt`, for example, `Packt.model.Actor`, `Pack.view.Login`, and so on. And the last argument passed to the command is the directory where the application will be created. In this case, it is inside a folder named `masteringextjs`, which is located inside the `htdocs` folder.

 Namespaces are used for scoping variables and classes so that they are not global, defining deeply their nested structures. Sencha has a good article about namespaces at `http://goo.gl/2iLxcn`.

After the command finishes its execution, we will have something like what is shown in the following screenshot:

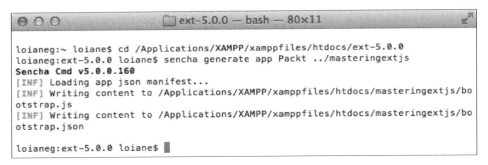

 The source code presented in this book was written with Ext JS 5.0 (so you will see the screenshots with version 5.0) and upgraded to 5.1 once it was released. So once you download its source code, it will be compatible with version 5.1. Upgrading the source code from 5.0 to 5.1 does not have any impact.

But why do we need to create a project structure like this one? The following is the structure used by Ext JS applications:

For more information about the Sencha generate app command, please consult http://docs.sencha.com/cmd/5.x/extjs/cmd_app.html.

Let's see what each folder does.

First we have the app folder. This is where we will create all the code for our application. Inside the app folder, we can find the following folders as well: controller, model, store, and view. We can also find the Application.js file. Let's have a detailed look at them. In the model folder, we will create all files that represent a Model, which is an Ext JS class that represents a set of fields, which means that an object that our application manages (actor, country, film, and so on). It is similar to a class on the server side with only the attributes of the class plus the getter and setter methods used to represent a table from the database.

On the `store` folder, we will create all the `Store` classes, which are caches of collections of Model instances. The `store` folder also has capabilities similar to DAO—classes used on server-side languages to perform CRUD operations on the database. As Ext JS does not communicate directly with databases, the `Store` classes are used to communicate with the server side or a local storage—used with a Proxy. Proxies are used by Store or Model instances to handle the loading and saving of Model data, and it is the place where we are going to configure how we want to communicate with the server (using Ajax and using JSON or XML, formatting the data so that the client and the backend understand each other).

On the `view` folder, we will create all `view` classes, also known as the **User Interface Components (UI Components)**, such as grids, trees, menus, forms, windows, and so on.

And finally, in the `controller` folder, we can create classes that will handle the events fired by the components (events fired because of the life cycle of the component or because of some *interaction* of the user with a component). We always need to remember that Ext JS is *event-driven*, and on the `Controller` classes, we will control these events and update any Model, View, or Store (if required). Some examples of events fired would be a click or mouseover of a button, an `itemclick` event of a row of a grid, and so on.

 We can also have `ViewController` classes inside the `view` folder. This is applied when we use the MVVM pattern, which we will discuss more in detail in the next chapter.

The MVC `app` folder structure has been created. Now, we will copy the Ext JS SDK (`extjs` folder) into the `masteringExtjs` folder, and we will also create a file named `app.js`. We will edit this file later in this chapter.

We also have the `Application.js` file. This is the entry point of our application. We'll come back to this later on.

The `masteringextjs` directory contains a few more files:

- `app.js`: This file inherits the code from the `Application.js` file. It is the point of entry of the application. This is the file that is called by Ext JS to initialize the application. We should avoid changing this file `app.json`: this is a configuration file for the application. In this file, we can add extra CSS and JS files, which should be loaded with the application, such as charts and locale-specific configurations. We will make some changes in this file throughout the book.

- `bootstrap.css`, `bootstrap.json`, and `bootstrap.js`: Created by Sencha Cmd, these files *should not be edited*. The CSS file contains the import of the theme used by the application (which is the so-called **Neptune theme** by default). After we make a build, the content of these files is updated with CSS definitions, and the JavaScript files will contain dependencies that need to be loaded prior to execution, custom `xtypes`, and other class system features.

- `build.xml`: Sencha Cmd uses Apache Ant (`http://ant.apache.org/`), which is a Java tool used to build Java projects. Ant uses a configuration file named `build.xml`, which contains all the required configurations and commands to build a project. Sencha Cmd uses Ant as the engine to build an Ext JS application on the background (while we simply need to use a command). This is the reason why we need to have the Java SDK installed to use some of the Sencha Cmd features.

- `index.html`: This is the index file of our project. This is the file that will be rendered by the browser when we execute our application. Inside this file, we will find the import of the `bootstrap.js` file. We should avoid making changes in this file as well because when we build the application, Sencha Cmd will generate a new `index.html` file in the `build` folder, discarding all the changes we might have made to the `index.html` file. If we need to include a JS or CSS file, we should define this within the `app.json` file.

- `ext`: Inside this folder, we can find all the Ext JS framework files (`ext-all`, `ext-all-debug`, and `ext-dev`), its source code, and also the `packages` folder, containing the locale definitions for our application and theme-related packages, among others.

- `overrides`: When we create the application, this folder is empty. We can add any class overrides and customizations we will need for our project.

- `packages`: Inside this folder, we can create our own packages. A package can be a new theme, for example. Its concept is similar to *gems* in Ruby or custom APIs in Java and .NET (for example, to use Apache Ant in a Java project, we need to include the Apache Ant `jar` file).

- `resources`: Inside this folder, we will place all the images of our application. We can also place other CSS files and font files.

- `sass`: Inside this folder, we can find some Sass files used to create themes. Any custom CSS for our application will be created inside this folder.

Let's gain firsthand knowledge now! We will now explore some of the concepts described previously during the development of our application to understand them better.

Looking out for changes with the watch command

Sencha Cmd has another command that is very useful while developing Ext JS applications. It is the watch command. We will use this command all the time while developing the application in this book.

Let's execute this command and see what it does. First, we need to change the directory to the masteringextjs folder (which is our application folder generated with Sencha Cmd). Then, we can execute the sencha app watch command. The following screenshot exemplifies the output of this command:

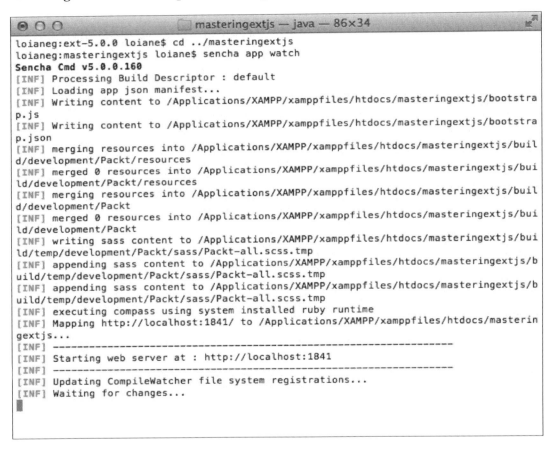

This command looks for any changes made inside the Ext JS application folder. If we create a new file or change any file, this command will know that a change has been made and will make an application build.

 You can minimize the terminal application and let the command be executed in the background. If we close the terminal, the command will no longer be alive, and we have to execute it again.

It is also going to start a web server at `http://locahost:1841`, where we can access our application as demonstrated in the following screenshot:

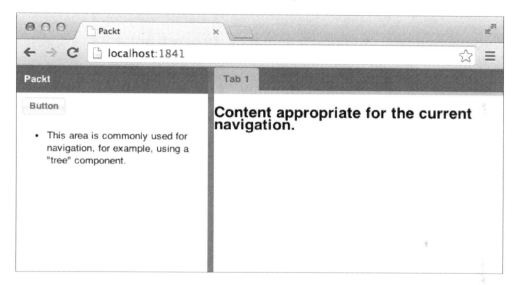

So this is how an application created with Sencha Cmd looks. Sencha Cmd also creates some files inside the `app` folder that we can change according to our needs. We will go through the files in the next chapter.

We can also execute the application from the Xampp `localhost` URL by accessing `http://localhost/masteringextjs`, as follows:

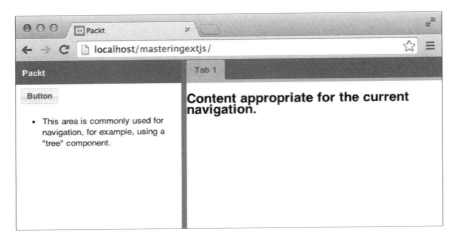

 The output from `http://localhost/masteringextjs` is exactly the same as accessing `http://locahost:1841`. You can use any of them. But be aware that `http://locahost:1841` will be alive only when we use the `sencha app watch` command. As we will use PHP and apply some other configurations, we will use `http://localhost/masteringextjs` throughout the book.

Applying the first changes in our app

We know that Sencha Cmd has created some files for us, but we do not want that screen to be the first one the user will see. We want the user to see the login screen and then go the main screen.

To make it happen, we need to make some changes inside the app.js file. If we open the file, we will see the following content:

```
Ext.application({
    name: 'Packt',

    extend: 'Packt.Application',

    autoCreateViewport: 'Packt.view.main.Main'
});
```

We are going to change the preceding code that was highlighted to the following code:

```
autoCreateViewport: false
```

This is the only change we will make in this file, because we should avoid changing it.

What this line does is create the `Packt.view.main.Main` component automatically after the application is initialized, but we do not want that happening. We want to display the splash screen first and then the login screen. That is why we are asking the application not to auto-render the viewport.

Note that the terminal where we have the `sencha app watch` command running will output a few lines, which means the application will be refreshed and the development build updated. This will happen every time we make a change and save it.

If we refresh the browser, we should see an empty page. This means we can start the development of our DVD Rental Store application.

Understanding the Application.js file

If we open the `app/Application.js` file, this is how it looks:

```
Ext.define('Packt.Application', { // #1
    extend: 'Ext.app.Application',

    name: 'Packt', // #2

    views: [ // #3

    ],

    controllers: [ // #4
        'Root'
    ],

    stores: [ // #5

    ],

    launch: function () { // #6
        // TODO - Launch the application
    }
});
```

The `app.js` file inherits all the behavior of the application from the `Application.js` file. This file is used as the entry point of the app.

On the first line of the preceding code, we have the `Ext.application` declaration (#1). This means that our application will have a single page (http://en.wikipedia.org/wiki/Single-page_application), and the parent container of the app will be the viewport. The viewport is a specialized container representing the viewable application area that is rendered inside the `<body>` tag of the HTML page (`<body></body>`).

Inside the `Ext.application`, we can also declare `views` (#3), `controllers` (#4), and `stores` (#5) used by the application. We will add this information in this file as we create new classes for our project.

We need to declare the `name` attribute of the application, which will be the namespace (#2) of the application. In this case, Sencha Cmd used the namespace we used in the `sencha generate app` command.

We can also create a `launch` function inside `Ext.application` (#6). This function will be called after all the application's controllers are initialized, and this means that the application is completely loaded. So this function is a good place to instantiate our main view, which in our case will be the login screen.

Do we need to use `Ext.onReady` when using `Ext.application`?

The answer is no. We only need to use one of the options. According to the Ext JS API documentation, `Ext.application` *loads Ext.app. Application class and starts it up with given configuration after the page is ready* and `Ext.onReady` *adds a new listener to be executed when all required scripts are fully loaded.*

If we take a look at the source code for `Ext.application`, we have:

```
Ext.application = function(config) {
    Ext.require('Ext.app.Application');
    Ext.onReady(function() {
        new Ext.app.Application(config);
    });
};
```

This means that `Ext.application` is already calling `Ext.onReady`, so we do not need to do it twice.

Hence, use `Ext.onReady` when you have a few components to be displayed, which are not in the MVC architecture (similar to the jQuery `$(document).ready()` function), and use `Ext.application` when you are developing an Ext JS MVC application.

The following diagram exemplifies all the high-level steps performed during the Ext JS application startup. Once the steps are executed, the application is completely loaded:

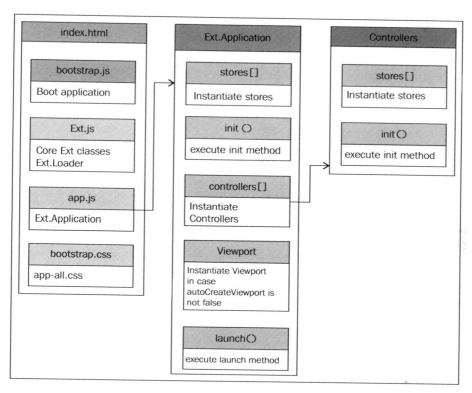

Now that we know how an Ext JS application is initialized, we can start building our app.

Creating the loading page

When working with large Ext JS applications, it is normal to have a short delay when loading the application. This happens because Ext JS is loading all the required classes to have the application up and running, and meanwhile, all the users see is a blank screen, which can be annoying for them. A very common solution to this problem is to have a loading page, also known as a splash screen.

So let's add a splash screen to our application that looks like what is shown in the following screenshot:

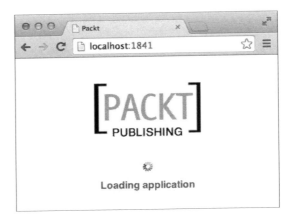

First, we need to understand how this splash screen will work. After the user loads the application, the splash screen will be displayed. The application will show the splash screen while it loads all the required classes and code so that the application can be used.

We already know that the application calls the launch function when it is ready to be used. So we know that we will need to remove the splash screen on the launch method. The question now is: where inside Ext.application can we call the splash screen? The answer is inside the init function. The init function is called when the application boots, so it gives some time to all required code to be loaded, and after that, the launch function is called.

Now that we know how the splash screen will work, let's implement it.

Inside Ext.application, we will implement a function called init after the launch function declaration:

```
init: function () {
    var me = this; // #1
    me.splashscreen = Ext.getBody().mask( // #2
        'Loading application', 'splashscreen'
    );
}
```

All we need to do is to apply a `mask` method (#2) into the HTML body of the application (`Ext.getBody()`). That is why we are calling the `mask` method passing the loading message (`Loading Application`) and applying a CSS style that will be a loading `GIF` file, and it is already part of the Ext JS CSS (`splashscreen`). The `mask` method will return an `Ext.dom.Element` class, which we will need to manipulate later (remove the `mask` method from the HTML body), and for this reason, we need to keep a reference to this `Ext.dom.Element` class, and we will store this reference as a variable part of `Ext.application` (`me.splashscreen`). The `me` variable is a reference to `this` (#1), which makes a reference to `Ext.application` itself.

With the code of the `init` method only, we will have a loading screen as follows:

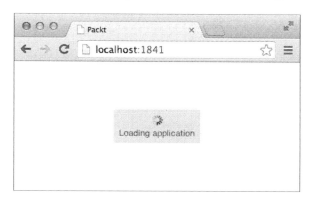

If this is all you need, that is OK. But let's go a little bit further and customize the loading screen, adding a logo image so that it can look like the first image of this topic, which is our final output.

To add the image to our splash screen, we need to create a CSS style. We could create a CSS file and then include it in our `index.html` file, but we will follow the best practices and create a `Sass` file inside the `sass` folder.

Ext JS has a better way to deal with custom CSS styles. When we are done implementing our application, we want to customize the theme, and we want to make a production build. The production build contains only the essential Ext JS SDK source code, which is required to execute the application, along with our application source code. This code will be obfuscated and optimized so that the user can download a file with minimal size. The production build will do the same with the CSS file as well; it will optimize and add only the required CSS from Ext JS components that are needed to execute the application. As of course, we want any custom CSS that we create to be optimized as well.

To do so, we are going to create our custom CSS inside the `sass/etc` folder using Sass (`http://sass-lang.com/`). So let's go ahead and create a file named `all.scss` inside the `sass/etc` folder.

Inside the resources, we will also create an `images/app` folder with the Packt logo image (you can copy the Packt logo image from this book's source code).

This is how our application structure will look after creating these files:

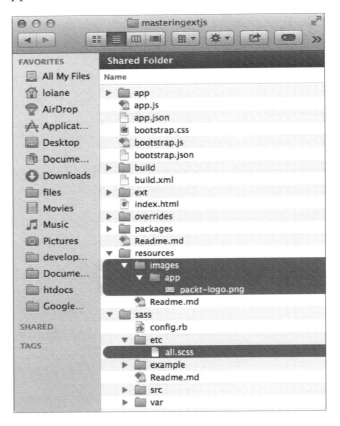

And the `all.scss` file will look like this:

```
.x-mask.splashscreen {
  background-color: white;
  opacity: 1;
}

.x-mask-msg.splashscreen,
.x-mask-msg.splashscreen div {
```

```
    font-size: 16px;
    font-weight: bold;
    padding: 30px 5px 5px 5px;
    border: none;
    background: {               // #1
      color: transparent;      // #2
      position: top center; // #3
    };
}

.x-message-box .x-window-body .x-box-inner {
  min-height: 110px !important;
}

.x-splash-icon {
  background-image: url('images/app/packt-logo.png') !important;
  margin-top: -30px;
  height: 70px;
}
```

It is plain CSS code, except for lines #1, #2, and #3, which is Sass code.

> If you are not familiar with Sass, it is a new way of writing CSS code. Sass uses the **don't repeat yourself** (**DRY**) principle, which means that you can use variables and nested syntax (as the one we used in #1) and import other Sass files (allowing you to create modular CSS), among other features. The Ext JS engine theme uses Sass and Compass (a Sass framework). Sass is an alternative to Less. To learn more about Sass, please visit http://sass-lang.com/.

Lines #1, #2, and #3 would be the same thing as:

```
background-color: transparent;
background-position: top center;
```

The preceding code is the CSS code generated after compiling the Sass file.

> When Sencha Cmd makes a build, the code from our all.scss file will be added to the single CSS file generated for our application, which contains the Ext JS CSS code and our code as well.

Now, let's go back to the `Application.js` file and continue to add some code to the `init` function.

We add the following code after the code we already have:

```
me.splashscreen.addCls('splashscreen');
```

We will add a new CSS style to the loading `<div>` tag. Note that the following styles from `app.css` will be applied: `.x-mask.splashscreen` and `.x-mask-msg. splashscreen div`. This will make the background white instead of gray, and it is also going to change the font of the "`Loading application`" message.

This is how the generated HTML will look:

```
Q  Elements  Network  Sources  Timeline  Profiles  Resources  Audits  Console  Sencha
<!DOCTYPE html>
▼<html>
  ▶<script id="tinyhippos-injected">...</script>
  ▶<head>...</head>
  ▼<body id="ext-element-1" class="x-body x-webkit x-chrome x-mac x-masked">
      <div role="presentation" class="x-mask x-mask-fixed splashscreen" style="top:0;left:0;" id="ext-element-3"></div>
    ▼<div role="presentation" class="x-mask-msg splashscreen" id="ext-element-2" style="right: auto; left: 528px; top: 78px;">
      ▼<div role="presentation" class="x-mask-msg-inner">
          <div role="presentation" class="x-mask-msg-text">Loading application</div>
        </div>
      </div>
<!DOCTYPE>
```

Now, we will add the following code in the `init` function:

```
Ext.DomHelper.insertFirst(Ext.query('.x-mask-msg')[0], {
    cls: 'x-splash-icon'
});
```

The preceding code will search for the first `<div>` tag that contains the `.x-mask-msg` class (`Ext.query('.x-mask-msg')[0]`) and will add a new `<div>` tag as a child with the class `x-splash-icon` that will be responsible for adding the logo image above the loading message.

And this is how the generated HTML will look:

```
Q  Elements  Network  Sources  Timeline  Profiles  Resources  Audits  Console  Sencha
<!DOCTYPE html>
▼<html>
  ▶<script id="tinyhippos-injected">...</script>
  ▶<head>...</head>
  ▼<body id="ext-element-1" class="x-body x-webkit x-chrome x-mac x-masked">
      <div role="presentation" class="x-mask x-mask-fixed splashscreen" style="top:0;left:0;" id="ext-element-3"></div>
    ▼<div role="presentation" class="x-mask-msg splashscreen" id="ext-element-2" style="right: auto; left: 528px; top: 78px;">
        <div class="x-splash-icon"></div>
      ▼<div role="presentation" class="x-mask-msg-inner">
          <div role="presentation" class="x-mask-msg-text">Loading application</div>
        </div>
      </div>
<!DOCTYPE>
```

After we execute the preceding code, we will have the output shown in the screenshot at the beginning of this topic.

Now we have the splash screen being displayed. We need to work on the `launch` function to remove the splash screen after all the code the application needs is loaded; otherwise, the loading message will be there indefinitely!

To remove the splash screen, the only code we need to add to the `launch` function is the following, which is about removing the mask from the HTML body:

```
Ext.getBody().unmask();
```

However, removing the mask abruptly is not nice because the user cannot even see the loading message. Instead of only removing the mask, let's give the user 2 seconds to see the loading message after the application is ready:

```
var task = new Ext.util.DelayedTask(function() { // #1
    Ext.getBody().unmask(); // #2
});

task.delay(2000); // #3
```

To do so, we use the `DelayedTask` class (#1), which is a class that provides the chance of a function to be executed after the given timeout in milliseconds (#3). So, in the case of the following task, we remove the mask from the HTML body (#2) after 2 seconds of timeout (2,000 milliseconds).

If we test the output right now, it works, but it is still not nice for the user. It would be even better if we could add an animation to the masking. So, we will add a fade out animation (which animates the opacity of an element—from opaque to transparent), and after the animation, we will remove the masking (inside the `Ext.util.DelayedTask` function). The following code is a demonstration of the explanation provided in this paragraph:

```
me.splashscreen.fadeOut({
    duration: 1000,
    remove:true
});
```

After we execute this code, notice that the loading message is still being displayed. We need to analyze the generated HTML to find out why.

Before we call the `fadeOut` function, this is the HTML of the loading message:

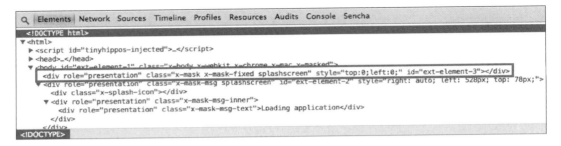

After we call the `fadeout` function, the HTML will be the following:

```
<!DOCTYPE html>
▼ <html>
  ▶ <script id="tinyhippos-injected">…</script>
  ▶ <head>…</head>
  ▼ <body id="ext-element-1" class="x-body x-webkit x-chrome x-mac x-masked">
    ▼ <div role="presentation" class="x-mask-msg splashscreen" id="ext-element-2" style="right: auto; left: 528px; top: 79px;">
        <div class="x-splash-icon"></div>
      ▼ <div role="presentation" class="x-mask-msg-inner">
          <div role="presentation" class="x-mask-msg-text">Loading application</div>
        </div>
      </div>
    <!DOCTYPE>
```

Only the first `<div>` tag with the `splashscreen` class was faded out. We need to also fade out the `<div>` tag with the `x-mask-msg splashscreen` class, which contains the logo and the loading message. To do so, we can use the next method, which will get the next sibling of the `splashscreen` node, as follows:

```
me.splashscreen.next().fadeOut({
    duration: 1000,
    remove:true
});
```

The output will be a pleasant animation that is shown to the user. Also note that the `splashscreen` `<div>` tag was removed from the generated HTML, which is as follows:

```
<!DOCTYPE html>
▼ <html>
  ▶ <script id="tinyhippos-injected">…</script>
  ▶ <head>…</head>
  ▼ <body id="ext-element-1" class="x-body x-webkit x-chrome x-mac x-masked">
    ▶ <div class="x-tip x-layer x-tip-default x-border-box" id="ext-quicktips-tip" data-sticky="true" style="display: none;">…</div>
        ""
  
        ""
    </body>
  </html>
<!DOCTYPE>
```

The complete code for the `launch` function will be the following:

```
launch: function () {
    var me = this;

    var task = new Ext.util.DelayedTask(function() {

        //Fade out the body mask
        me.splashscreen.fadeOut({
            duration: 1000,
            remove:true
        });

        //Fade out the icon and message
        me.splashscreen.next().fadeOut({
            duration: 1000,
            remove:true,
            listeners: { // #1
                afteranimate: function(el, startTime, eOpts ){//#2
                    console.log('launch') // #3
                }
            }
        });
    });

    task.delay(2000);
},
```

Downloading the example code

You can download the example code files from your account at
http://www.packtpub.com for all the Packt Publishing books you
have purchased. If you purchased this book elsewhere, you can visit
http://www.packtpub.com/support and register to have the
files e-mailed directly to you.

To make our splash screen even nicer, we will listen (#1) to the afteranimate event
(#2) of the fadeOut method so that we can display the initial component of our
application. We will show a login screen that we will implement in the next chapter.
For now, we will add a console message (#3) just to know where we need to call the
initial component. In Internet Explorer, console.log will not work; instead, you can
use window.console.log.

Notice that all the code we used to display the loading message mask and remove it is part of the Ext.dom.Element class. This class encapsulates a **Document Object Model (DOM)** element, where we can manage it using the class's methods. This class is a part of the Ext Core library, which is a part of the foundation of the Ext JS framework.

Summary

In this chapter, we explored the application we will implement throughout the chapters of this book in a lot of depth. We also covered all the requirements to create the development environment for this application. You learned how to create the initial structure of an Ext JS MVC application.

You also learned, through examples, how to create a splash screen (also known as the loading screen), manipulating the DOM using the Ext.dom.Element class. You learned the steps how to start up an Ext JS application and also learned the difference between the init and launch methods from Ext.application. We left Application.js ready to display its first screen, which will be a login screen, and which you will learn how to implement in the next chapter.

The Login Page

3

It is very common to have a login page for an application of which we want to control the access to the system by identifying and authenticating the user through the credentials presented by the user. Once the user is logged in, we can track the actions performed by the user. We can also restrain access to some features and screens of the system that we do not want a particular user to have access to or even a specific group of users.

In this chapter, we will cover:

- Creating the login page
- Handling the login page on the server
- Adding the Caps Lock warning message in the **Password** field
- Submitting the form when pressing the *Enter* key
- Encrypting the password before sending to the server

The Login screen

The **Login** window will be the first view that we are going to implement in this project. We are going to build it step-by-step, as follows:

- The user will enter the username and password to log in
- Client-side validation (username and password required to log in)
- Submit the login form by pressing *Enter*
- Encrypt the password before sending to the server
- Password Caps Lock warning (similar to Windows OS)
- Multilingual capability

Except for the multilingual capability, which we are going to implement in the next chapter, we will implement all the other features throughout this topic. So at the end of the implementation, we will have a **Login** window that looks as follows:

So let's get started!

Creating the Login screen

Under the app/view directory, we will create a new folder to organize all the source code related to the **Login** screen named login. Inside the login folder, we will also create a new file named Login.js. In this file, we will implement all the code that the user is going to see on the screen.

Inside view/login/Login.js, we will implement the following code:

```
Ext.define('Packt.view.login.Login', { // #1
    extend: 'Ext.window.Window',         // #2

    xtype: 'login-dialog',               // #3

    autoShow: true,                      // #4
    height: 170,                         // #5
    width: 360,
    layout: {
        type: 'fit'                      // #7
    },
    iconCls: 'fa fa-key fa-lg',          // #8
    title: 'Login',                      // #9
    closeAction: 'hide',                 // #10
    closable: false,                     // #11
    draggable: false,                    // #12
    resizable: false                     // #13
});
```

On the first line (#1), we have the definition of the class. To define a class, we use `Ext.define`, which (`define`) is a method call of the `Ext` singleton class, and which takes two arguments: the class name (#1) and the object literal with the configuration of the class (#2–#13).

We also need to pay attention to the name of the class. This is the formula suggested by Sencha in Ext JS MVC projects: *App Namespace + package name + name of the JS file*. In the previous chapter, we defined the namespace as `Packt` (the name of the application we passed as parameter for the `sencha generate app` command). If we open an existing file that was created by Sencha Cmd (the `app/view/main/Main.js` file) for example, we will note that the name of the class starts with `Packt`. So all the classes we are going to create through out this book will start with the namespace `Packt`.

We are creating a View for this project, so we will create the JS file under the `view` folder. For organization purposes, we created a subfolder named `login`. And then, the name of the file we created is `Login.js`; therefore, we will lose the `.js` and use only `Login` as the name of the View. Putting it all together, we have `Packt.view.login.Login`, and this will be the name of our class. It is very important that the class name follows the directory layout as explained; otherwise, we can get an error in the code saying Ext JS did not find the class. The following screenshot shows the dependency between the project directory layout and the class name:

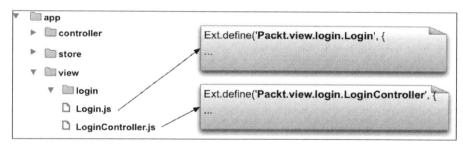

Then, we say that the `login` class will extend from the `Window` class (#2). Recapitulating what we have covered in *Chapter 1, Sencha Ext JS Overview*, we can use inheritance in Ext JS. The `login` class will inherit the behavior from the `Window` class (it is a subclass of the `Component` class). The `window` component represents a pop up that is rendered centralized in the browser.

For more information about the window component, please access `http://docs.sencha.com/extjs/5.0.0/apidocs/#!/api/Ext.window.Window`. And for more details on inheritance, please read `http://goo.gl/v4bmq8`.

We also assign this class: xtype (#3). The xtype class is a shorter name that can be used to instantiate the class instead of using its full name. We can also use the configuration alias instead of xtype.

The alias for a class that extends from a component always starts with widget, followed by the alias or xtype class we want to assign. If we want to use the alias configuration instead of xtype, we could use alias: 'widget.login-dialog' instead of xtype: 'login-dialog'. The result will be the same; it is just a matter of personal preference.

The naming convention for xtype and alias is lowercase. It is also important to remember that the alias must be unique in an application. In this case, we want to assign the xtype class login to this class so that later we can instantiate this same class using its alias (which is the same as xtype). For example, we can instantiate the Login class in five different ways:

- Option 1: Using the complete name of the class, which is the most used method:

  ```
  Ext.create('Packt.view.login.Login');
  ```

- Option 2: Using alias in the Ext.create method:

  ```
  Ext.create('widget.login-dialog');
  ```

- Option 3: Using Ext.widget, which is shorthand for Ext.ClassManager.instantiateByAlias:

  ```
  Ext.widget('login-dialog');
  ```

- Option 4: Using xtype as an item of another component:

  ```
  items: [
    {
      xtype: 'login-dialog'
    }
  ]
  ```

- Option 5: Using the new keyword:

  ```
  new Packt.view.login.Login();
  ```

In this book, we will use the options 1, 3, and 4 the most. Options 1, 2, 3, and 5 return a reference to the instantiated component.

Option number 5 is not a good practice. Although options 4 and 5 were the only way to instantiate classes until Ext JS 3, the other options were introduced in Ext JS 4, and option 5 became deprecated.

Although option 5 became deprecated with Ext JS 4 and later versions, we can still find some code in the Ext JS documentation and official Ext JS examples that use the new keyword. But do not get confused because of it. Option 5 should be avoided, always!

Then we have the `autoShow` configured to `true` (#4). Consider the following line of code:

```
Ext.create('Packt.view.login.Login');
```

When we execute the preceding code, an instance of the `Login` class will be created (and if we need to, we can store this reference in a variable to manipulate it later). As the `Login` class is a subclass of the `Window` class, it inherits all its behavior, and one if its behaviors is that the window is not displayed automatically when instantiated. If we want to display the `Window` class (or any of its subclasses in the application), we need to call the `show()` method manually, as follows:

```
Ext.create('Packt.view.login.Login').show();
```

An alternative to the preceding code is to have the `autoShow` configuration set to `true`. This way the `Window` class (or the `login` class in our case) will be automatically displayed when we instantiate it.

We also have the `height` (#5) and `width` (#6) of the window.

We set `layout` as `fit` (#7). Recapitulating, the `fit` layout is used when the parent container (in this case, `Login`) has only one child, and this child will occupy all the available space of the parent container. As our **Login** window will have two fields inside it (username and password), these two fields need to be placed inside the `form` subclass . In this case, the `form` subclass will be the child of the `Login` class.

We are setting `iconCls` (#8) to the **Login** window; this way, we will have an icon of a key in the header of the window (we will set up the icons later in this chapter). We can also give a `title` to the window (#9), and in this case, we chose `Login`.

There are also the `closeAction` (#10) and `closable` (#11) configurations. The `closeAction` will tell if we want to destroy the window when we close it. In this case, we do not want to destroy it; we only want to hide it. And the `closable` configuration tells us whether we want to display the *X* icon on the top-right corner of the window. As this is a **Login** window, we do not want to give this option for the user (the user can only try to submit the username and password to log in to the application).

What is the difference between the methods close, hide, and destroy? The close method closes the panel, and by default, this method removes it from the DOM and destroys the panel object and all its descendant components. The hide method hides the component, setting it to invisible (it can be made visible again by calling the show method). And the destroy method cleans up the object and its resources, but removes it from the DOM and frees the object so that it can be cleaned by the garbage collector.

We also have the draggable (#12) and resizable (#13) configurations. The draggable configuration controls whether the component can be draggable throughout the browser space. When the resizable configuration is set to true (its default value), the user can scroll over the corner of the component and resize it.

So far, this is the output we have—a single window with a blank icon in the top-left corner with the title **Login** (we will set up all the icons later in this chapter):

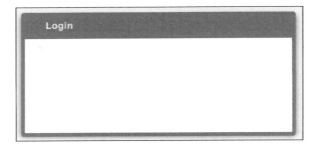

The next step is to add the form with the username and password fields. We are going to add the following code to the Login class (after line #13):

```
items: [
{
    xtype: 'form',              //#14
    bodyPadding: 15,            //#15
    defaults: {                 //#16
        xtype: 'textfield', //#17
        anchor: '100%',     //#18
        labelWidth: 60      //#19
    },
    items: [
        {
            name: 'user',
            fieldLabel: 'User'
        },
```

```
          {
                    inputType: 'password', //#20
                    name: 'password',
                    fieldLabel: 'Password'
          }
     ]
 ]
```

As we are using the `fit` layout, we can only declare one child `item` inside the `Login` class. So we are going to add a `form` (#14) inside the `Login` class. Note that here we are using option 4 presented earlier. When declaring items in Ext JS, this is usually the way we instantiate the components (using option 4). We added a body `padding` to the `form` body (#15), which is going to add a space between the form and the window border, making it look prettier.

As we are going to add two fields to the form, we probably want to avoid repeating some code. That is why we are going to declare some field configurations inside the `defaults` configuration of the `form` (#16); this way, the configuration we declare inside `defaults` will be applied to all items of the `form`, and we will need to declare only the configurations we want to customize. As we are going to declare two fields, both of them will be of the type `textfield` (#17).

The default layout used by the `form` component is the `anchor` layout, so we do not need to make this declaration explicit. However, we want both fields to occupy all the horizontal available space of the body of the form. That is why we are declaring the `anchor` as `100%` (#18).

While the `fit` layout allows you to render only one child component that will occupy all the available space within the parent container, the Anchor layout enables you to anchor child containers relative to the parent container dimensions. In this case, we want the text fields to occupy 100 percent of the horizontal space available in the form. If we wanted the text fields to occupy only 70 percent of the available horizontal space, we could set the `anchor` config to `70%`.

By default, the `width` attribute of the label of the `textfield` class is 100 pixels. This is too much space for a label `User` and `Password`, so we are going to decrease this value to `60 pixels` (#19).

And finally, we have the `user textfield` and the `password textfield`. The configuration `name` is what we are going to use to identify each field when we submit the form to the server.

There is only one detail missing: when the user types the password into the field, the system cannot display its value—we need to mask it somehow. That is why input Type is 'password' (#20) for the password field because we want to display bullets instead of the original value—and the user will not be able to see the password value.

> Other input types can be used with the textfield as well. Input types of HTML5, such as email, url, and tel can be used as well. However, if the application is being executed from an older browser (or a browser that does not support the input type), Ext JS automatically changes it to its default value, which is text. For more information about HTML5 input types and browsers that support each type, please visit http://www.w3schools.com/html/html5_form_input_types.asp.

Now we have improved our **Login** window a little more. This is the output so far:

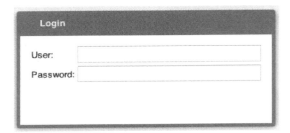

Client-side validations

The field component in Ext JS provides some client-side validation capability. This can save time and also bandwidth (the system will only make a server request when it is sure the information has the basic validation and we also do not need to wait for the server to validate the input). It also helps to point out to the user where they have gone wrong in filling out the form. Of course it is also good to validate the information again on the server side for security reasons, but for now we will focus on the validations we can apply to the form of our **Login** window.

Let's brainstorm some validations we can apply to the username and password fields:

- The username and password must be mandatory—how are you going to authenticate the user without a username and password?
- The user can only enter alphanumeric characters (A-Z, a-z, and 0-9) in both fields

- The user can only type between 3 and 25 chars on the `username` field
- The user can only type between 3 and 15 chars on the `password` field

So let's add into the code the ones that are common to both fields:

```
allowBlank: false,   // #21
vtype: 'alphanum',   // #22
minLength: 3,        // #23
msgTarget: 'under'   // #24
```

We are going to add the preceding configurations inside the `defaults` configuration of the `form` as they all apply to both fields we have. First, both need to be mandatory (#21), second, we can only allow the user to enter alphanumeric characters (#22), and the minimum number of characters the user needs to input is three (#23). Then, a last common configuration is that we want to display any validation error message under the field (#24).

And the only validation customized for each field is that we can enter a maximum of 25 characters in the **User** field:

```
name: 'user',
fieldLabel: 'User',
maxLength: 25
```

And a maximum of 15 characters in the **Password** field:

```
inputType: 'password',
name: 'password',
fieldLabel: 'Password',
maxLength: 15
```

After we apply the client validations, we will have the following output just in case the user went wrong in filling out the **Login** window:

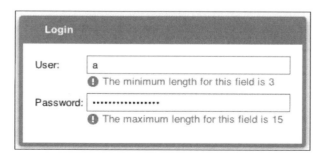

If you do not like the error message being displayed under the field, we can change the place where the error message appears. We just need to change the msgTarget value. The available options are: title, under, side, and none. We can also show the error message as a tooltip (qtip) or display them in a specific target (innerHTML of a specific component).

For the side option, for example, the red exclamation mark will be displayed on the side of the field, and when the user does a mouseover on it, the tooltip with the error message is displayed. Once the input is valid (the user enters more characters in the **User** field or deletes some characters from the **Password** field, the error message disappears automatically).

Creating custom VTypes

Many systems have a special format for passwords. Let's say we need the password to have at least one digit (0-9), one letter lowercase, one letter uppercase, one special character (@,#,$,%, and so on) and its length between 6 and 20 characters.

We can create a regular expression to validate that the password is being entered into the app. And to do this, we can create a custom VType to do the validation for us. To create a custom VType is simple. For our case, we can create a custom VType called customPass, as follows:

```
Ext.apply(Ext.form.field.VTypes, {
    customPass: function(val, field) {
        return /^((?=.*\d)(?=.*[a-z])(?=.*[A-
Z])(?=.*[@#$%]).{6,20})/.test(val);
    },
    customPassText: 'Not a valid password.  Length must be at
least 6 characters and maximum of 20. Password must contain one
digit, one letter lowercase, one letter uppercase, one special
symbol @#$% and between 6 and 20 characters.'
});
```

The name of our custom VType is customPass, and we need to declare a function that will validate our regular expression. And customPassText is the message that will be displayed to the user just in case the incorrect password format is entered.

To learn more about regular expressions, please visit http://www.regular-expressions.info/.

The preceding code can be added anywhere in the code, inside the init function of a Controller, inside the launch function of app.js, or even in a separate JavaScript file (recommended) where you can put all your custom Vtypes.

The VType is a singleton class that contains a set of commonly used field validation functions and provides a mechanism to create reusable custom field validations. For more information about this class and the default validations supported by Ext JS, please visit http://docs.sencha.com/extjs/5.1/5.1.0-apidocs/#!/api/Ext.form.field.VTypes.

Create a new file named CustomVTypes.js under the app directory. Add the preceding code to this file. Now, we need this file to be loaded with our application as well. But hold your instincts to manually include this JavaScript file in the index.html file. We are going to follow best practices!

Locate the following code around line 110 of the app.json file inside the masteringextjs folder:

```
"js": [
    {
        "path": "app.js",
        "bundle": true
    }
],
```

To make our CustomVTypes.js file automatically load with our application, we simply need to add the following highlighted code:

```
"js": [
    {
        "path": "app.js",
        "bundle": true
    },
    {
        "path": "app/CustomVTypes.js",
        "includeInBundle": true
    }
],
```

The includeInBundle configuration tells Sencha Cmd that this file needs to be added to the final .js file that is generated.

Only one file can have the bundle: true configuration. This means that it is the main file of the application.

Always remember to have the `sencha app watch` command running in a terminal window so that Sencha Cmd can make a new build every time we make changes to the code. In this case, `CustomVTypes.js` will be loaded without any further changes to the `index.html` file. Really cool!

Now, let's apply the custom `VType` to our code. Add the following code to the password field:

```
vtype: 'customPass',
msgTarget: 'side'
```

Also, change the message target for the password field. As the error message is quite long, it will not look nice with the message target `under`. This will be the result after we apply the custom `vType`:

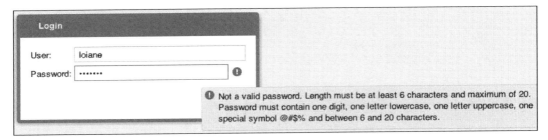

Adding the toolbar with buttons

Until now, we created the **Login** window, which contains a form with two fields and it is already being validated as well. The only thing missing is to add the two buttons, **Cancel** and **Submit**.

We are going to add the buttons as items of a `toolbar`, and the `toolbar` will be added on the `form` as a docked item. The `dockedItems` can be docked to either the *top*, *right*, *left*, or *bottom* of a panel (both form and window components are subclasses of a panel). In this case, we will `dock` the `toolbar` at the bottom of the form. Add the following code right after the items configuration of the form:

```
dockedItems: [
    {
        xtype: 'toolbar',
        dock: 'bottom',
        items: [
                xtype: 'tbfill' //#25
```

```
        },
        {

            xtype: 'button', //#26
            iconCls: 'fa fa-times fa-lg',
            text: 'Cancel'
        },
        {

            xtype: 'button', //#27
            formBind: true,  //#28
            iconCls: 'fa fa-sign-in fa-lg',
            text: 'Submit'
        }
    ]
  }
]
```

If we take a look back to the screenshot of the **Login** screen that we first presented at the beginning of this chapter, we will notice that there is a component for the translation/multilingual capability. And after this component, there is a space and then we have the **Cancel** and **Submit** buttons. As we do not have the multilingual component yet, we can only implement the two buttons, but they need to be at the right end of the form, and we need to leave that space. That is why we first need to add a `tbfill` component (#25), which is going to instruct the toolbar's layout to begin using the right-justified button container.

Then we will add the **Cancel** button (#26) and then the **Submit** button (#27). We are going to add an icon to both buttons (`iconCls`) that we will add to our CSS file later in this chapter.

We already have the client validations, but even with the validations, the user can click on the **Submit** button, and we want to avoid this behavior. That is why we are binding the **Submit** button to the form (#28); this way, the button will only be enabled if the form has no error from the client validation.

In the following screenshot, we can see the current output of the **Login** form (after we added the toolbar) and also verify the behavior of the **Submit** button:

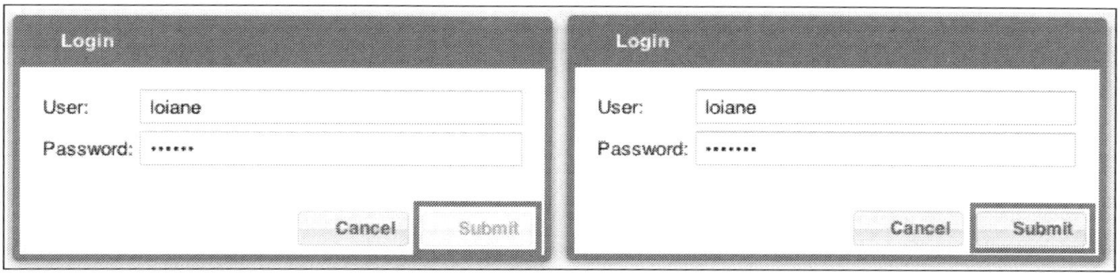

When we want to add a toolbar with buttons in a form, we can add it using the configuration `buttons` as well. For more information, please access `http://goo.gl/X38h8Q`.

Running the code

To execute the code we have created so far, we need to make a few changes in the `Application.js` file.

First, we need to declare the `views` we are using (only one in this case), as follows:

```
views: [
    'login.Login'
],
```

And the last change is inside the `launch` function. In the preceding chapter, we left a `console.log` message where we needed to instantiate our initial view; now we only need to replace the `console.log` message with the `Login` instance (#1):

```
me.splashscreen.next().fadeOut({
    duration: 1000,
    remove:true,
    listeners: {
        afteranimate: function(el, startTime, eOpts ){
            Ext.widget('login-dialog'); //#1
        }
    }
});
```

Now that `Application.js` is OK, and we can execute what we have implemented so far!

A quick overview about Ext JS dynamic class loading

Dynamic class loading was introduced in Ext JS 4. It provides an integrated dependency management capability, and it is very useful, especially when working on the development (local) environment (it also plays an important role in the final production build). This capability is also one of the reasons why option 5 for instantiating classes in Ext JS (using the keyword `new`) became deprecated and not a best practice.

What does dynamic loading mean? It means that we do not need to load all Ext JS SDK classes prior to load our application. For example, for the Login window, we are using the `Window`, `Form`, and `TextField` classes from the Ext JS SDK. To execute our application, we do not need the source code of the grid, tree, and charts. Do you agree?

Still on the Login window example, when our application is loaded, Ext JS will read that the `'login.Login'` view needs to be loaded. As all the application source code is inside the `app` folder, and the views are inside the `app/view` folder, the Ext JS loader will expect to find the `app/view/login/Login.js` file, and inside this file it expects to find the `'Packt.view.login.Login'` class definition (this is why it is very important to follow the naming conventions we introduced earlier). The Ext JS loader will then see that this class inherits from the `Ext.window.Window` class, and if this class was not loaded yet, it is going to figure out all its dependencies (from the `extend` and `requires` declarations—we will discuss `requires` in a bit) and load them until we have all the source code required to execute the application loaded (and it will do this recursively until all code is loaded).

For example, when you try to execute the application, open the Chrome Developer Tools (*Ctrl + Shift + I* or *Command + Shift + I*) or Firebug for Firefox (enable all panels) and open the **Network** tab. We will be able to see all files that were loaded for our application, as follows:

Q	Elements	**Network**	Sources	Timeline	Profiles	Resources	Audits	Console	NetBeans	Sencha

● ⊘ ▽ ≔ ▢ Preserve log

Name	Method	Status	Type	Initiator	Size	Time	Timeline
masteringextjs/	GET	304	text/html	Other	236 B	6 ms	●
bootstrap.js	GET	200	applicati...	localhost/:9	50.7 KB	117 ms	◐
bootstrap.json	GET	200	text/plain	bootstrap.js:558	147 KB	6 ms	○
Boot.js?_dc=1407863838178	GET	200	applicati...	bootstrap.js:511	38.5 KB	195 ms	◐
Ext.js?_dc=1407863838178	GET	200	applicati...	bootstrap.js:511	35.5 KB	193 ms	◐
Error.js?_dc=1407863838178	GET	200	applicati...	bootstrap.js:511	10.9 KB	207 ms	◐
Array.js?_dc=1407863838178	GET	200	applicati...	bootstrap.js:511	51.3 KB	208 ms	◐
Assert.js?_dc=1407863838178	GET	200	applicati...	bootstrap.js:511	5.5 KB	209 ms	◐
String.js?_dc=1407863838178	GET	200	applicati...	bootstrap.js:511	19.3 KB	210 ms	◐
Date.js?_dc=1407863838178	GET	200	applicati...	bootstrap.js:511	73.0 KB	306 ms	◐
Function.js?_dc=1407863838178	GET	200	applicati...	bootstrap.js:511	24.0 KB	306 ms	◐
Number.js?_dc=1407863838178	GET	200	applicati...	bootstrap.js:511	12.4 KB	310 ms	◐
Object.js?_dc=1407863838178	GET	200	applicati...	bootstrap.js:511	24.3 KB	310 ms	◐
Util.js?_dc=1407863838178	GET	200	applicati...	bootstrap.js:511	27.3 KB	310 ms	◐

346 requests | 5.0 MB transferred

We know that **5MB** is scary for only a **Login** screen, but we will solve this issue when we do the production build later on this book. We do not need to worry about it for now.

What will happen later when we do the production build is that Ext JS will know which classes from the SDK need to be included in the final JavaScript file, will concatenate everything into a single file, and will also obfuscate it. If you try to open any of the files listed in the preceding screenshot, you will be able to read the source code (and it will be pretty and indented as the development source code should be).

Adding Font Awesome support (Glyph icons)

Using icons on the application improves its look and feel, it makes the application look prettier, and users usually enjoy it. However, unless we get (or buy) icons with different sizes, the icons are 16 x 16 pixels big. With the introduction of **CSS3**, one of the new features is called **CSS3 Web Fonts** (http://www.w3schools.com/css/css3_fonts.asp), which allow us to use fonts that are not installed on the user's computer.

This feature allowed developers to create a new type of icons, called **Glyph icons**, which are not actually icons, but fonts where each character looks like an icon (similar to the *Webding* font, http://en.wikipedia.org/wiki/Webdings).

Using Glyph icons is great because we can change the size and color of the icon to match the application's theme. Whenever possible, we will use Glyph icons in our application. There is an open source and free font that is used widely by modern applications (HTML5 applications) called **Font Awesome**, and we are going to use this in our project as well.

So the first step is downloading the Font Awesome files from http://fortawesome.github.io/Font-Awesome/. Click on the **Download** button. The file that is going to be downloaded is a .zip file. Unzip it. Copy the fonts folder and paste it inside the resources folder of the masteringextjs application. Copy the scss folder and paste it inside the sass/etc folder. Rename the scss folder to fontAwesome. This is how the sass/etc and resource folders will look after the changes:

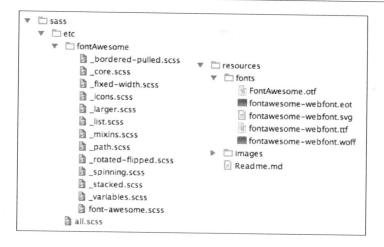

We are almost there! Open the `sass/etc/fontAwesome/_variables.scss` file, and change the variable `$fa-font-path` to the following value:

```
$fa-font-path: "../resources/fonts" !default;
```

This is to tell Sass where we placed the font files.

Now all we have to do is open the `sass/etc/all.scss` file and add the following code in the first line of the file:

```
@import "fontAwesome/font-awesome";
```

If you are running `sencha app watch` in the terminal application, you should note that the application was rebuilt and we are ready to see the icons in our application. The following is how the **Login** screen will look:

The next step is to add some action to the **Cancel** and **Submit** buttons.

 To learn more about Sass variables and import capabilities, please visit `http://sass-lang.com/guide`.

Creating the Login Controller

We have created the view for the **Login** screen so far. As we are following the MVC architecture, we are not implementing the user interaction on the `View` class. If we click on the buttons on the `Login` class, nothing will happen, because we have not implemented this logic yet. We are going to implement this logic now on the `Controller` class.

In Ext JS 5, we have two options to do this: use the default MVC architecture or use the MVVM architecture pattern (or a *hybrid* pattern).

Introducing the MVVM architecture

In the preceding chapter, we covered an introduction of the MVC architecture in Ext JS. Let's refresh our memory quickly of how MVC works:

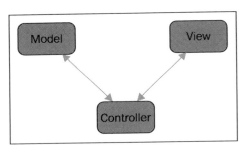

The **Model** represents the information that is being used by the application. The **View** is what the user will see on the screen—the components. In each interaction of the user with the application, the components will fire events. The **Controller** is where we are going to handle the events and execute any logic that is needed; the Controller is going to manage the information (**Model**) and also manage the **View** (and the interaction between the **View** and **Model**).

In Ext JS 5, Sencha introduced this new pattern called **Model View ViewModel (MVVM)**, which is shown in the following diagram:

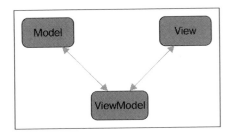

What happens in the MVVM is that using this pattern, it is much easier to control the **View** and the **Model** if they are bound. For example, consider that we have a data grid where we list some contacts. When we select a contact and click on the **Edit** button, we want the application to open a pop up about the title that will be the name of the contact and the pop up will also have a form that will display the contact details for editing. If we use the default MVC pattern, we will need to control the way the **View** (data grid, pop up, and form) interacts with the **Model** (contact information). The MVVM (which is based on the MVC) introduces a new abstraction entity that is the **ViewModel**. The **ViewModel** mediates changes between the **View** and the associated **Model**.

However, with this new pattern and new **ViewModel** abstraction, Sencha also introduced an abstraction for the controller, which is bound to the **View**, called the **ViewController**. The **ViewController** is very similar to the traditional controller of the MVC pattern, which is as follows:

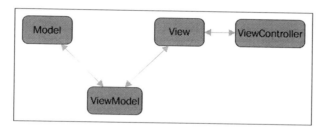

However, as we learned in *Chapter 2, Getting Started*, the controllers of the MVC pattern are created in the scope of the application, and they are unique instances (meaning a single instance of each controller of the application). As long as the application is running, the controllers are also alive.

The **ViewModel** and **ViewController** are part of the component (we learned about component in *Chapter 1, Sencha Ext JS Overview*). As long as the **View** is alive, they are also alive. When the **View** is destroyed, they also get destroyed. This means that we can save some memory (if we do not have many instances of the same **View** at once).

Do not worry if you do not understand all these concepts 100 percent right now. We will learn how to use them and how they work with some examples, and throughout this book we will use these different options of architecture so that we can learn how each one works, and maybe you can choose the one you like the most or the one that is going to fit your project best.

Creating the ViewController for Login View

Let's stop to think a little bit. Logging in is performed once during the application's lifetime. There are three things we can do in the application: log in to start using it, use its capabilities, or log out (because we clicked on the logout button or the session expired). Once we have logged in, we are in, and that is it.

In the previous topic we learned that the **ViewModel** and the **ViewController** are destroyed once the **View** is destroyed. So, instead of having a controller for the login alive during the application's lifetime, we can have a controller that will be alive only during the time that the login View is alive. For this reason, for the **Login** screen, we will use the **ViewController**.

The first step is creating the JavaScript file. Inside app/view/login, we will create the LoginController.js file. Inside this file, we will implement the following code, which is only a base of the ViewController class we are going to implement:

```
Ext.define('Packt.view.login.LoginController', { // #1
    extend: 'Ext.app.ViewController',           // #2
    alias: 'controller.login',                  // #3

    onTextFieldSpecialKey: function(field, e, options){ }, // #4

    onTextFieldKeyPress: function(field, e, options){ }, // #5

    onButtonClickCancel: function(button, e, options){ }, // #6

    onButtonClickSubmit: function(button, e, options){ }, // #7

    doLogin: function() { }, // #8

    onLoginFailure: function(form, action) { }, // #9

    onLoginSuccess: function(form, action) { } // #10
});
```

As usual, on the first line of the class, we have its name (#1). Following the same formula we used for the view/login/Login.js, we will have Packt (*app namespace*) + view (*name of the package*) + login (*name of the sub package*) + LoginController (*name of the file*), resulting in Packt.view.login.LoginController.

The ViewController classes need to extend from Ext.app.ViewController (#2) so that we will always use this parent class for our ViewController.

We also need to give an `alias` to this `ViewController` (#3). Aliases for ViewControllers start with `'controller'`, followed by the alias we want to assign (remember that the alias is always in lowercase).

For #4–#10, we have the signature of some methods we will implement until the end of this chapter. We will go through each of them later.

Binding the ViewController to the View

Now that we have the base of our ViewController ready, we need to bind the ViewController to its View, which is the `Login` View. Going back to the `Packt.view.login.Login` class, we are going to add the following configuration to the class:

```
controller: 'login',
```

The preceding configuration will bind the `ViewController` class to the `Login` class life cycle. Note that we are using the alias we defined in #3.

If you try to execute the code, it will throw an error. This is because Ext JS does not know which `ViewController` class has the `login` alias (since this alias is not a native of the framework; we are creating it). To make it work, we need to add the following code to the `login` class as well:

```
requires: [
    'Packt.view.login.LoginController'
],
```

This will tell the Ext JS loader that it also needs to be loaded when loading the `Login` class. Ext JS will load this class and all its dependencies. By the time Ext JS parses the `controller: 'login'` code, it will have registered the `login` alias for a controller and it is going to be OK.

Listening to the button click event

Our next step now is to start listening to the **Login** window events. First, we are going to listen to the **Submit** and **Cancel** buttons.

As we are using a `ViewController` class and not a Controller (MVC), we need to add listeners inside the `Login` class. First, let's do it for the **Cancel** button, as follows:

```
xtype: 'button',
iconCls: 'fa fa-times fa-lg',
text: 'Cancel',
listeners: {
    click: 'onButtonClickCancel'
}
```

This code means that when a user clicks on the **Cancel** button, the `onButtonClickCancel` method from the `Login ViewController` class will be executed. So let's implement this method! Back to the `LoginController` class, we already know that this is the method we are going to implement:

```
onButtonClickCancel: function(button, e, options){}
```

But how do we know which are the parameters the method can receive? We can find the answer to this question in the documentation. If we take a look at the click event in the documentation (`Button` class), this is what we will find:

---

click(this, e, eOpts)

Fires when this button is clicked, before the configured handler is invoked. Execution of the handler may be vetoed by returning `false` to this event.

Parameters

- this : Ext.button.Button

- e : Event

  The click event

- eOpts : Object

  The options object passed to Ext.util.Observable.addListener.

This is exactly what we declared. For all the other event listeners, we will go to the docs and see which are the parameters the event accepts, and then list them as parameters in our code. This is also a very good practice. We should always list out all the arguments from the docs even if we are only interested in the first one (or even none). This way, we always know that we have the full collection of the parameters, and this can come in very handy when we are doing maintenance on the application.

Make sure the documentation becomes your best friend while developing Ext JS applications. The Ext JS documentation is really good and user friendly.

Note that we also want to listen to the **Submit** button click. The `onButtonClickSubmit` method has the same signature as the `onButtonClickCancel` method. Let's go ahead and also add the listener to the **Submit** button, as follows:

```
xtype: 'button',
formBind: true,
iconCls: 'fa fa-sign-in fa-lg',
text: 'Submit',
listeners: {
    click: 'onButtonClickSubmit'
}
```

Let's do a quick test to see if everything is working as expected so far:

```
onButtonClickCancel: function(button, e, options){
    console.log('login cancel'); // #1
},

onButtonClickSubmit: function(button, e, options){
    console.log('login submit');   // #2
},
```

For now, we are only going to output a message on the console to make sure our code is working. So, we are going to output `'login submit'` (#2) if the user clicks on the **Submit** button, and `'login cancel'` (#1) if the user clicks on the **Cancel** button.

Let's go ahead and try it. Click on the **Cancel** button and then on the **Submit** button. This should be the output:

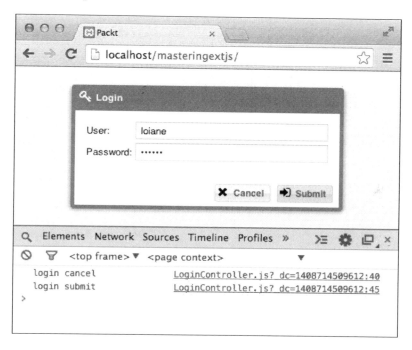

Cancel Button Listener implementation

Let's remove the `console.log` messages and add the code we actually want the methods to execute. First, let's work on the `onButtonClickCancel` method. When we execute this method, we want it to reset the **Login** form.

So this is the logic sequence we want to program:

- Get the form reference
- Call the `reset` method to reset the form

If we take a look at the parameters we have available on the `onButtonClickCancel` method, we have `button`, `e`, and `options`, and none of them provides us with the form reference. So what can we do about it?

The `ViewController` class has an interesting way of getting a reference of the `Login` class or any of its children, which uses the method `lookupReference(reference)` from the `ViewController` class. To be able to use this method, all we have to do is add a reference for the `form` in the `Login` `View` class:

```
xtype: 'form',
reference: 'form',
```

With this reference, we will be able to call the `this.lookupReference('form')` method directly to retrieve the form reference. With the form reference, all we have to do is call the method `reset()` from the `form` class. The complete code for the `onButtonClickCancel` method would be:

```
onButtonClickCancel: function(button, e, options){
    this.lookupReference('form').reset();
},
```

Submit Button Listener implementation

Now we need to implement the `onButtonClickSubmit` method. Inside this method, we want to program the logic to send the **User** and **Password** values to the server so that the user can be authenticated.

We can implement two programming logics inside this method: the first one is to use the `submit` method that is provided by the `Form Basic` class, and the second one is to use an Ajax call to submit the values to the server. Either way, we will achieve what we want to do. For this example, we will use the default form submit call.

These are the steps we need to perform in this method:

- Get the **Login** form reference
- Get the **Login** window reference (so we can close it once the user has been authenticated)
- Send Login information to the server

- Handle the server response, as follows:
  - ○ If the user is authenticated, display application
  - ○ If not, display error message

We already know how to get the form reference. This is how onButtonClickSubmit will look:

```
onButtonClickSubmit: function(button, e, options){
    var me = this;
    if (me.lookupReference('form').isValid()){ // #1
        me.doLogin();                 // #2
    }
},
```

So first, before doing anything, we will make sure the user has entered all the required information (user name and valid password (#1)). If everything is OK, then we call a helper method that will handle the authentication (#2), as follows:

```
doLogin: function() {
    var me = this,
        form = me.lookupReference('form');

    form.submit({
        clientValidation: true,        // #3
        url: 'php/security/login.php', // #4
        scope: me,          // #5
        success: 'onLoginSuccess',     // #6
        failure: 'onLoginFailure'      // #7
    });
},
```

First, just to make sure the data we are trying to submit is valid (we will call this doLogin method from another method as well, so to be sure we are sending valid data to server is never too much!), we set the clientValidation configuration as true to validate the information one more time (#3). Then we have the url that is going to be called (#4). The success (#6) and failure (#7) callbacks were declared as separate functions, which belong to the ViewController class, and that is why the scope is the ViewController class (#5).

We could implement the success and failure methods inside the submit call as well (as showed by the example in the documentation http://docs.sencha.com/extjs/5.0.0/apidocs/#!/api/Ext.form.Basic-method-submit). But we do not know how much code we will need to handle the authentication. Working with scoped callbacks is better because our code stays organized, with better readability.

If we try to run this code, the application will send the request to the server, but we will get an error as response because we do not have the login.php page implemented yet. That's OK because we are interested in other details right now.

With Firebug or Chrome Developer Tools enabled, open the **Network** tab and filter by the **XHR** requests. Make sure to enter a username and password (any valid value so we can click on the **Submit** button). This will be the output:

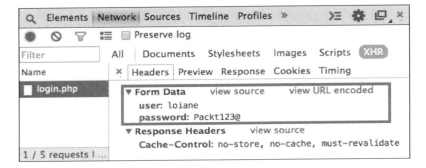

Note that the user and password are being sent as form data. This information is useful to handle the information on the server side (which in our case is the PHP code).

Whenever you have questions or you have no idea how you are going to handle the information sent by Ext JS to the server, open the debug tool of your browser and inspect the call. This helps a lot and also helps you to learn more about how Ext JS works when communicating with the server.

Creating the User and Groups tables

Before we start coding the `login.php` page, we need to add two tables to the Sakila database. These two tables are going to represent the users and also the group that the user can belong to. In our project, a user can belong to only one group, as shown in the following figure:

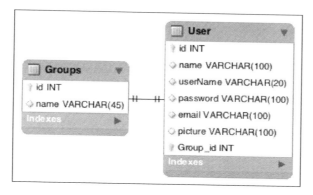

1. First, we are going to create the `Group` table, as follows:

```
CREATE   TABLE IF NOT EXISTS `sakila`.`Groups` (
  `id` INT NOT NULL AUTO_INCREMENT ,
  `name` VARCHAR(45) NOT NULL ,
  PRIMARY KEY (`id`) )
ENGINE = InnoDB;
```

2. Then, we are going to create the `User` table containing the indexes and also the `foreign key` to the `Group` table:

```
CREATE   TABLE IF NOT EXISTS `sakila`.`User` (
  `id` INT NOT NULL AUTO_INCREMENT ,
  `name` VARCHAR(100) NOT NULL ,
  `userName` VARCHAR(20) NOT NULL ,
  `password` VARCHAR(100) NOT NULL ,
  `email` VARCHAR(100) NOT NULL ,
  `picture` VARCHAR(100) NULL ,
  `Group_id` INT NOT NULL ,
  PRIMARY KEY (`id`, `Group_id`) ,
  UNIQUE INDEX `userName_UNIQUE` (`userName` ASC) ,
  INDEX `fk_User_Group1_idx` (`Group_id` ASC) ,
  CONSTRAINT `fk_User_Group1`
    FOREIGN KEY (`Group_id` )
    REFERENCES `sakila`.`Groups` (`id` )
    ON DELETE NO ACTION
    ON UPDATE NO ACTION)
ENGINE = InnoDB;
```

3. The next step is to insert some data into these tables:

```
INSERT INTO `sakila`.`Groups` (`name`) VALUES ('admin');
INSERT INTO `sakila`.`User` (`name`, `userName`,
`password`,
`email`, `Group_id`)
VALUES ('Loiane Groner', 'loiane',
'$2a$10$2a4e8803c91cc5edca222evoNPfhdRyGEG9RZcg7.qGqTjuCgXKda',
'me@loiane.com', '1');
```

As the password will be saved hashed on the database, the value $2a$10$2a4e 8803c91cc5edca222evoNPfhdRyGEG9RZcg7.qGqTjuCgXKda corresponds to the value Packt123@. We will be hashing our password for more security in the user administration module.

Now we are ready to start developing the login.php page.

Handling the Login page on the server

Since we have part of the Ext JS code to send the login information to the server, we can implement the server-side code. As mentioned in the first chapter of this book, we are going to use PHP to implement the server-side code. But if you do not know PHP, do not worry because the code is not going to be complicated, and we are going to use pure PHP as well. The goal is to focus on the programming logic we need to use on the server side; this way we apply the same programming logic to any other server-side language that you like to use (Java, .NET, Ruby, Python, and so on).

Connecting to the database

The first step is to create the file that is going to be responsible for connecting to the database. We are going to reuse this file in almost every PHP page that we are going to develop.

Create a new folder named php under the project's root folder, and under php, create a new folder named db. Then, create a new file named db.php:

```php
<?php
$server = "127.0.0.1";
$user = "root";
$pass = "root";
$dbName = "sakila";

$mysqli = new mysqli($server, $user, $pass, $dbName);

/* check connection */
if ($mysqli->connect_errno) {
```

```
        printf("Connect failed: %s\n", mysqli_connect_error());
        exit();
    }
?>
```

The connection is pretty straightforward. We simply need to inform the `server` (which is going to be `localhost`), the databases `username` and `password`, and also the database `name` that we want to connect to. And at last, we can check whether the connection was done successfully or any error occurred.

> For more information about MySQLi, please visit `http://php. net/manual/en/book.mysqli.php`.

Login.php

Finally, we can create the `login.php` file under the `php/security` folder. So let's start implementing it, as follows:

```
require("../db/db.php"); // #1
require("PassHash.php"); // #2

session_start();         // #3

$userName = $_POST['user']; // #4
$pass = $_POST['password']; // #5

$userName = stripslashes($userName); // #6
$pass = stripslashes($pass);         // #7

$userName = $mysqli->real_escape_string($userName); // #8
$sql = "SELECT * FROM USER WHERE userName='$userName'"; // #9
```

First, we need to *require* the `db.php` file to connect to the database (#1). We are also going to `require` the `PassHash.php` file (#2). This file contains the `check_password` method, which will compare the password entered by the user with the one that is stored in the database (hashed).

Then, we start a session (#3)—we are going to store the username on the session later.

The next step is to retrieve the `user` and `password` values sent by the form submit method from Ext JS (#4 and #5).

The `stripslashes` function removes the backslashes from the given string (#6 and #7). For example, if the user value is `"Loiane\'s"`, the return of `stripslashes` will be `"Loiane's"`.

 These two steps help a little bit to ensure the security of the application; however, they are not enough. It is very important to *sanitize* the user input in the server so that we do not store or try to execute SQL statements with malicious input. For the purpose of this book, we will not apply this technique to keep the server-side code simple, so even though you do not know PHP, you will be able to read and understand the logic behind it and implement something similar in the server-side language of your choice. However, be aware that in real-world applications, it is very important to apply this step, especially if you are releasing your application to the general public (not for internal use only).

There is a project called **Open Web Application Security Project (OWASP)**, which is free and open source that provides a set of libraries and APIs to apply security techniques in your application. There are subprojects available for .NET, Java, and PHP, tutorials on how to avoid XSS attacks and SQL injections, and how to prevent other security vulnerabilities. For more information, please visit https:// www.owasp.org.

Then, we prepare the `$username` variables for the SQL statement using the function `real_escape_string` (#8), which escapes special characters in a string for use in a SQL statement.

Next, we prepare the SQL query that is going to be executed (#9). It is a simple `SELECT` statement that is going to return a result matching the given `username`.

Let's continue with the next part of the code:

```
if ($resultDb = $mysqli->query($sql)) { //#10

    $count = $resultDb->num_rows; //#11

    if($count==1){ //#12

        $record = $resultDb->fetch_assoc(); //#13

        //#14
        if (PassHash::check_password($record['password'],$pass)){
            $_SESSION['authenticated'] = "yes"; //#15
            $_SESSION['username'] = $userName; //#16
```

```
                   $result['success'] = true; //#17
                   $result['msg'] = 'User authenticated!'; //#18
            } else{
                   $result['success'] = false; //#19
                   $result['msg'] = 'Incorrect password.'; //#20
            }
        } else {
          $result['success'] = false; //#21
          $result['msg'] = 'Incorrect user or password.'; //#22
        }
        $resultDb->close(); //#23
    }
```

Next, we need to execute the SQL query, and we are going to store the result set in the resultDb variable (#10). Then, we are going to store data according to whether the result set returned any rows within the result set (#11).

Now comes the most important part of the code. We are going to verify whether the result set returned any rows. As we passed the username, the number of rows returned within the result set must be exactly 1. So, if the number of rows is equal to 1 (#12), we need to see whether the hashed password stored in the database matches the password entered by the user, but first, we need to retrieve this information from the record that was fetched from the database (#13).

The PassHash class is responsible for hashing the password, making it a little bit more secure to save the hashed password in the database (instead of the plain password), for decrypting the hashed password from the database ($record['password']), and for comparing to the password the user entered in the login page (#14).

 For now, you can get the complete code for PassHash.php from the source code downloaded from this book. In *Chapter 6, User Management*, we will go through it line by line.

If the password entered by the user and the decrypted hash password from the database match, it means the user can be authenticated. We are going to store the username of the authenticated user (#16) in the Session and also the information that the user is authenticated (#15).

We also need to prepare the result that we are going to return to Ext JS. We are going to send back two pieces of information: the first one is about whether the user is authenticated (#17) — in this case "true" — and we can also send back a message (#18).

If the password entered by the user and the one from the database do not match, then we also need to return something to Ext JS. The success is going to be `false` (#19), and we are going to return a message so that we can display to the user (#20).

If the `username` does not exist in the database (number of rows returned within the result set is different from 1), we are also going to send back a message to Ext JS saying the username or password informed by the user is incorrect (#22). Therefore, the `success` information will be `false` (#21).

Then, we need to close the result set (#23).

Now, the third and last part of the code of `login.php`:

```
$mysqli->close(); // #23

echo json_encode($result); // #24
```

We need to close the database connection (#23), and we are going to encode the `result` that we are going to send back to Ext JS in the JSON format (#24).

And now, the `login.php` code is complete. We cannot forget to add `<?php` before the preceding code.

Handling the return of the server – logged in or not?

We already took care of the server-side code. Now, we need to go back to the Ext JS code and handle the response from the server.

Success and failure in Ext JS has two different concepts. The form handles it in a way and the Ajax request handles it in a different one. This can be a little bit confusing, so we are going to implement requests to the server using the form submit (as this example) and also the Ajax request so that we can learn how to implement the proper code using both ways.

For the form, the server needs to return the `success: true` information so that the callback to be executed is a successful one. For failure, the server needs to return `success: false`, which can be returned if any communication error might have occurred (page nor found, exception on server, and so on). For the Ajax request, it does not matter whether `success` is `true` or `false`; it is going to execute the success callback; only if any communication error occurs is it going to execute the failure callback.

It is good to remember that the content type that the server needs to return to Ext JS is `application/json` and in the JSON format.

Let's handle the success callback first. In the event of success, the `onLoginSuccess` method is going to be executed. In this case, we want to close the **Login** window and display the main screen of the application, as follows:

```
onLoginSuccess: function(form, action) {
    this.getView().close();                    //#1
    Ext.create('Packt.view.main.Main'); //#2
}
```

The `Window` class has a method called `close` that we can call to close the window. The question is how to get the reference of the `login` window class. The `ViewController` class is directly bound to it, and we can reference the `Login` class itself by calling the method `getView` of the `ViewController` class (#1). Then, we can create the main screen by instantiating the `Main` class (#2) that was created by Sencha Cmd when we created the application. We are going to reuse this class to create our main screen.

 With the preceding approach, there is a flaw with the security of the code. A smart user who understands how Ext JS works can access the main page using a code similar to the preceding one even if the user is not authenticated. A more secure way would be to redirect to a page that holds the application (calling the `Main` class directly). As we are working with an example here, that is OK. However, keep that in mind when developing a real application!

In the event of failure, there are two cases that we need to handle: the first one is if the user was not authenticated because the user does not exist or because the password is incorrect. The second one is if there is any communication failure (for example, error 404). Our `onLoginFailure` method will look like the following code:

```
onLoginFailure: function(form, action) {

    var result = Ext.JSON.decode(action.response.responseText, true);
//#3

    if (!result){ //#4
        result = {};
        result.success = false;
```

```
            result.msg = action.response.responseText;
    }

    switch (action.failureType) {
        case Ext.form.action.Action.CLIENT_INVALID:   //#5
            Ext.Msg.show({
                title:'Error!',
                msg: 'Form fields may not be submitted with invalid
                values',
                icon: Ext.Msg.ERROR,
                buttons: Ext.Msg.OK
        });
        break;
        case Ext.form.action.Action.CONNECT_FAILURE:   //#6
          Ext.Msg.show({
                title:'Error!',
                msg: 'Form fields may not be submitted with invalid
                values',
                icon: Ext.Msg.ERROR,
                buttons: Ext.Msg.OK
        });
         break;
        case Ext.form.action.Action.SERVER_INVALID:   //#7
            Ext.Msg.show({
                title:'Error!',
                msg: result.msg,   //#8
                icon: Ext.Msg.ERROR,
                buttons: Ext.Msg.OK
        });
    }
},
```

Before we dive into the failure callback, note that both onLoginFailure and onLoginSuccess receive two parameters: form and action. Where do they come from?

If we take a look at the documentation, specifically on the submit method of the Form class (Ext.form.Panel), we will see that this submit method is calling the submit method from the class Ext.form.Basic (which is the class that actually contains all methods to handle form actions). If we take a look at the submit method from the Ext.form.Basic class (http://docs.sencha.com/extjs/5.0/5.0.1-apidocs/#!/api/Ext.form.Basic-method-submit), we will see a code similar to ours as an example. If we read the description, it says that this submit method is a shortcut to the doAction method from the same class.

If we open the documentation for this method (`http://docs.sencha.com/
extjs/5.0/apidocs/#!/api/Ext.form.Basic-method-doAction`), we will be able
to see the parameters we used for the form submit call (`url`, `success`, and `failure`
callbacks, among others) and also the parameters that both success and failure
callbacks receive — `form` and `action` — as follows:

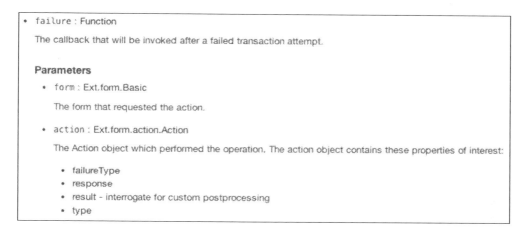

The `action` parameter contains four attributes inside it. For our failure callback, we
are interested in two of them: `failureType` and `response`. Let's analyze `response`
first. Add the following code (`console.log(action);`) to the first line of the failure
callback, and try to submit an incorrect user or password in the **Login** screen. Before
submitting to the server, open Chrome Developer Tools or Firebug to see what is
going to be logged, as follows:

Inside the response, note that there is `responseText` with JSON that we returned from the server. So, the first thing we are going to do is decode this JSON (#3). After we decode it, we will be able to access `result.success` and `result.msg`. We also need to be careful about one detail: we do not know what is going to be returned from the server. We always hope that is our `success` and `msg` information; however, we cannot be sure of it. If any other error is returned, it is also going to be returned inside `action.response.responseText`, and it cannot have the JSON format we are expecting (cannot be a JSON either). If this happens, `Ext.JSON.decode` will fail, and it will throw an exception. We can silence the exception (passing `true` as the second parameter to the `Ext.JSON.decode` function, and the `result` will have the value `null`), but we still need to handle it. And it is what we do when checking whether the `result` variable is `null` (#4). If it is null, we are instantiating the `result` and assigning some values (the `msg` will receive the error sent by the server).

After that, we will use the action `failureType` to see what type of error occurred. As `failureType` is code, Ext JS has some constants defined that are more developer friendly (`Ext.form.action.Action.CLIENT_INVALID`, for example). If `failureType` is `'client'` (#5), then we will display an error message in an alert pop up with an error icon. If a connection error happened with the server, then (#6) will handle it by displaying an error alert pop up as well. And if any exception or success is returned as false, (#7) will handle it. As we treated the return of the server to display the custom error message or any other message, we can simply display `result.msg` on the alert pop up (#8).

Try entering a wrong user or password again and see what happens. Change `login.php` url to `login.php` (or change to any other `url`), or inside the `db.php` file, enter the incorrect password to connect to the database to simulate an error, and here's what you will see:

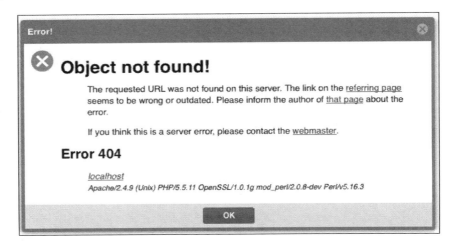

This way, we can handle all kind of server responses; not only the ones we are waiting for, but also any exceptions!

Reusing code by creating a Util class

Note that in (#5), (#6), and (#7) we are using the same error alert pop up, so code is repeated. Alert errors like this are used in different places of the application. As we are going to handle more Ajax requests and form submits in other screens of the application as well, the code in (#3) and (#4) will be repeated as well. For this reason, we can create a Util class that will encapsulate this code and provide us with the means to reuse it. Besides the reuse pro, it is also good to establish a pattern to be followed by the application, such as working out the JSON format that the server needs to return to Ext JS. This will make the application more organized, and it is also good when working in a team (usually each developer has their own pattern that they like to follow, and this way, we follow the same pattern for the same application, and it will not look as though it was implemented by different developers).

So let's go ahead and create our first Util class. We will name it Packt.util.Util. For this reason, we are going to create a new file named Util.js, and we are also going to create a new folder named util under the app folder, as follows:

```
Ext.define('Packt.util.Util', {

    statics : { //#1

        decodeJSON : function (text) { //#2
            var result = Ext.JSON.decode(text, true);
            if (!result){
                result = {};
                result.success = false;
                result.msg = text;
            }

            return result;
        },

        showErrorMsg: function (text) { //#3
            Ext.Msg.show({
                title:'Error!',
                msg: text,
                icon: Ext.Msg.ERROR,
                buttons: Ext.Msg.OK
```

```
        });
      }
    }
  });
```

All methods will be inside the `statics` declaration (#1). As we learned in *Chapter 1, Sencha Ext JS Overview*, we can simply call `Packt.util.Util.decodeJSON` for example, without needing to instantiate the `Packt.util.Util` class. The `decodeJSON` method (#2) contains the code to handle the JSON decoding, and the method `showErrorMsg` (#3) contains the code to display an error pop up alert with the content passed in the text parameter.

 Static methods do not require an instance of the class to be called. It is a concept of object-oriented programming.

Let's rewrite the `onLoginFailure` method by using the `Util` class, as follows:

```
onLoginFailure: function(form, action) {

    var result =
Packt.util.Util.decodeJSON(action.response.responseText);

    switch (action.failureType) {
        case Ext.form.action.Action.CLIENT_INVALID:
            Packt.util.Util.showErrorMsg('Form fields may not be
            submitted with invalid values');
            break;
        case Ext.form.action.Action.CONNECT_FAILURE:
        Packt.util.Util.showErrorMsg(action.response.responseText);
            break;
        case Ext.form.action.Action.SERVER_INVALID:
            Packt.util.Util.showErrorMsg(result.msg);
    }
},
```

Instead of 36 lines of code, now we have only 15, and the readability is better as well! In case we need to maintain this code, we can make the changes in the `Util` class, and the changes will be applied everywhere in the code that the class is being used! Best practices make our code really cool!

One last detail: we need to add the `Packt.util.Util` class in the `requires` declaration of the `ViewController` class as well:

```
requires: [
    'Packt.util.Util'
],
```

This is because of the dynamic loading we discussed earlier in this chapter. If we try to execute the preceding code without having the `Util` class loaded, we can get an error.

Enhancing the Login screen

Our **Login** screen is done. However, there are some enhancements we can apply to it to make it even better and also offer a better experience to the user.

The following list details the enhancements that we are going to apply in our **Login** screen:

- Apply a loading mask while authenticating
- Submit the form when the user presses *Enter*
- Displaying a Caps Lock warning message

Applying a loading mask on the form while authenticating

Sometimes, when the user clicks on the **Submit** button, there can be some delay while waiting for the server to send back the response. Some users will be patient, while some others will not. The ones that are not very patient will be able to click on the **Submit** button again, and this means making another request to the server. We can avoid this behavior by applying a loading mask to the **Login** window while awaiting the response.

First, we need to add the following code right before the `form.submit` call (inside the `doLogin` method):

```
this.getView().mask('Authenticating... Please wait...');
```

This will apply the mask to the **Login** screen.

Then, on the first line inside the `onLoginSuccess` and `onLoginFailure` functions, we need to add the following line of code:

```
this.getView().unmask();
```

And this will remove the mask from the **Login** window.

If we try to execute the code, we will have the following output:

Notice that the Login screen is not reachable and the user cannot click on the buttons again until the server sends back a response and removes the mask.

Form submit on Enter

For some forms, especially for the **Login** form, it is very natural for people to hit *Enter* when they are ready. This behavior is not automatic for Ext JS; therefore, we have to implement it.

The `textfield` component has an event to handle special keys, such as *Enter*. This event is called `specialkey`, and it is the one that we are going to listen to in our login controller. As we want to listen to this event for both text fields we have (**User** and **Password**), we can add the following code inside the defaults of the form from the **Login** window:

```
listeners: {
    specialKey: 'onTextFieldSpecialKey'
}
```

Next, we need to implement the `onTextFieldSpecialKey` method inside the `ViewController` class as well, as follows:

```
onTextFieldSpecialKey: function(field, e, options){
    if (e.getKey() === e.ENTER) {
        this.doLogin();
    }
},
```

First, we are going to verify that the key pressed by the user is *Enter*. If positive, we call the `doLogin` method we implemented earlier. Then, the form validation will be done and if the form is valid, it will try to log in. This will be the same as clicking on the **Submit** button.

Caps Lock warning message

The last enhancement we will apply to the form is the **Caps Lock** message. Sometimes the *Caps Lock* key is active, and when we input the password, we can input the correct password, but the system will say it is incorrect because it is case sensitive; warning the user about this is a nice thing to do.

The following screenshot presents the final result of the **Caps Lock** warning implementation:

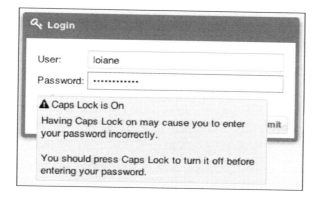

As you can see in the preceding screenshot, we will display the warning as a tooltip. So the first thing we need to do is go back to the `Application.js` launch function, and on the first line, we need to add the following code:

```
Ext.tip.QuickTipManager.init();
```

An alternative is using the configuration `enableQuickTips: true` inside `Aplication.js` as well. You can use either one, and the result will be the same.

Without the preceding code, the tooltips will not work in the application.

Ext JS has two concepts of tooltips. The first one is the Tooltip class, which does not have a built-in method of automatically populating the tooltip's text based on the target element; you must either configure a fixed HTML value for each tooltip instance or implement custom logic (inside an event listener). The second one is the QuickTip class, which automatically populates and configures a tooltip based on specific DOM attributes of each target element. Tooltips are enabled by default. QuickTips are managed by the QuickTipManager, which requires to be manually initiated.

The event that we are going to listen to is the keypress event, and we are only going to listen to this event fired by the password field. By default, the textfield component does not fire this event because it is a little bit heavy with regard to performance. As we want to listen to this event, we need to add a configuration (enableKeyEvents) to the password field (inside the view/login/Login.js file):

```
id: 'password',
enableKeyEvents: true,
listeners: {
    keypress: 'onTextFieldKeyPress'
}
```

We also need to add an id value to this field. Later, we will discuss the importance of avoiding using id in the components (since it is not a good practice), but in this case, there is nothing we can do about it. This is because when creating the Tooltip class, we need to set a target (in this case, the password field), and this target only accepts the id of the component, and not itemId.

Before we add the code to the Controller, we need to create the Tooltip class. We are going to create a new view called Packt.view.login.CapsLockTooltip, so we need to create a file named CapsLockTooltip.js under the app/view/login folder:

```
Ext.define('Packt.view.login.CapsLockTooltip', {
    extend: 'Ext.tip.QuickTip',

    xtype: 'capslocktooltip',

    target: 'password',
    anchor: 'top',
    anchorOffset: 0,
    width: 300,
    dismissDelay: 0,
    autoHide: false,
    title: '<div class="fa fa-exclamation-triangle"> Caps Lock is On</
div>',
```

```
      html: '<div>Having Caps Lock on may cause you to enter ' +
          'your password incorrectly.</div><br/>' +
          '<div>You should press Caps Lock to turn it off ' +
          'before entering your password.</div>'
});
```

In `Packt.view.login.CapsLockTooltip`, we declare some configurations that are going to set the behavior of the `Tooltip` class. For example, we have the following:

- `target`: This has the `id` value of the `password` field.

- `anchor`: This indicates that the tip should be anchored to a particular side of the target element (the `password id` field), with an arrow pointing back at the target.

- `anchorOffset`: This is a numeric value (in pixels) used to offset the default position of the anchor arrow. In this case, the arrow will be displayed 60 pixels after the tooltip box beginning.

- `width`: This is the numeric value (in pixels) to represent the `width` of the tooltip box.

- `dismissDelay`: This is the delay value (in milliseconds) before the tooltip automatically hides. As we do not want the tooltip to be automatically hidden, we set the value to `0` (zero) to disable it.

- `autoHide`: Set it to `true` to automatically hide the tooltip after the mouse exits the target element. And as we do not want it, we set it to `false`.

- `title`: This is the title text to be used as the title of the tooltip.

- `html`: This is the HTML fragment that will be displayed in the tooltip body.

Note that on the title, we added a class to the `<div>` tag. This will display a warning icon from Font Awesome that we configured earlier.

 To see all icons from Font Awesome that are available to be used in the application, please visit `http://fortawesome.github.io/ Font-Awesome/cheatsheet/`.

And at last, we need to make some changes in the `ViewController` class. First, in the `requires` declaration, we will add the `CapsLockTooltip` class:

```
requires: [
    'Packt.view.login.CapsLockTooltip',
    'Packt.util.Util'
],
```

Next, we are going to implement the `onTextFieldKeyPress` method, as follows:

```
onTextFieldKeyPress: function(field, e, options){

    var charCode = e.getCharCode(),
        me = this;

    if((e.shiftKey && charCode >= 97 && charCode <= 122) ||  //#2
        (!e.shiftKey && charCode >= 65 && charCode <= 90)){

        if(me.capslockTooltip === undefined){                    //#3
            me.capslockTooltip = Ext.widget('capslocktooltip'); //#4
        }

        me.capslockTooltip.show(); //#5

    } else {

        if(me.capslockTooltip !== undefined){  //#6
            me.capslockTooltip.hide();          //#7
        }

    }

},
```

First, we need to get the `code` of the key that the user pressed (#1). Then, we need to verify that the *Shift* key is pressed and if the user pressed one of the small alphabet keys (a-z), or if the *Shift* key is not pressed and the user pressed one of the capital alphabet keys (A-Z) (#2). If the result of this verification is true, this means that the *Caps Lock* is active. If you want to check the values of each key, you can go to `http://www.asciitable.com/`.

If the *Caps Lock* is active, we will verify that there is a reference of the `CapsLockTooltip` class (#3). If there is not, we will create a reference using its `xtype` (#4) and store it in a variable named `capslockTooltip`. This variable will be created as part of the `ViewController` class, so if this method is executed again, we can access it. Then, we display it by executing the method shown (#5).

If the *Caps Lock* is not active, we need to verify that there is a reference to the `CapsLockTooltip` class (#6). If positive, we will `hide` the tooltip because the *Caps Lock* is not active.

The Caps Lock warning code is now complete. We can save the project and test it.

Summary

In this chapter, we covered the details on how to implement a login page step by step. We covered how to create the login View and the `Login ViewController` class. We applied client validations on the form to make sure we send acceptable data to the server. We covered how to do a basic login using PHP, and we covered important concepts of how to handle the data that the server is going to send back to Ext JS.

We learned about some enhancements that we can apply to the **Login** screen, such as submitting the form when the user hit *Enter*, displaying a Caps Lock warning in the password field, and also how to apply a load mask on the form while it is sending data and waiting for information from the server.

We also added support to Font Awesome that will be used throughout our project.

In the next chapter, we will continue to work on the **Login** screen. We will learn how to add the multilingual capability and also implement the Logout and Session Monitor capabilities.

4

The Logout and Multilingual Capabilities

In this chapter, we are going to implement the multilingual capability of the system. This feature will allow the system to display the translation of the labels according to the language selected by the user (using some HTML5 features as well).

We will also learn how to implement the logout capability so that the user can end the session, and also for security reasons, we will learn how to implement a session timeout warning for the user, in the case of inactivity (not using the mouse or keyboard for a while).

Also, after the user is authenticated, we need to display the application. In this chapter, we will learn how to implement the base of the application.

So, in this chapter, we will cover:

- The base of the application
- The logout capability
- Activity monitoring and session timeout warnings
- Structuring the application to receive the multilingual capability
- Creating the change language component
- Handling the change language component at runtime

While we cover all the application capabilities, we will cover some Ext JS components as well.

The base of the application – view/main/Main.js

When we implemented the `success` function in the **Submit** button listener on the login controller, we mentioned the `Packt.view.main.Main` class. We are going to reuse this class (it was automatically created by Sencha Cmd when we created the project) as the base of our application. Before we start with the hands-on approach, let's take a look at what is going to be the result of the application by the end of this chapter:

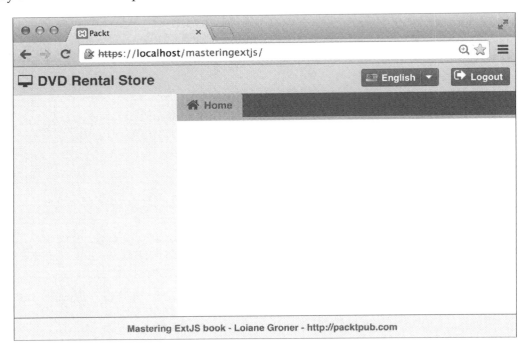

The Viewport

Whenever we construct an application entirely with Ext JS (because we do have the option of using a single component rendered to a `<div>` tag if we want to, in a manner similar to what is done in jQuery), we need to use a component that is going to be the base of the application. This component is the Viewport. The Viewport is a specialized container representing the viewable application area (the browser viewport). The Viewport renders itself to the document body, and automatically sizes itself to the size of the browser viewport and manages window resizing. There might only be one Viewport created in an application.

Before we create the Viewport, if we click on the **Submit** button of the **Login** screen, we will see a grayish screen, even though we are calling `Ext.create('Packt.view.main.Main');` inside the `LoginController` class. This means `Packt.view.main.Main` is being created, but nothing is being displayed on the screen. This is because the `Main` class is not being rendered as a child of any component, and it is also not being rendered to the HTML body. But we are going to change this behavior by changing it to a Viewport.

Open the `app/view/main/Main.js` file. In the second line of code, you will find the following snippet:

```
extend: 'Ext.container.Container'
```

The `Main` class that was created by Sencha Cmd is extending the `Container` component. The `Container` component is the simplest container component in the Ext JS API. It supports adding and removing items to it, and it is also the parent class to many other components, such as Panel, Window, and TabPanel. We are going to change `Ext.container.Container` to `Ext.container.Viewport` so that we can use the `Main` class as the base class of our application. Save the code, refresh the browser, and give it a try. The next time you click on the **Submit** button, you should see the original code created by Sencha Cmd after you are logged in.

Using the Viewport plugin

Extending the `Ext.container.Viewport` class is the classic and traditional way of having a Viewport in Ext JS applications. Ext JS 5 introduces a new way of using a Viewport by using the Viewport plugin (`Ext.plugin.Viewport`).

 To learn more about Ext JS plugins, please read `http://www.sencha.com/blog/advanced-plugin-development-with-ext-js/`.

To use the plugin, first roll back the changes we made in the preceding topic (the `Main` class will continue to extend `Ext.container.Container`) and add the following code after the `extend` code:

```
Ext.define('Packt.view.main.Main', {
    extend: 'Ext.container.Container',

    plugins: 'viewport',

    xtype: 'app-main',
```

Using the `plugins` configuration has the same result as extending the `Viewport` class. This plugin transforms any component into a Viewport, making it fill all the available space in the browser. The advantage of this plugin is that we can still reuse this class in other contexts, for example, inside a window.

We know that the **ptype** (plugin type) of the Viewport plugin is **viewport** by accessing the documentation:

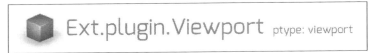

 Always remember that the documentation needs to be your best friend while developing Ext JS applications!

Organizing the main screen using the Border layout

As we learned in *Chapter 1, Sencha Ext JS Overview*, the Border layout can be used to organize the children of a parent container into five regions: north, south, west, east, and center.

The center region is the only one that is mandatory to have. The other ones are optional. Looking at the following screenshot, we can see that we are going to organize our main screen into four regions: **center**, **north**, **south**, and **west**:

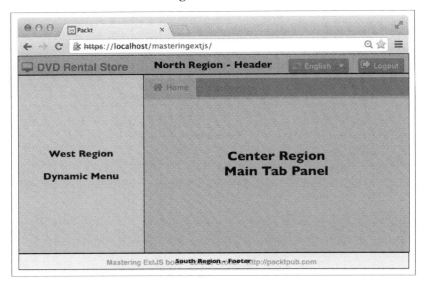

Let's take a look at the `items` configuration of the `Main` class (you can replace the code that was generated by Sencha Cmd with the following code):

```
items: [{
    region: 'center',    // #1
    xtype: 'mainpanel'
},{
    xtype: 'appheader', // #2
    region: 'north'
},{
    xtype: 'appfooter', // #3
    region: 'south'
},{
    xtype: 'container', // #4
    region: 'west',
    width: 200,
    split: true
}]
```

In the `center` region, we have `mainpanel` (#1). In *Chapter 5, Advanced Dynamic Menu*, we are going to create a dynamic menu that will give the options to the user to open the screens the user is entitled to. Each screen the user opens will be created as a tab in `mainpanel`. We will create it in a minute.

In the `north` region, we have the header (#2), and in the `south` region, we have the footer (#3). We will also work on them in a minute.

In the `west` region, we have `container` (#4), which we will use in the next chapter to render the dynamic menu. For now, we will leave the space reserved for it.

It is important to know that for the `center` region, we do not need to specify `width` or `height`. The container that is being rendered in the `center` region is going to use whatever space is left in the Border layout. For the `south` and `north` regions, you are required to specify `height`. We will do this when we create `Header` and `Footer`. The `south` and `north` regions are going to use all the available horizontal space that is available in the screen — limited by `height` — which is why `width` is not required. For the `west` and `east` regions, it is required to specify `width`. As we are only using the `west` region, we specified `200` pixels (#4).

Creating the main TabPanel component

We need to create the mainpanel component that we are using in the center region of the Main class. To do so, we are going to create a new file named Panel.js inside the app/view/main folder, and we are going to write the following code inside it:

```
Ext.define('Packt.view.main.Panel', { // #1
    extend: 'Ext.tab.Panel',           // #2
    xtype: 'mainpanel',                 // #3

    activeTab: 0,                       // #4

    items: [
        {
            xtype: 'panel',                        // #5
            closable: false,                       // #6
            iconCls: 'fa fa-home fa-lg tabIcon',   // #7
            title: 'Home'          // #8
        }
    ]
});
```

As usual, we will start with the name of the class. The class name convention is *app namespace* + *folder* (inside app) + *filename* (without the .js extension), which will result in Packt.view.main.Panel (#1). The main.Panel class is extending the TabPanel component (#2).

In line #3, we have xtype of the main.Panel class. This is the xytpe class we used to instantiate this class inside the Main class. In line #4, we have the activeTab configuration. When we set a tab to active, the TabPanel component is going to display the contents of the tab, and it is also going to highlight it.

As we learned in *Chapter 1, Sencha Ext JS Overview*, the TabPanel component is a container that has tabs as children organized by the Card layout, which means that the user will see the content of one active tab at a time. Each child declared inside the items configuration is an instance of the tab class (Ext.tab.Tab), and it can be of any type as we have in line #5. So as not to display an empty screen, we are displaying a 'Home' tab (#8) that is a panel (#5), which means it can have toolbars and other components inside it as well. This Home tab cannot be closed (#6); otherwise, the user will see a blank space in the middle of the main screen, and we do not want that. We are also setting a Font Awesome icon in the format of home in line #7 for it to look prettier.

You can use this **Home** tab to display announcements or to behave like a dashboard, where the user will see a summary of all the pending tasks.

Creating the footer

The next step is creating the footer of the main screen. We are going to create a new file named `Footer.js` inside `app/view/main` with the following code inside it:

```
Ext.define('Packt.view.main.Footer', {
    extend: 'Ext.container.Container',    //#1
    xtype: 'appfooter',                   //#2

    cls: 'app-footer',                    //#3

    height: 30,                           //#4

    layout: 'center',                     //#5

    items: [
        {
            xtype: 'component',              //#6
            width: 350,                      //#7
            componentCls: 'app-footer-title', //#8
            bind: {
                html: '{footer}'             //#9
            }
        }
    ]
});
```

`Footer` is going to extend from the `Container` class (#1). The `Container` class is the lightest component that we can create that can have items inside it. We should give preference to use it whenever possible. We will discuss this in greater detail later. Then, we declare the `xtype` class (#2), which is the alias we are using to instantiate this class in the `Main` class.

 Always remember that the convention for aliases (`xtype`) is to use all letters in lowercase. If you would like to, you can separate words with "-" (a hyphen) depending on your personal preference.

If we look at the first image of this chapter, we will note that the footer has a top border. We add a style on line #3 that adds this border to the footer. The `cls` configuration allows us to add extra CSS to a component in Ext JS. It is available to all components. We will add the style to our CSS in a minute.

As we are declaring Footer in the south region of the Main class, you are required to set the height parameter. We can do this inside the Footer class or inside the Main class when declaring the south region. In this case, we are setting it inside the Footer class (#4).

Inside the Footer class, we want to have only one component in this example, which is text (you can use a copyright message), and we are going to display it using HTML. We also want this text to be centered. For this reason, we can use the center layout (#5). To use the center layout, the parent container needs to have only one child component (because it inherits from the fit layout, which only supports a single child as well). It is also required to declare the width parameter of the child component (#7); in this case, the text we are going to display is approximately 350 pixels wide.

In Ext JS 4, the Center layout was used as a UX plugin shipped with the Ext JS SDK. In Ext JS 5, this layout was promoted to the native API, but it kept backwards compatibility. In the layout configuration, you can use center (introduced in Ext JS 5) and also keep using ux.center (from Ext JS 4) if you are migrating an application from Ext JS 4 to 5.

To render the HTML, we are going to use the lightest and simplest component as possible, which is component (#6). As we also want to apply some CSS to our text, we are going to use the componentCls (#8) class, which is a CSS class that is added to a component's root-level element.

Note that there is no text declared anywhere inside the Footer class. Instead, we are binding the html configuration to a value (#9) named footer. This is also part of the new MVVM architecture that we are also going to use in this chapter. In the preceding chapter, we only used the View and ViewController classes for the login capability. In this chapter, we are going to use the complete feature: View, ViewController, and ViewModel from the MVVM architecture (Sencha Cmd already generated these classes when we created the project, so we better reuse them!). For now, keep in mind that this is part of the ModelView binding that we will dive into in the next topic.

A quick word about modular CSS

Let's discuss another way of adding CSS to our application. We already know that the best practice to add CSS to our application is to add using Sass inside the sass/etc folder as we did in the previous examples. However, there are some styles that we create to apply to specific components, and we are not going to reuse them throughout the application. Instead of adding these CSS styles to our all.scss file and having a big file that can give us a headache later if we need to maintain it, we can use a more modular CSS approach to create specific CSS for our Ext JS views.

Inside the `sass` folder, create a new folder named `src` (if it has not been created by Sencha Cmd automatically), and inside `src`, create a new folder named `view`. Inside `view`, create a new folder named `main`. We will have the directory `sass/src/view/main`. Inside this directory, create a file named `Footer.scss` with the following content inside it:

```scss
$packt-footer-text-color: rgb(11, 103, 196); //#1

.app-footer-title {
  color: $packt-footer-text-color; //#2
  font-size: 12px;
  font-weight: bold;
}

.app-footer {
  border-top: 1px solid darken($packt-footer-text-color, 15); //#3
}
```

In line #1, we declare a Sass variable with a bluish color (the same blue color as the `TabPanel` background). We are reusing this variable in lines #2 and #3 in the styles we created to use in our `Footer` class.

 In line #3, we use the `darken` function from Sass, which accepts a color and a number from 0-100, the percentage to which we want to make the color darker. For more information, please refer to the Sass documentation at `http://goo.gl/JsAnVz`.

The `view/main/Footer.scss` file has the same path as the `view/main/Footer.js` file. Note that this way, it is easier to maintain the styles specific to the `Footer` class. We will do the same for the `Header` class in the next topic. We separate the CSS into modules for it to be easier to read and maintain, and when we do the build, all the CSS will be concatenated into a single production CSS file—this is called modular CSS. See, developing applications with Ext JS is not all about Ext JS; we can apply the knowledge from other frontend technologies as well!

Creating the Header class

Next, we are going to create the `Header` class. The `Header` class contains the logo of the application along with the application name, the dropdown that offers the translation capability, and the **Logout** button. To create the header, we are going to create a new file, `Header.js`, inside the `app/view/main` folder with the following code:

```javascript
Ext.define('Packt.view.main.Header', {
    extend: 'Ext.toolbar.Toolbar', //#1
```

```
    xtype: 'appheader',                //#2

    requires: [
        'Packt.view.locale.Translation' //#3
    ],

    ui: 'footer',                      //#4

    items: [{
            xtype: 'component',        //#5
            bind: {                    //#6
                html: '{appHeaderIcon}'
            }
        }, {
            xtype: 'component',
            componentCls: 'app-header-title', //#7
            bind: {                          //#8
                html: '{appName}'
            }
        }, {
            xtype: 'tbfill'            //#9
        }, {
            xtype: 'translation'       //#10
        }, {
            xtype: 'tbseparator'       //#11
        }, {
            xtype: 'button',           //#12
            itemId: 'logout',          //#13
            text: 'Logout',
            reference: 'logout',       //#14
            iconCls: 'fa fa-sign-out fa-lg buttonIcon', //#15
            listeners: {
                click: 'onLogout'  //#16
            }
        }
    ]
});
```

Our Header class is going to extend the Toolbar class (#1). The Toolbar class is usually used inside panels and its subclasses (grid, form, tree) to organize buttons, but it can also be used to hold other components as we are going to do in this example. We will cover more about toolbars in other chapters as well. We are also declaring an xtype class for the Header class that we are making a reference to in the Main class (#2).

Whenever we use an `xtype` class created by ourselves, Ext JS does not understand what component we are trying to instantiate. For this reason, we require the class we are referring to. For example, in line #3, we reference the class of the translation component we are instantiating using its `xtype` class in line #10. We are going to develop this component later in the chapter.

 Note that in the `Main` class, we did not use `requires` yet. We need to go back and add the required `Header`, `Footer`, and `main.Panel` classes.

The `ui` configuration allows us to use a specific theme for a component. The `Toolbar` component has the configuration `ui: 'footer'` (#4), which gives the toolbar a transparent background. The `footer` value is included in the Ext JS SDK, and it makes the toolbar transparent. We are going to create some custom `ui` configurations when we discuss themes later in this book.

The two first children items of the `Header` class are the icon (#5) and the application name. For the icon, we are going to use Font Awesome to display an icon in the format of a desktop. For the title of the application, we will use the same approach we used in the case of the `Footer` class. We are also using a `componentCls` configuration (#7) to style it. We get both values (icon-#6 and application name-#8) from the ViewModel, which we will cover in a minute.

The next item is a toolbar fill (#9). This component will align the `translation` (#10) and `logout` buttons (#13) to the right, filling the `Toolbar` class with space in the middle (between the application title and the buttons).

 Instead of `{ xtype: 'tbfill' }`, we could also use `'->'` as a shortcut.

We also have the `logout` button declared on line #12. We are going to assign `itemId` so that we can reference this button globally by the application. We will need it when we work with the session monitor capability. The `itemId` needs to be unique in its scope; in this case, it needs to be unique within this class, but it is going to be even better if it is unique at the application level.

As we are going to use the `ViewController` class to handle the logout, we will declare a `reference` (#14) to make it easier to retrieve the button reference inside the `ViewController` class, and we are also going to declare the listener (#16), which means that the `onLogout` function from the `ViewController` class is going to be executed when we click on the **Logout** button.

We are also setting an icon to the `Logout` button from Font Awesome (#15). By default, the icon will have the color black. The button text is white, and we want the icon to have the same color as the text. For this reason, we add a custom style (`buttonIcon`).

At last, we have the toolbar separator declared on line #11. This simply adds a separator ("|") between the buttons.

 Likewise, `tbfill`, the toolbar separator, also has a shortcut. Instead of `{ xtype: ' tbseparator' }`, we could also use `'-'`.

Creating the Header CSS

Just as we did with the `Footer` class, we are also going to create a filename, `Header.scss`, inside the `sass/view/main` folder with the following content inside it:

```
$packt-header-text-color: #2a3f5d;

.app-header-logo {
  color: $packt-header-text-color;
}

.app-header-title {
  padding: 5px 0 5px 3px;
  color: $packt-header-text-color;
  font-size: 18px;
  font-weight: bold;
}
```

The `app-header-logo` was created to customize the color of the icon to be the same as the application title. We are using the Sass variable inside both styles. The text color of the title is a dark blue.

Customizing the Font Awesome icon colors

By default, the Font Awesome icons will be displayed in black. But we want some of the icons to have the same color as our theme. We can do this customization using CSS as well.

We have declared two styles to customize the Font Awesome icons until now. The first one was inside the `Panel` class (`tabIcon`), and the second one is the **Logout** button (`buttonIcon`). So we also need to add these styles to our CSS. To follow the modular CSS approach, let's create a new file, `iconColors.scss`, under `sass/etc` with the following content:

```
$packt-button-icon-color: #fff;
$packt-tab-icon-color: rgb(11, 103, 196);

.tabIcon {
  color: $packt-tab-icon-color;
}

.buttonIcon {
  color: $packt-button-icon-color;
}
```

 We will get used to using Sass variables to make our life easier if we decide to customize the Ext JS theme later!

Then, all we need to do is import this file in the `all.scss` file:

```
@import "fontAwesome/font-awesome";
@import "iconColors";
```

The main screen and MVVM

Now, it's time to put everything together. Let's take a look at how the `Main` class looks with the complete code:

```
Ext.define('Packt.view.main.Main', {
    extend: 'Ext.container.Container',
    plugins: 'viewport',
    xtype: 'app-main',

    requires: [ //#1
        'Packt.view.main.Header',
        'Packt.view.main.Footer',
        'Packt.view.main.Panel',
        'Packt.view.main.MainController',
        'Packt.view.main.MainModel'
    ],
```

```
        controller: 'main', //#2
        viewModel: {
            type: 'main' //#3
        },

        layout: {
            type: 'border'
        },

        items: [{
            region: 'center',
            xtype: 'mainpanel'
        },{
            xtype: 'appheader',
            region: 'north'
        },{
            xtype: 'appfooter',
            region: 'south'
        },{
            xtype: 'container',
            region: 'west',
            width: 200,
            split: true
        }]
    });
```

We need to add the `requires` declaration of all the classes we created (and we are referencing them by their `xtype` classes) and also the `Main` ViewModel and `Main` ViewController class that were already created by Sencha Cmd.

The `controller` (#2) and `viewModel` (#3) declarations were already added by Sencha Cmd when we created the project. We are simply reusing them by referencing their types.

The main ViewModel

If we open the `MainModel.js` file inside the `app/view/main` folder, we will see some content inside it already. We are going to add more content to it, and the file is going to look as follows:

```
Ext.define('Packt.view.main.MainModel', { //#1
    extend: 'Ext.app.ViewModel', //#2

    alias: 'viewmodel.main', //#3
```

```
data: {
    name: 'Packt', //#4
    appName: 'DVD Rental Store', //#5
    appHeaderIcon: '<span class="fa fa-desktop fa-lg app-
    header-logo">', //#6
    footer: 'Mastering ExtJS book - Loiane Groner -
    http://packtpub.com' //#7
    }
});
```

Let's start with the name of the class (#1). The naming convention for ViewModel suggested by Sencha is the name of the view (Main) + "Model", resulting in MainModel. A ViewModel extends from the ViewModel class (#2) introduced in Ext JS 5, along with the MVVM architecture. The alias (#3) of a ViewModel is defined by "viewmodel." + the name of the type we want to assign. In this case, Sencha already created this class for us with the type main. That is why we can reference this alias in the View class using the following code:

```
viewModel: {
    type: 'main'
}
```

The data configuration allows us to populate values in the ViewModel class. The name field (#4) was created by Sencha Cmd, so we are going to keep it (you can remove it if you want). The appName (#5) and appHeaderIcon (#6) properties are being used by Header and footer (#7) is being used by the Footer class.

MainModel is bound to the Main class (View). Because Header and Footer are items of the Main component, they can also reference MainModel.

This is the simplest way in which we can create the ViewModel class, with prepopulated data. We will provide other advanced examples throughout this book, but we need to start with baby steps!

 For more information about ViewModel, data binding, and how to bind different data types, please read the following Sencha guide: http://goo.gl/qta6kH.

Logout capability

As the user has the option to log in to the application, the user can also log out from it. Inside the Header class, we have already declared the logout button. The only thing pending is to implement the listener inside MainController.

As the `MainController` class was created by Sencha Cmd, we are reusing it. The file already has some code in it. Let's remove any listener created by Sencha. `MainController` will look like this:

```
Ext.define('Packt.view.main.MainController', {
    extend: 'Ext.app.ViewController',

    requires: [
        'Ext.MessageBox'
    ],

    alias: 'controller.main',

    //we will insert code here
});
```

In the `Header` class, we declared the `logout` button, its reference, and its listener. So we need to implement the `onLogout` function, as follows:

```
onLogout: function(button, e, options){

    var me = this;          //#1
    Ext.Ajax.request({
        url: 'php/security/logout.php',  //#2
        scope: me,                       //#3
        success: 'onLogoutSuccess',      //#4
        failure: 'onLogoutFailure'       //#5
    });
},
```

The `me` (#1) variable makes a reference to `this`, which is the `MainController` class. We will make an Ajax call (#2) to `php/security/logout.php` (we will create this file soon). We will handle the `success` (#4) and `failure` (#5) callbacks in separate functions that are declared inside the `MainController` class as well. That is why the scope is set to the `MainController` class (#3) itself.

 We could declare the `success` and `failure` callbacks directly inside the Ajax request. But then, our code will be very long, which would decrease its readability. This way, the code stays organized and easier to read. This is always a best practice to be followed.

Handling the logout on the server

To handle the logout capability on the server, we will create a new PHP page named
`logout.php` under the `php/security` folder. The code is very simple:

```php
<?php

session_start(); // #1

$_SESSION = array(); // #2

session_destroy(); // #3

$result = array(); // #4

$result['success'] = true;
$result['msg'] = 'logout';

echo json_encode($result); // #5
```

First, we need to resume the current session (#1), then we need to unset all of
the session variables (#2), and next we need to destroy the session (#3). Lastly,
we need to send the information back to Ext JS that the session has been destroyed
(#4 and #5).

Ajax request success versus failure

We have already taken care of the server-side code. Now, we need to go back to the
Ext JS code and handle the response from the server. But first, we need to understand
a very important concept that usually confuses most Ext JS developers.

In *Chapter 3, The Login Page*, we mentioned that the ways that the form submit and
Ajax requests in Ext JS handle the *success x failure* are a little different, and this is
what confuses most developers.

The `Ext.Ajax` class is responsible for Ajax requests done by Ext JS. If we look at the
documentation, this class has three events: `beforerequest`, `requestcomplete`, and
`requestexception`, which are explained as follows:

- The event `beforerequest` is fired before the request
- The event `requestcomplete` is fired when Ext JS is able to get a response
  from the server
- The `requestexception` event is fired when an HTTP error status is returned
  from the server

Now, let's go back to the `Ext.Ajax.request` call. We can pass some options to the request, including the `url` property we want to connect to, parameters, and other options including the `success` and `failure` functions. Now, this is where the misunderstanding begins. Some developers understand that if the action happened successfully on the server, we usually return `success = true` from the server. If something goes wrong, we return `success = false`. Then, on the `success` function, `success = true` is handled, and on the `failure` function, `success = false` is handled. This is *wrong*, and it is not how Ext JS Ajax requests work; however, *that is exactly how form requests work* (as we learned in *Chapter 3, The Login Page*). See how it gets confusing?

For Ext JS Ajax requests, `success` is when the server returns a response (`success` `true` or `false`; it does not matter), and `failure` is when the server returns an HTTP error status. This means that if the server was able to return a response, we will handle this response on the `success` function (and we will need to handle it whether the `success` information is `true` or `false`), and on the `failure` message, we need to inform the user that something went wrong and the user should contact the system administrator.

We will implement the `failure` callback function first. So, inside the `ViewController` class, we will add the following code:

```
onLogoutFailure: function(conn, response, options, eOpts){
    Packt.util.Util.showErrorMsg(conn.responseText);
},
```

What we are going to do is display an alert to the user with an error icon and an **OK** button with the HTTP status error information.

To reproduce an error so the `requestexception` event can be fired, we can rename the `logout.php` file to something else (for example, `logout_.php`) only for testing purposes. And then, we can execute the code, and we will have the following output:

And this is all we need for the `failure` function. Note that we are reusing the `Packt.util.Util` class that we developed in *Chapter 3, The Login Page,* in this chapter again! See how it is nice to reuse code?

> We are reusing code and saving some lines of duplicated code. We are also creating a pattern of how to handle a few things in our project. This is very important when working in a project, especially when working in a team. This way, the project will look like a single person and not that multiple people developed it, which is really good. This is also a best practice to be followed. Reusing code is also part of what is called *minimizing the payload size,* which is one of the best practices while developing with JavaScript and also a concern of web development. To learn more about this, please visit `https://developers.google.com/speed/docs/best-practices/payload`.

To make the code work, remove the following code from the `MainController` class:

```
requires: [
    'Ext.MessageBox'
],
```

Write the following code in the preceding code's position:

```
requires: [
    'Packt.util.Util'
],
```

Now, let's focus on the `success` callback function:

```
onLogoutSuccess: function(conn, response, options, eOpts){
    //#1
    var result = Packt.util.Util.decodeJSON(conn.responseText);

    if (result.success) { //#2
        this.getView().destroy(); //#3
        window.location.reload(); //#4
    } else {

        Packt.util.Util.showErrorMsg(result.msg); //#5
    }
}
```

The first thing we need to do is decode the JSON message (#1) that we received from the server. If we log the `conn` parameter sent to the `success` function (`console.log(conn)`), this will be the output we will get on the console:

```
▼ Object {request: Object, requestId: 2, status: 200, statusText: "OK", getResponseHeader: function…}
  ▶ getAllResponseHeaders: function () {
  ▶ getResponseHeader: function (header) {
  ▶ request: Object
    requestId: 2
    responseText: "{"success":true,"msg":"logout"}"
    responseXML: null
    status: 200
    statusText: "OK"
  ▶ __proto__: Object
```

The `conn.responseText` property is where the information we want to retrieve is present, the `success` and `msg` values. Recall that in *Chapter 3*, *The Login Page*, we discussed the possibility of `responseText` containing an exception other than the JSON we are expecting. So, for this reason, we are going to reuse the `decodeJSON` function we created (#1) so that we can properly handle any results.

In the case of `success` (#2), we are going to `destroy` the `Main` class (#3), which is our Viewport (this is good to release the browser's memory and make the objects available for the JavaScript garbage collector). As the Viewport contains all the other components of our application, it is going to destroy them as well. Then, we will reload the application displaying the **Login** screen again (#4).

If `success` is `false` (or any error occurred), we will display an error alert with the error message (#5).

Client-side activity monitor

Let's enhance our application a little bit more. It is very important to let the users know that web applications have a timeout and they cannot leave it open all day long—mainly for security reasons. Server-side languages also have a timeout. Once the user is logged in, the server will not be available forever. This is for security reasons. That is why we need to add this capability to our application as well.

We are going to use a plugin to do this. The plugin is called `Packt.util.SessionMonitor` and is based on the Activity Monitor plugin from the Sencha Market (`https://market.sencha.com/extensions/extjs-activity-monitor`). After an interval (a default of 15 minutes of inactivity), the plugin will display a message to the user asking whether the user wants to keep the session alive. If yes, then it will send an Ajax request to the server to keep the server session alive. If the user does not do anything after the message is displayed for 60 seconds, the application will logout automatically.

You can get the source code of this plugin from `https://github.com/loiane/masteringextjs/blob/master/app/util/SessionMonitor.js`. It works in Ext JS 4 and Ext JS 5.

At line 53 inside `Ext.ComponentQuery.query` at the preceding URL, we will change the `logout` button selector to `button#logout`, which is the selector we have for our `logout` button (that is why we created `itemId` for the `logout` button).

Also, we will change the `url` property of the Ajax request on line 42 to `php/sessionAlive.php` at the preceding URL.

If we want to change the inactivity interval, we only need to change the `maxInactive` configuration.

To start monitoring the session, we only need to add this line of code inside the `onLoginSuccess` method of `LoginController` right after we instantiate the `Main` class:

```
onLoginSuccess: function(form, action) {
    Ext.getBody().unmask();
    this.getView().close();
    Ext.create('Packt.view.main.Main');
    Packt.util.SessionMonitor.start();
}
```

We cannot forget to add `'Packt.util.SessionMonitor'` to requires in `LoginController` as well.

In the `php/sessionAlive.php` file, we will have the following code:

```
<?php
session_start();
```

That is only to keep the server session alive and also to reset the session timer back to 15 minutes.

If we run this code and wait for the inactivity time (15 minutes—of course we can change the `maxInactive` parameter to wait for less time), we will see a message like this one:

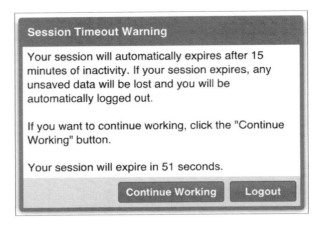

Ext JS does not provide this capability natively. But as we can see, it is very easy to implement, and we can reuse this plugin for all Ext JS projects that we work on.

The multilingual capability

Sometimes you want to ship the project or product that you are working on overseas, and so having the translation capability is very important. After all, not everyone understands or speaks the same language that you do. And this is what we are going to implement in this topic: a multilingual component that we can use to translate the labels of this project. So at the end of this topic, this is going to be our output:

The idea is to store the user language preference locally, so the next time the user loads the application, the preferred language will be automatically set. And when the user changes the language, the application needs to be reloaded, so the new translations can be loaded into the memory.

Creating the change language component

If we take a look at the screenshot we showed at the beginning of this topic, we can notice that the multilingual component is a button, and when we click on the arrow, a menu pops up with the available languages.

The button with the arrow is a split button component, which has a Menu, and each language option is a Menu Item of the Menu. So, let's go ahead and create a new class named `Packt.view.locale.Translation` containing the characteristics we described.

 Whenever we name a `View` class (also known as Ext JS widgets or components), it is nice to give a name that can quickly remind us what the class does. For example, by naming the class `locale.Translation`, we quickly know that the class provides capabilities localizing the application.

We need to create a new file named `Translation.js` under the `app/view/locale` folder with the following code inside it:

```
Ext.define('Packt.view.locale.Translation', {
    extend: 'Ext.button.Split',     //#1
    xtype: 'translation',           //#2

    menu: {                     //#3
        xtype: 'menu',      //#4
        items: [
            {
                xtype: 'menuitem', //#5
                iconCls: 'en',
                text: 'English'
            },
            {
                xtype: 'menuitem', //#6
                iconCls: 'es',
                text: 'Español'
            },
            {
```

```
                    xtype: 'menuitem', //#7
                    iconCls: 'pt_BR',
                    text: 'Português'
                }
            ]
        }
    });
```

So, the class that we created is extending from the split button class (#1). A split button class is one that provides a built-in drop-down arrow that can fire an event separately from the default click event of the button. Typically, this would be used to display a drop-down menu that provides additional options to the primary button action. And we are also assigning the xtype class to this class (#2) that we used to instantiate it in the Header class.

Then, on menu (#3) configuration, we need to create an instance of the menu class (#4) followed by menuitems of the menu class, which are going to represent each locale option. So we have: an option to translate to English (#5) — and it will also show the American flag (en); an option to translate to Spanish (#6) — and it will also show the flag of Spain (es); and also an option to translate to Portuguese (#7) — and it will also display the flag of Brazil (pt_BR).

We can add as many options as we need to. For each translate option, we only need to add new menuitems of the menu class.

Adding the CSS – country flags

The next step now is to add the CSS for iconCls, which we used in the translation component of the application CSS. To keep our code more organized (and leave room to add more languages and more flag icons if needed), we are going to create a new file named flagIcons.scss inside the sass/etc folder with the following content:

```
.pt_BR {
  background-image:url('images/app/flags/br.png') !important;
}

.en {
  background-image:url('images/app/flags/us.png') !important;
}

.es {
  background-image:url('images/app/flags/es.png') !important;
}
```

Note that the name of the style (pt_BR, en, and es) is the same as the iconCls property we used for each menuitem. This is very important.

Inside the all.scss file, we need to import this file we created. Add the following code on the second line (right after we imported the Font Awesome file):

```
@import "flagIcons";
```

But what about the icons? Font Awesome does not have flag icons. We are going to use the Flag set from FamFamFam (http://www.famfamfam.com/), which are free to use for any purpose (*Creative Commons License*). Create the folder flags under the directory resources/images/app, and copy and paste the flag icons. You might need to rename them to comply with the names we are using in this example.

Using the translation component

Now, the translation component is ready (only what is going to be displayed to the user). We are going to use the translation component in two places of our project: on the **Login** screen and before the **Logout** button on Header (which is already in place).

Let's add it to the **Login** screen. Open the Packt.view.login.Login class again. On the toolbar, we will add it as the first item so that it can look exactly as we showed in the screenshot at the beginning of this topic:

```
items: [
  {
      xtype: 'translation'
  },
  {
      xtype: 'tbfill'
  },
  //...
]
```

We cannot forget to add the class to the requires declaration of the **Login** screen class:

```
requires: [
    ' Packt.view.locale.Translation '
],
```

If we reload the application (do not forget to have `sencha app watch` executed on the terminal while we make all these changes), we are going to be able to see what we have developed until now.

Creating the multilingual files

We need to store the translations somewhere in our project. We are going to store the translations for each language on a JavaScript file inside the `resources/locale` folder. As we are going to use `iconCls` as the ID to load the translation files, we need to create three files: `en.js`, `es.js`, and `pt_BR.js`. Inside each file, we will create a JavaScript object named `translations`, and each attribute of this object will be a translation. All translation files must be the same; the only thing that will be different is the value of each attribute that will contain the translation.

For example, the following code is for the `en.js` file:

```
translations = {
    login: "Login",
    user: "User",
    password: "Password",

    cancel: "Cancel",
    submit: "Submit",
    logout: 'Logout',

    capsLockTitle: 'Caps Lock is On',
    capsLockMsg1: 'Having Caps Lock on may cause you to ',
    capsLockMsg2: 'enter your password incorrectly.',
    capsLockMsg3: 'You should press Caps Lock to turn it ',
    capsLockMsg4: 'off before entering your password.'
};
```

The following code is for `pt_BR.js`, which contains the Brazilian Portuguese translations:

```
translations = {
    login: "Login",
    user: "Usuário",
    password: "Senha",

    cancel: "Cancelar",
    submit: "Enviar",
    logout: 'Logout',
```

```
    capsLockTitle: 'Caps Lock está ativada',
    capsLockMsg1: 'Se Capslock estiver ativado, isso pode fazer ',
    capsLockMsg2: 'com que você digite a senha incorretamente.',
    capsLockMsg3: 'Você deve pressionar a tecla Caps lock para ',
    capsLockMsg4: 'desativá-la antes de digitar a senha.'
};
```

The following code is the `es.js` code, which contains the Spanish translations:

```
translations = {
    login: "Login",
    user: "Usuario",
    password: "Contraseña",

    cancel: "Cancelar",
    submit: "Enviar",
    logout: 'Logout',

    capsLockTitle:'Bloq Mayús está Activado',
    capsLockMsg1:'Tener el Bloq Mayús activado puede causar que ',
    capsLockMsg2:'introduzca su contraseña de forma incorrecta.',
    capsLockMsg3:'Usted debe presionar Bloq Mayús para apagarlo ',
    capsLockMsg4:'antes de escribir la contraseña.'
};
```

As we can see, the files are the same; however, the translation is different. As the application grows, we will add more translations to it, and it is a good practice to maintain the files organized in the same way to facilitate changing any translation in the future.

Applying the translation on the application's components

To apply the translations on the components that we have developed until now is very simple: we need to use the `translations` dictionary we created instead of the string that is going to represent the label.

For example, in the `Packt.view.view.Login` class, we have the title of the window, the `fieldLabel` of the `username` and `password`, and the text of the **Cancel** and **Submit** buttons. The labels are hardcoded, and we want to get the translation from the translation files.

So, we need to replace the `title` of the :**Login** window with the following:

```
title: translations.login,
```

We need to replace the `fieldLabel` of `username textfield` with the following:

```
fieldLabel: translations.user,
```

We need to replace the `fieldLabel` of `password textfield` with the following:

```
fieldLabel: translations.password,
```

We need to replace the `text` of the **Cancel** button with the following:

```
text: translations.cancel
```

We need to replace the `text` of the **Submit** button with the following:

```
text: translations.submit
```

And so on. We can also apply the translation for the **Logout** button and also to the `CapsLockTooltip` class.

HTML5 local storage

Our idea for the `translate` component is to store the language preference of the user somewhere. We could use cookies for this, but what we want is very simple, and cookies are included with every HTTP request. We want to store this information for the long term and also use something that can be persisted beyond a page refresh or the fact that the user closed the browser. And the perfect option is to use local storage, one of the new features of HTML5.

Ext JS has support for local storage; it can be used with **LocalStorageProxy**, but we need something simpler, and using the HTML5 feature itself on the code is simpler. And it also demonstrates that we can use other APIs along with the Ext JS API.

Local storage is not supported by every browser; it is only supported by IE 8.0+, Firefox 3.5+, Safari 4.0+, Chrome 4.0+, Opera 10.5+, iPhone 2.0+, and Android 2.0+. We will build a nice page warning the user to upgrade the browser later on in this book. We will also use other HTML5 features along with Ext JS in other screens as well. So, for now, we need to know that this code, which we will implement now, does not work on every browser.

 For more information about HTML5 storage, please visit `http://diveintohtml5.info/storage.html`.

We want this code to be loaded right before we instantiate the Ext JS application. So, for this reason, we are going to add it right before `Ext.define('Packt.Application', {` in the `app/Application.js` file:

```
function loadLocale(){

    var lang = localStorage ? (localStorage.getItem('user-lang') ||
'en') : 'en',
        file = Ext.util.Format.format("resources/locale/{0}.js",
lang);

    Ext.Loader.loadScript({url: file, onError: function(){
        alert('Error loading locale file. Please contact system
administrator.');
    }});
}

loadLocale(); //#1
```

So, first, we are going to verify that `localStorage` is available. If it is available, we are going to check whether there is an item named `user-lang` stored on `localStorage`; if not, English will be the default language. Even if `localStorage` is not available, English will be set as the default language.

Then, we create a variable named `file` that is going to receive the path of the translation file that must be loaded by the application.

 Ext JS has a class, `Ext.util.Format`, that contains a static method format that concatenates the string and the values passed as tokens, which in this case is `lang`. It is cleaner than doing manual string concatenation in JavaScript.

After we have the `url` formatted, we are going to load it using `Ext.Loader`. The `loadScript` method loads the specified script URL and calls the supplied callbacks (if any). It accepts `onLoad` and `onError` callbacks. In our case, there is no need for a success callback (`onLoad`). If there is any error while loading the locale file, the application will not load, so the `onError` callback is interesting and needed in this case so that the user can contact support in the event of an error (try renaming the `en.js` file to simulate an error).

To avoid creating global variables (since this is not a good JavaScript practice), we wrapped our code in a function. Therefore, we need to call the function (#1) right before `Ext.define('Packt.Application'`.

By the time our application is loaded, it will have all the translations available.

Handling change language in real time

Now comes the final part of the code of the `translation` component. When the user selects a different language, we need to reload the application so that the `loadLocale` function is executed again and load the new language chosen by the user.

To do so, we will create a new Controller in our application just to handle the translation component. The question here is: do we use MVC (which we will cover in the next chapter) or MVVM now? The answer depends on your personal preference. For this capability, we will continue using MVVM, or better, the ViewController, for a simple reason: both files (`TranslationController.js` and `Translation.js`) are located in the same directory (`app/view/locale`). And this means that it is easier to copy and paste this component to use it in other projects (we can copy the `locale` folder altogether).

So we need to create a new class named `Packt.view.locale.TranslationController`, and to create this class, we need to create a new file named `TranslationController.js` under the `app/view/locale` folder. In this controller, we will need to listen to two events: one fired by the `translation` component itself and the other one fired by `menuitems`:

```
Ext.define('Packt.view.locale.TranslationController', {
    extend: 'Ext.app.ViewController',
    alias: 'controller.translation'
});
```

Let's go back to the `Translation.js` file and add `TranslationController` as the ViewController so that we can start listening to the events:

```
requires: [
    'Packt.view.locale.TranslationController'
],

controller: 'translation',
```

The split button has two events, which are the `click` (fired because it is a button) and the `arrowclick` events, fired when the user clicks on the arrow. We are not interested in either event. Inside the split button, there is a `Menu` class with `menuitems`, and each `menuitem` represents a locale file. The `MenuItem` component also fires the `click` event when clicked on. So we can add the `click` listener to each `MenuItem`—or even better, add a `defaults` configuration to `menu`, as follows (which is going to be applied to all items):

```
xtype: 'menu',
defaults:{
```

```
    listeners: {
        click: 'onMenuItemClick'
    }
},
```

Now, we can go back to `TranslationController` and implement the `onMenuItemClick` method, as follows:

```
onMenuItemClick: function(item, e, options){

    var menu = this.getView(); //#1

    menu.setIconCls(item.iconCls); //#2
    menu.setText(item.text);        //#3

    localStorage.setItem("user-lang", item.iconCls); //#4

    window.location.reload(); //#5
}
```

First, we will get the reference to the `translation` component (#1). Then, we will update the split button `iconCls` and `text` with `iconCls` and `text` of the selected Menu Item (#2 and #3). Next, we will update the new language selected by the user on `localStorage` (#4), and finally, we will ask the browser to reload the application (#5).

The early life of the ViewController

There is still one detail missing. When we load the application, the `translation` component does not have text or an icon configured. We also need to take care of this. We could listen to the `beforerender` or `render` events to update these two properties before the component is displayed to the user, but there is a very important detail: the ViewController is created very early in the component's life cycle, and for this reason, it is not possible to listen to these events.

There are three methods that we can use that can execute some tasks during the key points of the component's life cycle according to the Sencha documentation:

- `beforeInit`: This method can be overridden in order to operate on the view prior to its `initComponent` method being called. This method is called immediately after the controller is created, which occurs during `initConfig` called from the component constructor.

- `Init`: This is called shortly after `initComponent` has been called on the view. This is the typical time to perform initialization for the controller now that the view is initialized.

- **initViewModel**: This is called when the view's ViewModel is created (if one is defined).

As we want the `translation` component to have `iconCls` and `text` when it is rendered, we can use the `init` method in `TranslationController` to execute this logic for us:

```
init: function() {
    var lang = localStorage ? (localStorage.getItem('user-lang') ||
'en') : 'en',
        button = this.getView();

    button.setIconCls(lang); //#1

    if (lang == 'en'){         //#2
        button.setText('English');
    } else if (lang == 'es'){
        button.setText('Español');
    } else {
        button.setText('Português');
    }
}
```

First, we will verify that there is `localStorage`, and if positive, we will get the language that was stored. If there is no `localStorage`, or the preferred language was not stored yet (the first time the user uses the application or the user has not changed the language yet), the default language will be `English`. Then, we will set the `iconCls` of the split button as the flag of the selected language (#1).

If the selected language is English, we will set the split button `text` as "English" (#2), and if the selected language is Spanish, we will set the split button `text` as "Español" (#8); otherwise, we will set the text as "Português" (Portuguese).

This controller is also available in the MVC architecture. You can take a look at the differences between the MVC and MVVM implementation at http://goo.gl/ajaIao.

If we execute the application, we can change the preferred language and see that the result is a translated application, as follows:

Using locale files to translate Ext JS

As usual, there is one last thing missing. We are translating only the labels of the application. Form errors and other messages that are part of the Ext JS API are not translated. Ext JS provides locale file support. All we need to do is add the JavaScript locale file on the HTML page. To do so, we are going to add the following code inside the `loadLocale` function in the `Application.js` file:

```
var extJsFile = Ext.util.Format.format("ext/packages/ext-
locale/build/ext-locale-{0}.js", lang);
Ext.Loader.loadScript({url: extJsFile});
```

> The name of `iconCls` used for the flag and translation files (`en.js`, `es.js`, `pt_BR.js`) are due to the name of the locale files used by Sencha. So make sure you verify what name Sencha is using before naming your own file.

And now, if we try to execute the application again, we will be able to see that all the Ext JS messages will also be translated. For example, if we change the translation to Spanish, the form validation errors will also be in Spanish:

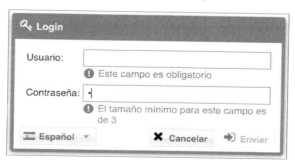

Now, the locale support of the application is completed!

 You might want to review the label size (use the `labelWidth` configuration to change its default size of 100 pixels) and the message targets for the screens after applying locale support. For example, the label **Contraseña** needs more width in the screen than **Password**.

After applying the locale, change `labelWidth` to `70` inside the `Login` class. You can change `msgTarget` to `'side'` or increase the `height` of the window so that the form validation messages can be properly displayed in other languages as well.

Summary

We covered how to implement the base of the application we are going to implement throughout this book using the Border layout, and you learned how to implement a **Logout** button (on the Ext JS side and also on the server side). We also covered the Client Activity Monitor and Session Timeout capabilities.

And finally, you learned how to build a `translation` component using HTML5 features along with Ext JS, which is able to translate all the labels of the application and also change the preferred language at runtime. You also learned how to use the Ext JS locale support used to translate the framework's messages and labels.

We made a great advance in this chapter regarding the implementation of our application. We created new files and our application is growing. We will continue to create more files and components in the next chapters of this book.

In the next chapter, we will learn how to build a dynamic menu using Accordion panels and trees.

5
Advanced Dynamic Menu

We already have the login capability that we implemented throughout *Chapter 3, The Login Page*, and the base of the application, that we implemented in *Chapter 4, The Logout and Multilingual Capabilities*. In the base of our application there is one missing piece, which is the menu. So the next thing we are going to develop is the dynamic menu.

Once the user has been authenticated, we are going to display the base screen of the application, which consists of a Viewport with a Border layout. On the left-hand side of the Viewport, we are going to display a menu. This menu will be dynamic, and the items that will be displayed on the menu depend on the permissions that the user has, which is why we call it a dynamic menu.

One of the options is to render all the screens of the system and then, depending on the user roles, we can hide or show them. However, this is not the approach we are going to use in this book. We are going to render and display only the screens the user has access to. The approach we are going to use is to dynamically render a menu according to the user entitlements.

So in this chapter, we will learn how to display a dynamic menu using different Ext JS components and layouts (that we have not covered yet). To summarize, in this chapter, we will cover:

- Creating a dynamic menu with the Accordion layout and TreePanel
- Using the Model association to load the data from the server
- Handling the dynamic menu on the server
- Opening a menu item dynamically
- Using the MVC architecture

An overview of the dynamic menu

So the first component that we are going to implement in this chapter is the dynamic menu. We could use only a TreePanel to display the menu, but we do like a challenge and we want to offer the best experience to the user. So, we are going to implement a dynamic menu using the Accordion layout and TreePanels, which results in a more advanced dynamic menu.

Our system consists of modules, and each module has subitems, which are the screens of our system. An accordion panel will represent the menu itself with all the modules; this way, the user can expand to see the options of each module at a time. And for the options of each module, we will use a TreePanel; each option of the menu will be a node from the TreePanel.

So, at the end of this topic, we will have a dynamic menu like the following screenshot:

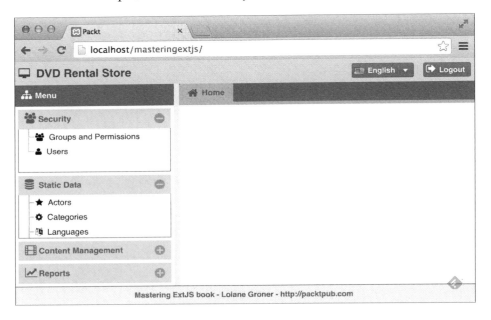

Before we get started with the dynamic menu, let's take a quick look at how the Ext JS TreePanel component works and how the Accordion layout works. Understanding these two concepts first will make it easier to understand how the dynamic menu is implemented.

Ext JS TreePanel

A TreePanel is the perfect component to display hierarchical data in an application. This is the reason why we will use it to display the menu. The following image exemplifies a TreePanel and its pieces:

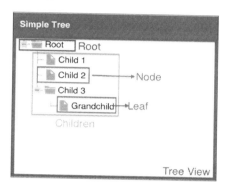

As we learned in *Chapter 1, Sencha Ext JS Overview*, the TreePanel extends from the `Ext.panel.Table` class, and so does the GridPanel. The `Ext.panel.Table` class extends from the `Panel` class. All the `Panel` classes have a *shell*, which is the panel itself, which allows us to set a title and add toolbars and also add child items.

The piece that is responsible for displaying the data is called the View, which is of the type `Ext.view.View`, and it is placed inside the `Panel` container. There are two ways that we can set data to a TreePanel: predefined using the `root` configuration or using a Store.

The Store behaves as our **Data Access Object (DAO)**. In this example, we will load data from the server, so we will use a Store. The Store loads a collection of objects that we call `Model` (`Ext.data.Model`). In the case of the TreePanel, these models are decorated with `NodeInterface` (`Ext.data.NodeInterface`).

For more information about the decorator pattern, please access `http://en.wikipedia.org/wiki/Decorator_pattern`.

We can choose to show or hide `Root` of the TreePanel. In the preceding image, `Root` is visible (the node called `Root`).

Each **Node** of a TreePanel can have **Children** (in as many nested levels as needed). When a **Node** does not have any child, we call it a **Leaf**.

We will dive more into the TreePanel when we implement the menu later in this chapter. For now, these are the concepts that we need to be familiar with.

Accordion layout

The Accordion layout manages multiple panels in an expandable accordion style such that by default only one panel can be expanded at any given time (this can be changed by setting the `multi` configuration as true). Only Ext panels and all subclasses of `Ext.panel.Panel` can be used in an Accordion layout container.

We could implement the dynamic menu using only a TreePanel, but we do like a challenge! Besides, from the UI point of view, having the modules separated by an Accordion layout container looks prettier than a simple TreePanel, as we can see in the following image:

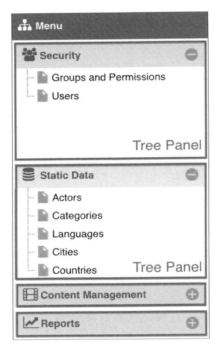

The menu itself is a panel that uses the Accordion layout. A TreePanel represents each module of the menu (note that you can expand or collapse each module due the capabilities of the Accordion layout). We are going to load the required data to display this menu from the server, and we are going to load the data from the database according to the user entitlements. That is why we call it a dynamic menu.

An important note on this approach: we are creating a TreePanel for each module for navigation. Creating many objects at the same time has some disadvantages, such as memory consumption. We can also create a single TreePanel and display all the modules as nodes with children. For more information about JavaScript, and memory consumption and its problems, please read `https://developer.chrome.com/devtools/docs/javascript-memory-profiling`.

So now that we are familiar with all the concepts, we can start with the menu!

The database model – groups, menus, and permissions

We have already created the `user` and `groups` tables. To store the information of the menu and its options and also the permission that each group has, we need to create two more tables: the `menu` and `permissions` tables, as shown by the following screenshot:

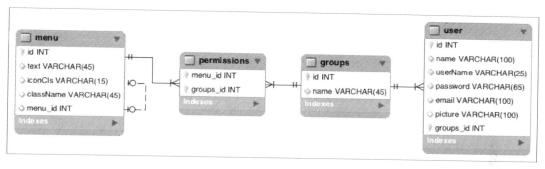

On the `menu` table, we will store all the `menu` information. As each option of the `menu` table will be a node of a TreePanel, we will store the information in a way that represents a TreePanel. So, we have an `id` field to identify the node, a `text` field as the text that is going to be displayed on the node (in our case, we will store the attribute of the translations file since we are using a multilingual capability), `iconCls` representing the `css` class that will be used to display the icon for each node, `className` representing the `alias` (`xtype`) of the class that we are going to instantiate dynamically and open at the central tab panel of the application, and finally the `menu_id` field representing the `root` node (if it has one—the module nodes will not have a `menu_id` field, but the module items will).

Then, as the menu table has an **N:N** relationship with the groups table, we need to create the permissions table that will represent this relationship. We will learn more about how to assign a user to a group in the next chapter.

 If you are not familiar with database relationships, the following link provides a good tutorial: http://goo.gl/hXRsPx.

So to create the new table, we will use the following SQL script:

```sql
USE `sakila` ;

CREATE  TABLE IF NOT EXISTS `sakila`.`menu` (
  `id` INT NOT NULL AUTO_INCREMENT ,
  `text` VARCHAR(45) NOT NULL ,
  `iconCls` VARCHAR(15) NULL ,
  `className` VARCHAR(45) NULL ,
  `menu_id` INT NULL ,
  PRIMARY KEY (`id`) ,
  INDEX `fk_menu_menu1_idx` (`menu_id` ASC) ,
  CONSTRAINT `fk_menu_menu1`
  FOREIGN KEY (`menu_id` )
  REFERENCES `sakila`.`menu` (`id` )
    ON DELETE NO ACTION
    ON UPDATE NO ACTION)
  ENGINE = InnoDB;

CREATE  TABLE IF NOT EXISTS `sakila`.`permissions` (
  `menu_id` INT NOT NULL ,
  `groups_id` INT NOT NULL ,
  PRIMARY KEY (`menu_id`, `groups_id`) ,
  INDEX `fk_permissions_groups1_idx` (`groups_id` ASC) ,
  CONSTRAINT `fk_permissions_menu1`
  FOREIGN KEY (`menu_id` )
  REFERENCES `sakila`.`menu` (`id` )
    ON DELETE NO ACTION
    ON UPDATE NO ACTION,
  CONSTRAINT `fk_permissions_groups1`
  FOREIGN KEY (`groups_id` )
  REFERENCES `sakila`.`groups` (`id` )
    ON DELETE NO ACTION
    ON UPDATE NO ACTION)
  ENGINE = InnoDB;
});
```

And we also need to populate the `menu` and `permissions` tables with some data. We can use the following SQL code to create all the modules and menu options that we are going to develop throughout this book. We are also going to grant the user we created in the preceding chapter access to all menu options, as this user is *admin*. Here's the code that encapsulates what we discussed in this paragraph:

```
INSERT INTO `menu` (`id`,`text`,`iconCls`,`className`,`menu_id`)
VALUES
(1,'menu1','fa fa-group fa-lg',NULL,NULL),
(2,'menu11','xf0c0','panel',1),
(3,'menu12','xf007','panel',1),
(4,'staticData','fa fa-database fa-lg',NULL,NULL),
(5,'actors','xf005','panel',4),
(6,'categories','xf013','panel',4),
(7,'languages','xf1ab','panel',4),
(8,'cities','xf018','panel',4),
(9,'countries','xf0ac','panel',4),
(10,'cms','fa fa-film fa-lg',NULL,NULL),
(11,'films','xf1c8','panel',10),
(12,'reports','fa fa-line-chart fa-lg',NULL,NULL),
(13,'salesfilmcategory','xf200','panel',12);

INSERT INTO `permissions` (`menu_id`,`groups_id`) VALUES
(1,1), (2,1), (3,1), (4,1), (5,1), (6,1), (7,1),
(8,1), (9,1), (10,1), (11,1), (12,1), (13,1);
```

Throughout this book, we are going to create the screens of our application, and we will need to run some update queries. For now, whenever we click on any menu option, the application is going to open an empty panel so that we can test it.

Note that `className` is set to `Panel` for all options. We will update the records in the database accordingly throughout the next chapters.

The dynamic menu – an MVC approach

We have covered the MVC architecture concept in *Chapter 2, Getting Started*, already, but let's do a quick overview one more time.

The Model represents the data we want to manipulate. It is a representation of the tables we have in the database. A Model instance represents a single data row of a table. The Store will be responsible for loading the collection of models from the server. A Store is usually bound to a View. A View is the component with which the user is seeing the screen (we have created a few so far; for example, a GridPanel provides a visual representation of data found in a Store.). And the Controller is what keeps everything together. The Controller will capture the events from the View and will execute some logic based on it. The Controller can also redirect the logic to the Model or the Store, making all the pieces communicate with each other, behaving like a mediator.

In the previous chapters, we used the MVVM architecture. We saw an example using the View and ViewController only and an example with View, ViewModel (predefined data), and ViewController. We have also learned that the ViewController is bound to its View's component life cycle, which means it is created when the View is created, and it is destroyed when the View is destroyed. With the MVC approach, the Controllers are alive as long as the application is running in the browser.

While in the ViewController, we can easily retrieve the view's reference or any of its children's references as well (using the `reference` configuration), in the Controller, we need to define what events from what components we want to listen to, and there is another approach to retrieve the components references.

MVC is not better than MVVM or vice versa. It depends on the application, the type of screen you are developing, the use case, and also your personal preference (why not?). That is why we are going to use all the possibilities in this book in the examples. This way, you can learn all of them (MVVM, MVC, and hybrid architecture) and use the one you like the most!

Creating the models

When working with the MVC architecture, we usually create the models first.

So first, we will create a class named `Packt.model.menu.Accordion`. To do that, we need to create the directory `app/model/menu` and also create a file named `Accordion.js`. With this Model, we will be able to represent each of the accordion panels we want to create (that will be represented by a TreePanel). So, for each module (or TreePanel), we want to set a title and also an icon.

The following code snippet shows the implementation of the `Packt.model.menu.Accordion` class:

```
Ext.define('Packt.model.menu.Accordion', {
    extend: 'Ext.data.Model',
```

```
    fields: [ //#1
        { name: 'id', type: 'int'}, //#2
        { name: 'text' },
        { name: 'iconCls' }
    ]
});
```

The main configuration for a Model is called `fields` (#1). In this configuration, we can declare all the `fields` for the Model (which would be similar to the columns of a table from the database). The class `Ext.data.field.Field` represents each field. Each field can have `name` and it can also have `type`. The available types are `string`, `int`, `number`, `boolean`, `date`, and `auto` (when no type is defined, and in this case, the field does not try to convert the value to any of the default types). The fields `text` and `iconCls` have the type `auto`.

Every Model needs a field that works as its unique identifier. In this case, we are defining the field `id` (#2) as our unique field. If the unique identifier of the Model is not called `id`, we need to configure this information in the Model as well by using the `idProperty` configuration. For example, if our ID was named `accordionId`, we would declare it normally, and inside the Model, we would add `idProperty: 'accordionId'` so that the Model would know that the field is the identifier.

> The `Model` and `Field` classes also have other features. Please refer to them to see all their capabilities in the Ext JS documentation, which is very complete and full of examples. Please take a look at `http://docs.sencha.com/extjs/5.0/apidocs/#!/api/Ext.data.Model` and `http://docs.sencha.com/extjs/5.0/apidocs/#!/api/Ext.data.field.Field`.

We also need a Model to represent the menu option, which consists of the Tree nodes of the TreePanel. To do so, we will declare the following Model:

```
Ext.define('Packt.model.menu.TreeNode', {
    extend: 'Ext.data.Model',

    fields: [
        { name: 'id', type: 'int'},
        { name: 'text' },
        { name: 'iconCls' },
        { name: 'className' },
        { name: 'parent_id', mapping: 'menu_id'} //#1
    ]
});
```

The `TreeNode` Model declared three fields present in the `NodeInterface` class, which are `id`, `text`, and `iconCls`. The `className` value is going to be used as `xtype` to instantiate the class that represents the screen of the menu option. We will talk more about this later. Then, we have the `parent_id` field. In the JSON, when we load data from the server, we will have the `menu_id` property instead of `parent_id`. We can use the `mapping` configuration to make this link (#1). This is nice because our Ext JS models do not need to be exactly like what is coming from the server (but it makes our life easier if they are the same).

Working with the hasMany association

There are two different ways of working with associations in Ext JS. The first one is using `Ext.data.association.Association` introduced in Ext JS 4. And the second one is using the `reference` configuration introduced in Ext JS 5. Ext JS 5 maintains backwards compatibility with the Model associations from Ext JS 4, although these Ext JS 4 features are marked as legacy code in the sources.

In this example, we are going to use the hasMany association introduced in Ext JS 4. Later in this book, we will see another example using `reference`, and we will be able to compare the difference and choose when to use one or the other.

To use the hasMany association, inside the `Accordion` Model, we first need to add the `hasMany` configuration:

```
hasMany: {
    model: 'Packt.model.menu.TreeNode',
    foreignKey: 'parent_id',
    name: 'items' //#1
}
```

This means that a new field named `items` (#1) will be created for the `Accordion` Model. For each instance of the `Accordion` Model, a method named `items()` will also be available to retrieve the `TreeNode` Model instances.

We cannot forget to add the `requires` declaration to the beginning of the `Accordion` Model as well, as shown in the following code:

```
requires: [
    'Packt.model.menu.TreeNode'
],
```

Creating the store-loading menu from the server

Now that we have the Model defined, we can move on and create the Store. We will create a new class named `Packt.store.Menu`, so we need to create a new file named `Menu.js` under the `app/store` folder with the following content:

```
Ext.define('Packt.store.Menu', {
    extend: 'Ext.data.Store',

    requires: [
        'Packt.util.Util' //#1
    ],

    model: 'Packt.model.menu.Accordion', //#2

    proxy: {
        type: 'ajax',              //#3
        url: 'php/menu/list.php', //#4

        reader: { //#5
            type: 'json',
            rootProperty: 'data'
        },
        listeners: {
            exception: function(proxy, response, operation){ //#6
                Packt.util.Util.showErrorMsg(response.responseText);
            }
        }
    }
});
```

There are two important things we need to declare in the Store: the `model` and the `proxy` properties. The `model` tells the Store what type of data the Store needs to load from the server (or client storages), and the `proxy` tells the Store how and where to get the data.

This Store is going to use the model `Packt.model.` (#2). Instead of using the `model` configuration, it is also possible to declare the fields directly inside the Store using the `fields` configuration (it would be a copy from `fields` from the Model). In this case, the Store would use a so-called "anonymous model".

The Store is going to communicate with the server through the proxy using an Ajax request to the provided `url`. The `reader` (#5) tells the proxy how to decode the information from the server and transform it into a collection of the specified models. This Store is expecting a JSON format with `rootProperty` (known in Ext JS 4 as `root`) named `data`, as follows:

```
{
    "data":[
        {
            "id":"1",
            "text":"menu1",
            "iconCls":"fa fa-group fa-lg",
            "items":[
                {
                    "id":"2",
                    "text":"menu11",
                    "iconCls":"xf0c0",
                    "className":"panel",
                    "menu_id":"1",
                    "leaf":true
                },
                {
                    "id":"3",
                    "text":"menu12",
                    "iconCls":"xf007",
                    "className":"panel",
                    "menu_id":"1",
                    "leaf":true
                }
            ]
        }
    ]
}
```

 Because we declare the associations in the previous topic, the Store knows how to decode a nested JSON and create the respective Model instances.

And, of course, exceptions can occur! For this reason, we can add `exception` `listener` (#6) in `proxy` so that we can display an error message to the user. As we are using the `Util` class we created, we also need to add this class in the `requires` declaration (#1).

We can listen to events from views and stores in the Controller; however, the Store does not have any exception event. For this reason, `listener` needs to be added directly to `proxy`. This is an optional step, but if an error occurs, nothing will happen in the UI (Ext JS will output an error message in the browser's console, but users do not use the application with the developer tools console opened). That is why it is a good practice to have `exception listener` declared inside every proxy we use. We will develop a more elegant approach, but for now, we will use it like this.

 Instead of declaring `proxy` inside the Store, we can declare it inside the Model. You can declare `proxy` in the place of your preference. However, if you declare `proxy` on the Model and on the Store, when using the Store's `sync()` method, it will call the `proxy` instance declared on the Store; else the Model's `proxy` will be used.

Now that we know the data format that we need to retrieve from the server, let's implement it!

Handling the dynamic menu on the server

As we declared on the `Packt.store.Menu` Store, we need to create a new file named `menu/list.php` under the `php` folder. The following is the programming logic that we need to follow:

1. Get the user that is logged in from the session.
2. Open a connection with the database.
3. Select the menu `id` instances from the `permission` table so that we know what permissions the user from the session has.
4. Select the modules that the user has permission to access—`menu_id` is `null`.
5. For each module, select the nodes (menu options) that the user has access to.
6. Encode the result in the JSON format and wrap it in the `data` root (as specified by the Store).

So let's get our hands on the code. The following code was organized in functions, so we can organize the code exactly as listed in the preceding set of instructions:

```php
<?php
require('menuFunctions.php'); // #1

session_start(); // #2
```

```
$userName = $_SESSION['username']; // #3

$permissions = retrievePermissions($userName); // #4
$modules = retrieveModules($permissions);        // #5
$result = retrieveMenuOptions($modules, $permissions); // #6

echo json_encode(array( // #7
    "data" => $result
));
```

As the code was organized in functions, let's create another file called menuFunction.php inside the php/menu folder as well. As we are going to code the functions inside this file, we need to require this file inside menu/list.php (#1).

Then, we will get the user that is logged in to the session (#2). So we will get the entitlements for the user that is logged in, increasing the security a little bit.

Then, we will do as listed. For each function to which we open the connection with the database, we will retrieve the user's permissions (#4), then we will retrieve the modules the user has permission to access (#5), and then based on the module, we retrieve the menu options the user also has access to (#6).

At last, we will encode the result array in the JSON format (#7), and it is going to produce the JSON listed in the preceding topic.

Fetching the user permissions

Now, let's dive into each function declared inside the menuFunctions.php file. The first one is the function used to retrieve the user's permissions as listed here:

```
function retrievePermissions($userName){

    require('../db/db.php'); // #8

    $sqlQuery = "SELECT p.menu_id menuId FROM User u "; // #9
    $sqlQuery .= "INNER JOIN permissions p ON u.groups_id =
    p.groups_id ";
    $sqlQuery .= "INNER JOIN menu m ON p.menu_id = m.id ";
    $sqlQuery .= "WHERE u.username = '$userName' ";

    $permissions = [];

    if ($resultDb = $mysqli->query($sqlQuery)) { // #10
        while($user = $resultDb->fetch_assoc()) { // #11
            $permissions[] = $user['menuId'];
```

```
        }
    }

    $resultDb->free(); // #12
    $mysqli->close();   // #13

    return $permissions; // #14
}
```

First, we will open the connection with the database (#8), and then we prepare the SQL query to get the `id` instances from the `menu` table that the user has access to (#9). We are using `JOIN` because the only information we have is `username`, and we need to pass through the `groups` table to get to the `permissions` table.

We execute the SQL query (#10), and we create an array with the menu `id` that the user has permission to use (#11).

In the end, we free the result set (#12), close the database connection (#13), and we return the `permissions` array (#14).

Fetching the modules the user is entitled to

Now let's take a look at the function that will retrieve the modules based on users' permissions:

```
function retrieveModules($permissions){

    require('../db/db.php');

    $inClause = '(' . join(',',$permissions) . ')'; // #15

    $sqlQuery = "SELECT id, text, iconCls FROM menu WHERE menu_id
    IS NULL AND id in $inClause"; // #16

    $modules = [];

    if ($resultDb = $mysqli->query($sqlQuery)) { // #17
        while($module = $resultDb->fetch_assoc()) {
            $modules[] = $module;

        }
    }
    $resultDb->free();
    $mysqli->close();

    return $modules; // #18
}
```

To be able to retrieve the modules the user has access to, we need to know what modules (records from the menu table that do not have a menu_id parent menu) the user has permission to access. In our SQL query (#16), there is an IN clause to fetch all modules. As we have the permissions array, we can use the join PHP function (#15) that will return a string with all the array values separated by the "," delimiter we informed. Then, we concatenate with "( )" and we are good to go.

The next step is executing the SQL query (#17), and with the results from the database, we create an array with the modules that the user has access to, and at the end of the function, we return this information (#18).

The modules variable represents the Accordion Model class we created.

Fetching the menu options based on modules and permissions

After we have retrieved the permissions and modules the user has access to, it is time to retrieve the last piece to create the data for the dynamic menu, which is retrieving the menu options. The code is presented as follows:

```php
function retrieveMenuOptions($modules, $permissions){

    require('../db/db.php');

    $inClause = '(' . join(',',$permissions) . ')'; // #1

    $result = [];

    foreach ($modules as $module) { // #2

        $sqlQuery = "SELECT * FROM menu WHERE menu_id = '"; // #3
        $sqlQuery .= $module['id'] ."' AND id in $inClause";

        if ($resultDb = $mysqli->query($sqlQuery)) { // #4

            $count = $resultDb->num_rows; // #5
            if ($count > 0){ // #6
                $module['items'] = array(); // #7
                while ($item = $resultDb->fetch_assoc()) {
                    $module['items'][] = $item; // #8
                }
            }
            $result[] = $module; // #9

        }
    }
    $resultDb->close();
    $mysqli->close();
```

```
        return $result; // #10
    }
```

For each `module` that the user has access to (#2), we will retrieve the menu options (#3). To do so, we need the ID of the module and also the `permissions` (#1). As each module might have several menu options, a user might not have permission to access all of them.

Next, we execute the query (#4) and retrieve the number of records returned by the database (#5). If this number is positive (#6), we create the `items` array ((#7), the `hasMany` association) and we fetch each item adding it to the `module['items']` array (#8).

Each `$item` variable inside `module['items']` represents the `TreeNode` model.

At the end of it, we add `$item` to the `result` variable (#9) and return it (#10). This `result` variable is the one that will be wrapped inside the `data` root and encoded as JSON to be returned to Ext JS.

The database for the `menu` fits perfectly to what Ext JS needs. We designed the `menu` table according to Ext JS expectations, and in a way that would be easier for us to retrieve the information. The preceding server-side code also fits perfectly to what Ext JS needs. Unless we have the chance to design the database ourselves in a project that we are starting from scratch, we will probably have a different design; therefore, the server-side code to retrieve the information will be a little different too. There is no problem at all. It does not matter how the database looks or the server-side code you need to write to retrieve the information. However, Ext JS is expecting a specific format to be sent back to the frontend code, and unfortunately, we need to send the information in this specific format (the JSON listed before). If the information we retrieved from the database is not in the format that Ext JS expects (the same format as our preceding code), all we need to do is parse and transform it, which means there will be an extra step in our server-side code before we send it back to Ext JS.

Creating the menu with the Accordion layout and TreePanel

We can go back to the Ext JS code and start implementing the dynamic menu View component now. First, we need to create a new folder under `app/view/menu` and create a new file named `Accordion.js`, as follows:

```
Ext.define('Packt.view.menu.Accordion', {
    extend: 'Ext.panel.Panel',
    xtype: 'mainmenu', // #1
```

```
        width: 250, // #2
        layout: {
            type: 'accordion', // #3
            multi: true          // #4
        },
        collapsible: true, // #3
        split: true,       // #4
        iconCls: 'fa fa-sitemap fa-lg', // #5
        title: translations.menu  // #6
    });
```

This class is going to be a panel and it is going to wrap the TreePanels that will be the menus. It is going to use the Accordion layout (#3); this way, the user can expand or collapse the desired module. As the default behavior, all modules will be expanded (#4). If only the first module should be expanded at a time, we can comment line #4.

As we are going to use this class in the west region of the Main class, we are going to declare xtype (#1).

Be very careful when declaring xtype. Always remember to create a unique xtype and not any that is already being used by Ext JS components. For example, let's say there is an xtype property you might want to use, but if we go to the documentation and use the quick search, we will see this xtype property is already in use by Ext JS, as shown below:

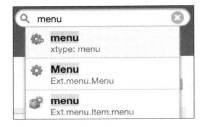

As this panel will be rendered in the west region, we need to set a width (#2) — remember that whenever we are using the Border layout, we need to specify a width for the west and east regions. We will also allow the user to resize the west region (#4) and collapse (#3) so that there is more space for the screen in the center.

At last, to prettify, we are declaring a Font Awesome icon (#5) and a title property (#6). We cannot forget to add the following entry in the locale/en.js file and its translations:

```
menu: 'menu',
```

You can get the Spanish and Portuguese translations by downloading the source code bundle from this book or downloading from the GitHub repository https://github.com/loiane/masteringextjs.

Next, we need to create a TreePanel to represent each module. We will create a new class named `Packt.view.menu.Tree`; therefore, we need to create a new file named `Tree.js` under `app/view/menu`:

```
Ext.define('Packt.view.menu.Tree', {
    extend: 'Ext.tree.Panel',
    xtype: 'menutree',

    border: 0,
    autoScroll: true,
    rootVisible: false
});
```

This class is a TreePanel. We do not want a `border` property for our module, and the `root` property will not be visible. As we can see, we are not setting many attributes. We will set the missing information dynamically on the Controller.

The last step is going back to the `Main` class and adding `Accordion` to the `west` region. To do so, first we cannot forget to add the class `'Packt.view.menu.Accordion'` to `requires` and change the `west` region code to the following:

```
{
    xtype: 'mainmenu',
    region: 'west'
}
```

We removed all the configurations (`width`, `split`) and replaced `xtype` with `menu.Accordion`. When we execute the application, we will be able to see the `west` region with a panel now. The creation of the dynamic menu is pending though, and we will take care of it next.

Creating the menu Controller

We already have all the views, models, and stores and also have the server-side covered. Now the only thing left is to implement the Controller, which is where all the magic will happen. So, let's go ahead and create a new file named `Menu.js` under the `app/controller` folder:

```
Ext.define('Packt.controller.Menu', {
    extend: 'Ext.app.Controller',
```

```
       init: function(application) {

    this.control({ // #1
            "menutree": { // #2
                itemclick: this.onTreePanelItemClick // #3
            },
            "mainmenu": {
                render: this.renderDynamicMenu // #4
            }
        });
    }
});
```

 In the MVC approach, all controllers are created inside the app/
controller folder, while in the MVVM approach, ViewController is
created in the same folder as the View.

The init function is called when the application boots, and it is called before the
application's launch function is. We can use this function to execute any logic before
the first View (Login or Viewport) is created. Inside this function is also the place
where we want to set up the events we want this Controller to listen to using the
control function (#1).

In this Controller, we want to listen to two events. The first one is we want to
render the dynamic menu (#4) when the Viewport (Main class) has been rendered.
The second one is whenever the user clicks on a menu option (a node from the
TreePanel — #2), we want to open the screen inside the center panel (#3).

To listen to an event inside the control method, we need to define three things: the
selector, the event we want the Controller to listen to, and the method to be executed.
It has the following format:

```
"{selector}": {
    event1: this.methodToBeExecuted1,
    event2: this.methodToBeExecuted2
}
```

Finding the selector is the most challenging part. The scope in this case is not the View as in the ViewController, but the application. For selectors, we usually use the xtype component. It helps when it is an xtype component we created for the application and not an Ext JS xtype such as 'tree'; for example, 'menutree' is much better because we narrow down the possibilities (there might be several TreePanels within the application, but we know that only the TreePanels from the dynamic menu have menutree as xtype). We have to remember that if we use the selector 'tree' (xtype for TreePanel), the Controller will listen to the event from all TreePanels of the application, so it is good to be as specific as we can be.

We can listen to as many events from a selector as we want to. We simply need to separate the events by a ",".

For example, let's implement the renderDynamicMenu method first. We use mainmenu as the selector. This is the xtype component for the view.menu.Accordion class, which is being rendered in the west region of the Main class (Viewport). So, when this component is rendered, the Controller is going to execute the renderDynamicMenu method. Let's declare this method inside the Menu Controller:

```
renderDynamicMenu: function(view, options) {
    console.log('menu rendered');
}
```

We can always start the implementation of an event listener in the Controller by adding a console.log or alert message to make sure the method is being executed.

 Remember to always go to the documentation to verify the parameters that are being passed to the event so that we can declare them. For the render event, it is usually the component itself and options.

Let's declare onTreePanelItemClick as well so that we can test this Controller:

```
onTreePanelItemClick: function(view, record, item, index, event,
options){ },
```

The method signature is enough so that we do not get any errors.

We need to add this Controller in Application.js as well. So, go back to Application.js and add the highlighted code shown as follows:

```
controllers: [
    'Root',
    'Menu'
],
```

If we execute the application, we will get the output as shown in the following screenshot:

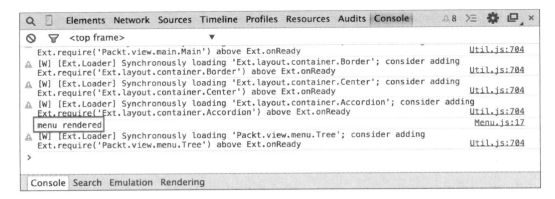

This means that it is working as we expect. Do not worry about the other warning messages; we will take care of them later in this book (the important thing is not getting error messages).

So let's go ahead and add the required business logic.

Rendering the menu from nested JSON (the hasMany association)

We need to add the logic that will be responsible for creating the dynamic menu with the information that will be received from the server. We will add the following code inside the `renderDynamicMenu` method:

```
var dynamicMenus = [];  //#1

view.body.mask('Loading Menus... Please wait...');  //#2

this.getMenuStore().load(function(records, op, success){ //#3

    Ext.each(records, function(root){ //#4

        var menu = Ext.create('Packt.view.menu.Tree',{ //#5
            title: translations[root.get('text')],      //#6
            iconCls: root.get('iconCls')                //#7
        });
```

```
            var treeNodeStore = root.items(),        //#8
                nodes = [],
        item;

            for (var i=0; i<treeNodeStore.getCount(); i++){ //#9
                item = treeNodeStore.getAt(i);                 //#10

                nodes.push({                          //#11
                    text: translations[item.get('text')],
                    leaf: true,                       //#12
                    glyph: item.get('iconCls'),    //#13
                    id: item.get('id'),
                    className: item.get('className')
                });
            }
        menu.getRootNode().appendChild(nodes); //#14
            dynamicMenus.push(menu); //#15
        });
    view.add(dynamicMenus); //#16
    view.body.unmask();        //#17
});
```

The first thing we are going to do is create an empty array so that we can add all the modules to it (#1). As we are going to make a request to the server and as initially the menu in the west region is going to be empty, it is nice to add a loading message (#2) just in case there is any delay with the server response (*Ajax is asynchronous*). The view was passed as a parameter to the event and is a reference to the Packt.view. menu.Accordion class instance.

Then, we need to load the Menu Store (#3), which is responsible for loading the nested JSON from the server (#1). Note that we are using this.getMenuStore() to retrieve the Store, which means this is a method from the Controller. We need to declare the menu Store inside the stores configuration in the Controller so that it will generate this method for us:

```
stores: [
    'Menu'
],
```

In this case, there is no need to declare the complete name of the Store—only what is after `'Packt.store'`. Because of the MVC architecture, Ext JS knows that it needs to look for a file named `Menu.js` inside the `app/store` folder. As the name of the Store is `Menu`, the Controller will generate a method named `get` + `Menu` + `Store` (`getMenuStore`) once the Store is loaded (that is why we are going to handle the creation of the dynamic menu inside the load callback). For each `record` returned from the Store (#4), we will create a TreePanel (`Packt.view.menu.Tree`—#5) to represent each module. We will set the `title` property (getting the `title` property from the locale file (#6). In the database, we will store the key from the `en.js` file in the column `text` and set `iconCls` (#7) for it to look prettier (a Font Awesome icon).

Ext.create or Ext.widget

In *Chapter 2, Getting Started,* when we instantiated a class for the first time in this book, we discussed the options we can use when we need to instantiate a `component` class. Just to remind you, we can use `Ext.create` passing the complete name of the class as an argument, or we can use `Ext.widget` passing the class alias as an argument (there are other ways as well, but these two are more commonly used). It is a matter of preference, but you can use any of the ways we mentioned in *Chapter 2, Getting Started.*

So, with this code, we are able to display each TreePanel representing each of the modules (with no menu option). The next step is getting the data to display inside the TreePanel. This data is available in the JSON already through the `hasMany` association we configured. Because of the `hasMany` association, a method named `items` (name of the association we configured) will be created for each Model instance inside the Store. The `items` method returns a Store with the `hasMany` data in it (#8).

When we are not sure whether the method was created or not, we can always inspect the Model instance in the console. For example, if we output `console.log(this)` inside the `load` callback, we will get the Store outputted in the browser's console. Inspect the `data` configuration, and inside the `data` configuration, we will find `items`, which contains the Model collection as shown in the following screenshot:

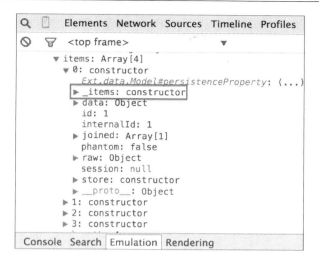

For each `Packt.model.menu.TreeNode` Model instance from the Store (#9 and #10), we will push a new node (#11) into an array. When adding the new node, we set the `text` and `leaf` (#12) that are properties from the `NodeInterface` class. We are adding `id` and `className` that are not part of the `NodeInterface` class.

To add all the nodes created, we need access to the `Root` node of the TreePanel. As `Root` is also a node (decorated with the `NodeInterface` class), it has a method called `appendChild`, which can be used to append nodes to a specific node (in this case, `Root`). So, we add all the nodes we created at once (#14).

To avoid many changes in the DOM, which is not a good practice, we are going to create an array with all the menus we created (#15). And then, we will add all the menus at once (#16) to the `Accordion` panel (this will avoid browser reflow).

Minimizing browser reflow is a technique used to increase performance. We could do the insertions inside the loops, but this would increase DOM manipulation, which is very expensive. With simple changes in the code to add whatever needs to be added at once, we can increase the performance a little bit. For more information, please visit `https://developers.google.com/speed/articles/reflow`.

At last, we remove the `mask` from the `Accordion` menu (#17).

If we execute the code, the menu will be rendered.

Using glyphs in TreePanel – working with overrides

There was a piece from the code that we did not cover in the previous topic, which is line #13, the `glyph` configuration in the node. We know that we can use icon fonts, such as Font Awesome, with Ext JS, but the support is still limited. It is not possible to use Font Awesome icons in TreePanel nodes. However, there is an override we can use that will allow us to do that.

This is the first time we are mentioning the term **glyph** in this book. It is basically the same thing as the font icon we have been using until now, but it has an alternative configuration for it. For example, we used a key icon in the `Login` class, and we set `iconCls` as follows:

```
iconCls: 'fa fa-key fa-lg'
```

We could have used the `glyph` configuration instead as an alternative:

```
glyph:'xf084@FontAwesome'
```

The preceding code could also be written as follows:

```
glyph:'xf084'
```

But we need to configure the `glyphFontFamily` configuration inside the `Packt.Application` class in `Application.js`, as follows:

```
glyphFontFamily: 'FontAwesome'
```

And then, we can remove `'@FontAwesome'` from the `glyph` configuration.

 Font Awesome provides a cheat sheet with the CSS names and glyph codes at `http://fortawesome.github.io/Font-Awesome/cheatsheet/`.

The Font Awesome `iconCls` is not going to work for the Tree nodes, but as mentioned before, we can apply an override. An override is a way of changing the behavior of the Ext JS class. It would be similar to modifying the prototype of a JavaScript object—the new behavior is applied to all the instances of that class.

Even though Ext JS is open source, we should avoid changing the source code directly (despite the open source code philosophy). Changing the source code can be an issue when upgrading the framework version in the future. Using overrides is more elegant.

The override we are going to use can be found at `http://www.sencha.com/forum/showthread.php?281383-Glyph-support-on-treepanels`.

We are going to create the override inside the file `app/overrides/tree/ColumnOverride.js`. We cannot forget to change the name of the override to `Packt.overrides.tree.ColumnOverride` (the first line of code).

Then, inside `Application.js`, we are going to add the following code to make sure it is loaded when the application is loaded and the override is applied, as follows:

```
requires: [
    'Packt.overrides.tree.ColumnOverride'
],
```

We can also add this `require` declaration inside the `Packt.view.menu.Tree` class to remind us that we are using an override as well, but it is optional.

This is what the `menu` table looks like at this moment. The modules have the Font Awesome CSS, and the menu options have the glyph codes (`iconCls` column), as follows:

id	text	iconCls	className	menu_id
1	menu1	fa fa-group fa-lg	NULL	NULL
2	menu11	xf0c0	panel	1
3	menu12	xf007	panel	1
4	staticData	fa fa-database fa-lg	NULL	NULL
5	actors	xf005	panel	4
6	categories	xf013	panel	4
7	languages	xf1ab	panel	4
8	cities	xf018	panel	4
9	countries	xf0ac	panel	4
10	cms	fa fa-film fa-lg	NULL	NULL
11	films	xf1c8	panel	10
12	reports	fa fa-line-chart fa-lg	NULL	NULL
13	salesfilmcategory	xf200	panel	12

You can use only the glyph codes throughout the application. We are using both to show it is possible to use both. From now on, you can use the approach you prefer.

Menu locale support

We also need to add the keys to the en.js file (and other locale files as well). For the menu, these are the entries needed:

```
menu1 : 'Security',
menu11 : 'Groups and Permissions',
menu12 : 'Users',
staticData: 'Static Data',
actors: 'Actors',
categories: 'Categories',
languages: 'Languages',
cities: 'Cities',
countries: 'Countries',
cms: 'Content Management',
films: 'Films',
reports: 'Reports',
salesfilmcategory: 'Sales by Film Category'
```

 Note the keys are the same entries as the text column from the menu table.

Opening a menu item programmatically

After the menu is rendered, the user will be able to select an option from it. The logic behind the method is: when the user selects an option from the menu we need to verify that the tab has already been created on the tab panel. If yes, we do not need to create it again; we only need to select the tab on the tab panel and make it active. If not, then we need to instantiate the screen selected by the user. To do so, the Controller will execute the following method:

```
onTreePanelItemClick: function(view, record, item, index, event,
options){
    var mainPanel = this.getMainPanel(); // #1

    var newTab = mainPanel.items.findBy( // #2
        function (tab){
            return tab.title === record.get('text'); // #3
    });

    if (!newTab){ // #4
        newTab = mainPanel.add({                 // #5
            xtype: record.get('className'), // #6
```

```
        closable: true,              // #7
        glyph: record.get('glyph'),  // #8
        title: record.get('text')    // #9
    });
}
    mainPanel.setActiveTab(newTab); // #10
}
```

First, we need to get the reference of the tab panel (#1). We are using `this.getMainPanel()`, which was created by the Controller.

There are three ways of getting object references inside Controller methods. The first one is using the parameters passed to the method. The second one is using the `ComponentQuery` (that we have not discussed yet), and the third one is using `refs`.

For this example, we are going to use `refs`. We need to add the following code inside the Controller:

```
refs: [
    {
        ref: 'mainPanel',
        selector: 'mainpanel'
    }
],
```

We can configure the selector we want the Controller to search for and the name of the reference. In this case, the Controller will create a method called `get +` `mainPanel` (in the `ref` name, the first letter becomes a capital letter) resulting in `getMainPanel`. This is equivalent to `reference` used by the ViewController.

Then, we need to verify that the selected menu option was already created (#2), and we will do it comparing the tab `title` with the `text` configuration of the selected node (#3).

If it is not a new tab, we will add it to the tab panel, passing as an instance to the `add` method (#5). So we will get the `xtype` configuration of the component we are going to add from the node `className` (#6), and the tab can be `closed` (#7); it will have the same `glyph` as its node (#8) and will also have the same `title` as the node (#9 — menu option).

Then, we will set it as the active tab. If the screen is already rendered, we will only change the `active` tab to the screen that the user selected from the menu (#10).

The dynamic menu functionality is now complete!

Summary

In this chapter, we learned how to implement an advanced dynamic menu using an Accordion layout and also TreePanels for each module of the application. We learned how to handle the dynamic logic on the sever side and also how to handle its return on the Ext JS side loading a Store to build the menu dynamically. And finally, we have also learned how to open an item from the menu programmatically and display it on the center component of the application. We also used the MVC architecture for the first time.

In the next chapter, we will learn how to implement screens to list, create, and update users and also how to assign a group to the user.

6
User Management

In the previous chapters, we developed mechanisms to provide login and logout capabilities and client-side session monitoring, and we also implemented a dynamic menu based on the user permissions. However, all the users, groups, and permissions were added manually to the database until now. We cannot do this every time we need to grant access to the application to a new user or change the user permissions. For this reason, we will implement a screen where we can create new users and grant or change the permissions. So in this chapter, we will cover:

- Listing all the users from the system
- Creating, editing and deleting users
- Picture preview of a file upload (user's picture)

Managing users

So the first module we are going to develop is user management. In this module, we will be able to see all the users that are registered on the system, add new users, edit, and delete current users.

When the user clicks on the **Users** menu option, a new tab will open with the list of all users from the system as shown in the following screenshot:

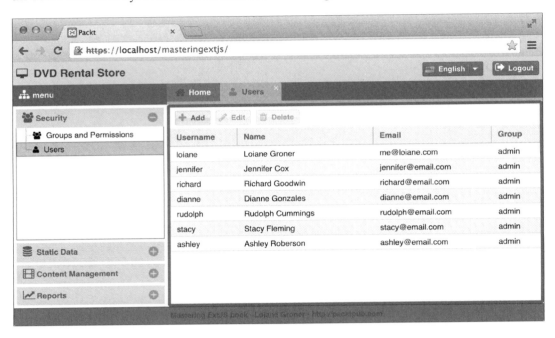

When the user clicks on the **Add** or **Edit** button, the system will display a window so that the user can create a new user or edit a current user (based on the record selected on the GridPanel). The **Edit** window will look like the following screenshot:

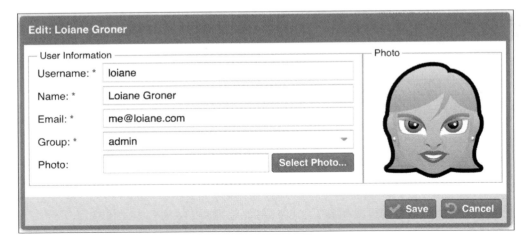

Some capabilities of creating or editing a user: we can edit the **User Information** such as **Name**, **Username**, and so on and we can also upload a **Photo** representing the user. But there is an extra feature; using the HTML5 API, we are going to display a preview of the **Photo** right after the user selects the picture from the computer and before the user uploads to the server.

Listing all the users using a simple GridPanel

We need to implement a screen similar to the first screenshot present in this chapter. It is a simple GridPanel. So to implement a simple GridPanel, we need the following:

- A Model to represent the information that is stored on the user table
- A Store to load the information and a Proxy to tell Ext JS to read the information from the server
- A GridPanel component representing the View
- A ViewController to listen to the events, as we are going to develop this module using MVVM

Creating a User Model

So the first step is to create a Model to represent the user table. We are going to create a new file named User.js under the app/model/security directory. This Model is going to represent all the fields from the user table, except the password field, because as the password is something very personal to the user, we cannot display the user's password to any other user, including the administrator. So the User Model is going to look like the following:

```
Ext.define('Packt.model.security.User', {
    extend: 'Packt.model.security.Base', //#1

    fields: [
        { name: 'name' },
        { name: 'userName' },
        { name: 'email' },
        { name: 'picture' },
        { name: 'groups_id' , type: 'int'}
    ]
});
```

And as we mentioned before, all the fields from the user table are mapped into this Model, except the password field.

In line #1 we are not extending the default Ext.data.Model class. We are extending a class that we created. Let's see its declaration next.

Working with schemas

When we designed the database tables, we also added a foreign key to the user table. This means the user table has a relationship with the groups table. Ext JS 5 introduced the concept of schemas. A schema (Ext.data.schema.Schema) is a collection of related entities and their respective associations. We know that the User and Group Model classes are related entities, so we can create a schema to represent them.

So let's see what's inside the Packt.model.security.Base class:

```
Ext.define('Packt.model.security.Base', {
    extend: 'Ext.data.Model',

    requires: [
        'Packt.util.Util'
    ],

    idProperty: 'id',

    fields: [
        { name: 'id', type: 'int' } //#1
    ],

    schema: {
        namespace: 'Packt.model.security', //#2
        urlPrefix: 'php',                  //#3
        proxy: {
            //proxy code here
        }
    }
});
```

The security.Base model will work as a super Model that the User and Group (which will be defined later in this chapter in the section *Declaring the User ViewModel*) classes and contains the common code for both models.

The first thing the User and Group Model classes have in common is the id field (#1). So to reuse this field in both classes, we can declare it here.

Next, `config` is the `schema`. Inside the `schema`, we can configure some options. The first one is `namespace` (#2). In some cases, we want to use a short name for the Model entities. We will use the short name of the `User` and `Group` classes when declaring associations and in the **ViewController** later. The short name is also known in Ext JS as `entityName` of the Model (we can declare this `config` in the Model as well). By default, `entityName` is the full class name, but this is exactly what we are trying to avoid. However, if `namespace` is used (in a `schema` declaration), the common portion can be discarded, and we can derive a shorter name. For example, the full name of the `User` class is `Packt.model.security.User`, and its schema namespace is `Packt.model.security`, so `entityName` will result in `User`. Using only `User` instead of `Packt.model.security.User` is much better.

We also have the `urlPrefix` (#3), which is the URL prefix used for all requests to the server. We are going to use this information when configuring `proxy` (in *Chapter 5, Advanced Dynamic Menu*, we used `proxy` inside the Store; now we are going to use it inside the Model).

Next, we are going to configure `proxy` as follows. As we are using `proxy` inside the schema declaration, the configuration will be available for all classes extending the `Packt.model.security.Base` class:

```
type: 'ajax',
api :{
    read  : '{prefix}/{entityName:lowercase}/list.php', //#4
    create: '{prefix}/{entityName:lowercase}/create.php',
    update: '{prefix}/{entityName:lowercase}/update.php',
    destroy: '{prefix}/{entityName:lowercase}/destroy.php'
},
reader: {
    type: 'json',
    rootProperty: 'data'
},
writer: { //#5
    type: 'json',
    writeAllFields: true,
    encode: true,
    rootProperty: 'data',
    allowSingle: false
},
listeners: { //#6
    exception: function(proxy, response, operation){
        Packt.util.Util.showErrorMsg(response.responseText);
    }
}
```

When we want to specify a different `url` for each of the CRUD operations, instead of using the `url` config we use the `api` config. Inside the `api` config, we define a `url` config for each CRUD action. When using schemas, we can use a template in the `proxy` to configure the URLs. For example, we use `prefix`, which refers to `urlPrefix` that we configured before. The `entityName` attribute refers to the Model `entityName` (and in this example, we also ask to transform the `entityName` to lowercase). In line #4, for the `User` Model class, the read `url` will be `php/user/list.php`. This is very useful when we want to follow a pattern and share (reuse) the `schema` configuration between different models.

We learned how to configure `reader` already. We can also specify `writer` (#5) when we want to send information to the server (create, update, or delete records). In this case, we are telling Ext JS we want to send a JSON back to the server. The `writeAllFields` configuration specifies whether we want the Model (and all its fields) to be sent to the server or only the fields that were modified (plus the `id` field). To make our life easier on the server-side code, we set `writeAllFields` as true. Just as with `reader`, we are also going to configure `rootProperty` to be a wrapper of the records. Then, we have the `encode` configuration set to `true` to send record data (all record fields if `writeAllFields` is `true`) as a JSON-encoded HTTP parameter named by the `rootProperty` configuration. The encode option should only be set to `true` when `rootProperty` is defined, because the values will be sent as part of the request parameters as opposed to a raw post. And at last, we have `allowSingle` set to `false`. This will force `proxy` to get all the modified records (to be created, updated, or deleted) and send them in an array (wrapped by `rootProperty` if configured). This will make `proxy` send only one request to the server (one request for creating, updating, or deleting records) instead of one request for each modification.

At last, we have the proxy `exception listener` (#6), which we are already familiar with from previous chapters.

Defining store-less grids with Users GridPanel

The next step is to create the views we are going to use to manage the users of our application. But before we get our hands on the code, we need to keep one thing in mind; when we implement the **Manage Groups** module and on the **Edit Group** screen, we want to display all the users that belong to that group. And for that, we will need to use a **Users** grid as well. So that being said, we need to create a component that will list the users (in this case all the users from the application) that we can reuse later. For this reason, the component that we are going to create will only contain the list of users and will not contain the **Add/Edit/Delete** buttons. We will add a toolbar with these buttons and also wrap the **Users** grid in another component.

So we are going to create a GridPanel. To do so, let's create a new class named `Packt.view.security.UsersGrid`. To create this class, we will create a new file named `UsersGrid.js` under the `app/view/security` directory:

```
Ext.define('Packt.view.security.UsersGrid', {
    extend: 'Ext.grid.Panel',
    alias: 'widget.users-grid',   //#1

    reference: 'usersGrid', //#2

    columns: [   //#3
        {
            width: 150,
            dataIndex: 'userName',   //#4
            text: 'Username'
        },
        {
            width: 200,
            dataIndex: 'name',
            flex: 1,                 //#5
            text: 'Name'
        },
        {
            width: 250,
            dataIndex: 'email',
            text: 'Email'
        },
        {
            width: 150,
            dataIndex: 'groups_id', //#6
            text: 'Group'
        }
    ]
});
```

As usual, we are going to start with `xtype`. An alternative to `xtype` is using the `alias` (#1). When using `xtype`, we can declare it directly (for example `xtype: 'user-grid'`). When using `alias`, we need to specify what type of alias we are creating. For components we use "`widget.`" and for plugins, we use "`plugin.`", followed by the `xtype`.

Let's go ahead and also create `reference` so that we can refer to this component later in the ViewModel (#2).

Whenever we declare a grid, there are two mandatory configurations we need to specify. The first one is the `columns` (#3) configuration, and the second one is the `store` configuration.

The `columns` (#3) configuration is an array of column definition objects that define all columns that appear in the grid. Each column definition provides the header `text` (text configuration) for the column, and a definition of where the data for that column comes from ((`dataIndex`) #4).

As a Grid is going to display a collection of data represented by a Model, each column needs to have the `dataIndex` (#4) configured matching the Model field that it represents.

We can define a `width` for each column. But we do not know the monitor resolution the user will be using, and we might end up with some extra space. We can choose a column to use all the available space by specifying the `flex` configuration (#5).

At last, on line #6, we have a column with `dataIndex groups_id` (#6), which will render the `groups_id` foreign key from the `groups` table. When we display associated data in a grid, we do not want to display the foreign key, but the description or name of the information. For now, we will leave the `groups_id` configured, but we will come back here and change this.

The `store` configuration is also required when declaring a Grid. But this configuration is missing in this class. Ext JS 5 introduced the ViewModel, and because of this new architecture and the data-binding concept, we can declare a store-less Grid and configure this later.

The Users screen

Now that we have the **Users** GridPanel ready, we still need to create another component that is going to wrap the **User** GridPanel and will also contain the toolbar with the **Add/Edit/Delete** buttons. The simplest component that supports Docked Items is the panel.

We are going to create a new class named `Packt.view.security.User` that is going to extend from the `Ext.panel.Panel` class. To do so, we need to create a new file named `User.js` under the `app/view/security` directory, as follows:

```
Ext.define('Packt.view.security.User', {
    extend: 'Ext.panel.Panel',
    xtype: 'user',

    requires: [
        'Packt.view.security.UsersGrid' //#1
    ],
```

```
        controller: 'user',  //#2
        viewModel: {           //#3
            type: 'user'
        },

        frame: true,          //#4

        layout: {             //#5
            type: 'vbox',
            align: 'stretch'
        },

        items: [
            {
                xtype: 'users-grid',  //#6
                flex: 1               //#7
            }
        ]
    });
```

In this class, we will have only one component being rendered in the panel's body for now. It is the users-grid (#6). And as we are using its xtype to instantiate it, we need to make sure the UsersGrid class is already loaded, and that is why we need to add the class in the requires declaration (#1).

Later, we are going to create a window (popup) with a form that is going to allow us to create or edit a user. Because of some ViewModel concepts and limitations, we will add the window as an item of this class. For this reason, we are not going to use the Fit Layout (renders a single child), but we are going to use the VBox layout (#5).

The VBox layout aligns the child items vertically. It divides the available vertical space between the child items using the flex configuration (#7). In this example, the window will be displayed as a popup, so the Grid will continue being the only child component.

When using the VBox layout, we can also define the alignment of the items. We are going to use align: 'stretch'. According to Ext JS documentation, the possible options are the following:

- begin: Child items are aligned vertically at the top of the container
- middle: Child items are vertically centered in the container
- end: Child items are aligned vertically at the bottom of the container
- stretch: Child items are stretched vertically to fill the height of the container
- stretchmax: Child items are stretched vertically to the height of the largest item

To add a border around the screen, we are going to set `frame:true` (#4). We are also specifying a `controller` (#2) and a `ViewModel` (#3) for this `View` that we are going to create later in this chapter.

 There is also the `border` configuration that we can set for any panel subclass. The `border` configuration when specified as `false` (default value) renders the panel with zero width borders. The `frame` configuration when specified as `true` applies a frame to the panel.

Working with docked items

The next step is to add the toolbar with the **Add**, **Edit**, and **Delete** buttons, so we are going to `dock` this toolbar on the `top`, and we are going to declare it inside the `dockedItems` declaration of the `Packt.view.security.User` class:

```
dockedItems: [
    {
        xtype: 'toolbar',
        dock: 'top', //#1
        items: [
            {
                xtype: 'button',
                text: 'Add',
                glyph: Packt.util.Glyphs.getIcon('add'), //#2
                listeners: {
                    click: 'onAdd' //#3
                }
            },
            {
                xtype: 'button',
                text: 'Edit',
                glyph: Packt.util.Glyphs.getIcon('edit'),
                listeners: {
                    click: 'onEdit'
                }
            },
            {
                xtype: 'button',
                text: 'Delete',
                glyph: Packt.util.Glyphs.getIcon('destroy'),
                listeners: {
                    click: 'onDelete'
                }
```

```
            }
        ]
    }
]
```

Inside the `dockedItems` configuration, we can add a component or a collection of components to be added as docked items to the panel or any of its subclasses. The docked items can be docked to either the `top`, `right`, `left`, or `bottom` of a panel. We can have as many as needed, and it is usually used to declare toolbar inside a panel (or any of its subclasses).

In this example, we are adding a toolbar at the `top` (#1) of the panel. The toolbar has three buttons. For each button, we are going to configure an icon with the help of a `glyph` (#2) and also the event listener we are going to create inside the ViewController (#3).

If we take another look at line #2, we can see that we have not implemented the `Packt.util.Glyphs` class yet. Let's work on it before we dive into the ViewModel and ViewController code.

Working with singletons – Ext JS class system

Let's enjoy the opportunity to create a new utility class for our project and dive into some class system concepts of Ext JS.

We already know we can use the Font Awesome CSS in the `iconCls` configuration of a button (or any other component that supports it), and we also learned we can use the `glyph` configuration as an alternative. The con of using `glyph` is declaring code as value (`xf067`), and if we decide to read this code in the future or another developer decides to maintain it, it is not very helpful; after all, what does `'xf067'` mean?

We can take advantage of the Ext JS class system—most specifically the `singleton` classes—to create a utility class that will take care of this for us. Let's take a look at the code of the `Packt.util.Glyphs` class:

```
Ext.define('Packt.util.Glyphs', {
    singleton: true, //#1

    config: { //#2
        webFont: 'FontAwesome',
        add: 'xf067',
        edit: 'xf040',
        destroy: 'xf1f8',
        save: 'xf00c',
        cancel: 'xf0e2'
    },
```

```
constructor: function(config) { //#3
    this.initConfig(config);
},

getGlyph : function(glyph) { //#4
    var me = this,
        font = me.getWebFont(); //#5
    if (typeof me.config[glyph] === 'undefined') {
        return false;
    }
    return me.config[glyph] + '@' + font;
}
});
```

The idea is to declare the glyph code inside configurations of the class (#2) and use them as a key to retrieve a glyph code. Packt.util.Glyphs.getIcon('add') is easier to understand than 'xf067'. We can reuse it throughout the application, and if we want to change the code for the **Add** button, we can change the Glyphs class, and the code is changed for the entire application.

Let's understand the previous code. We started declaring a class, but in line #1, we have singleton:true. This means the class will be instantiated as a singleton, which means only one instance of this class can be created.

 To learn more about singletons, please visit http://en.wikipedia. org/wiki/Singleton_pattern.

Next, we have the config of the class (#2). Inside config, we can declare the attributes of the class. For each attribute, Ext JS is going to generate a getter method and a setter method. For example, the webFont attribute can be retrieved as this.getWebFont() as showed in line #5.

The method getGlyph (#4) will be the responsible for returning a string with the glyph code + '@' + name of the font. If the glyphFontFamily is set, we do not need to specify the font.

In line #3, we have constructor. A class constructor is the class method that gets invoked immediately when a new instance of that class is created. Inside the constructor, we call the initConfig method. Calling initConfig inside the constructor initializes the configuration for the class.

This class can be modified if we need to work with different font icons.

We cannot forget to add the `requires` in the classes where we are going to use this class:

```
requires: [
    //other requires
    'Packt.util.Glyphs'
],
```

Panel versus Container versus Component

Before we continue, let's take a look back on what we have learned so far. We have created a few views. In some of them we used the component class, in others we used container, and in others, still we used panel. Can you tell the difference between them? When do you use component, container, or panel?

The component is the base class for all Ext JS components (widgets). It has built-in support for basic hide/show, enable/disable, and size control behavior. Visually speaking, there is no style. We can set HTML content and set styles using one or more `'cls'` configurations.

The container is the base class that can contain other components (`items` configuration). It is also the base class that uses the layouts we are covering in this book (border, fit, VBox, anchor, accordion, and so on).

The panel class is a container with more capabilities. The panel has a header that we can set a title and add tools (useful buttons, such as collapse and expand, among others) to and it also support docked items (toolbars).

So, whenever you want to create a new Ext JS widget, you need to ask yourself, "What do I need to have in this widget?". If it is HTML content, we use a component. If we need to have items, or if we need a container to organize the layout of the children items, we can use a container. If we need to set a `title` or have a toolbar inside it, then we use a panel. Because the panel class has more capabilities, it is also a heavier component.

 Using the right widget can also help to boost the application performance.

In this example, we could `move` the toolbar inside the `UserGrid` class. To organize the layout, we could transform the `User` class in a container. If we only wanted to display the `UserGrid` class, we would not need the `User` class at all. This could avoid a bad practice called over-nesting. Over-nesting is using an additional container that does not do anything besides containing another component.

Declaring the User ViewModel

As we use the MVVM architecture, we declare the Model, and then we declare the View. The next step would be declaring the ViewModel. To do so, we are going to create the class `Packt.view.security.UserModel`, which is the ViewModel for the `Packt.view.security.User` class.

 Note the naming convention we are using. The View name is User, so the ViewModel will be the name of the View + 'Model'.

Let's take a look at the `ViewModel` class:

```
Ext.define('Packt.view.security.UserModel', {
    extend: 'Ext.app.ViewModel',

    alias: 'viewmodel.user',

    stores: { //#1
        users: { //#2
            model: 'Packt.model.security.User',
            autoLoad: true //#3
        }
    }
});
```

You learned that we can set the predefined data in the `ViewModel` class in *Chapter 3, The Login Page*. Now we are configuring ViewModel to load data from a `store` (#1) that we are declaring and creating (#2) at the same time. The Store `users` (this would be the Store ID) is a collection of the Model User, and we are also asking the Store to load automatically (#3) (we do not need to call the method load manually).

 As the ViewModel will be created when the View is created, the Store will be loaded when the View is created as well. It is a different approach than declaring the Store as a standalone Store with `autoLoad true` — in this case, the Store will be created when the application is loaded and will retrieve the information from the server as well.

Instead of creating the Store inside the ViewModel, we could create the file representing the Store inside the store package and make a reference here. This Store also does not have a proxy since we declared it inside the Model (specifically inside the schema for reuse purposes).

Working with ViewModel data binding

Let's go back to the UsersGrid class. We have not declared a store, which is required. We will do it using data binding and referencing the user's Store created in the ViewModel.

Inside the UsersGrid class, we are going to add the following code:

```
bind : '{users}',
```

This means the UsersGrid will be bound to the users Store. As the UsersGrid is a child component of the User class that refers the User ViewModel, the UsersGrid class will also have access to the ViewModel.

Next, we will go back to the User view class to add another data binding. We will add the following code to the **Edit** and **Delete** buttons:

```
bind: {
    disabled: '{!usersGrid.selection}'
}
```

We want the **Edit** and **Delete** buttons to be enabled only when the user selects a row from the Grid. If no row is selected, there is no point in clicking on the **Edit** or **Delete** buttons. So we are going to enable or disable the button according to this constraint. It is bound with the usersGrid (reference of the UsersGrid class) and the attribute selection of the Grid.

We also cannot forget to add the ViewModel to the requires from the User class:

```
requires: [
    //other requires
    'Packt.view.security.UserModel'd
],
```

Our code is complete so far. Time to listen to some events!

Creating the User ViewController

The next step is creating the ViewController for the User class, so we are going to create the Packt.view.security.UserController class.

 Note the naming convention we are using. The View name is User, so the ViewController will be the name of the View + 'Controller'.

Let's add the following code to the ViewController class. It contains the method signature of all events and internal methods we are going to create:

```
Ext.define('Packt.view.security.UserController', {
    extend: 'Ext.app.ViewController',

    alias: 'controller.user',

    requires: [
        'Packt.util.Util'
    ],

    onAdd: function(button, e, options){},

    onEdit: function(button, e, options){},

    createDialog: function(record){},

    getRecordsSelected: function(){},

    onDelete: function(button, e, options){},

    onSave: function(button, e, options){},

    onSaveSuccess: function(form, action) {},

    onSaveFailure: function(form, action) {},

    onCancel: function(button, e, options){},

    refresh: function(button, e, options){},

    onFileFieldChange: function(fileField, value, options) {}
});
```

Before we dive into each method, go back to the User View, and add the ViewController to the `requires` declaration as well so that we can run and test what we coded so far:

```
requires: [
    //other requires
    'Packt.view.security.UserController'
],
```

To be able to execute the code, we also need to execute UPDATE on the database:

```
UPDATE `sakila`.`menu` SET `className`='user' WHERE `id`='3';
```

This will update the `className` column from `menu` `table` to match the `xtype` configuration we created for the User class, which is the View we want to be opened when a user clicks on the **Users** option from the menu.

Reloading the project, we will be able to see the list of all users from the application:

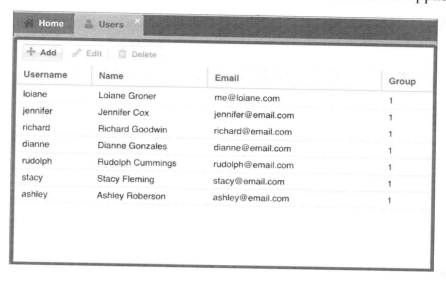

Adding and editing a new user

Now that we are capable of listing all the users of the application, we can implement the **Add** and **Edit** buttons capability. But before we start adding new event listeners to the controller, we need to create the new view that we are going to display to the user to edit or add a new user.

Creating the Edit View – form within a window

This new view is going to be a window since we want to display it as a popup, and inside this window, we will have a form with the user's information, and then, we will have a toolbar at the bottom with two buttons: **Cancel** and **Save**. It is very similar to the Login window that we developed in *Chapter 3, The Login Page*, but we will add new capabilities to this new form, such as file upload and also a preview file using HTML5 features.

The view we are going to create looks like the following screenshot:

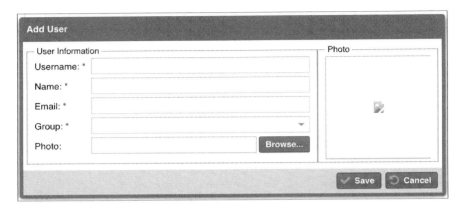

So, let's get started and create a new class named `Packt.view.security.UserForm` that is going to `extend` from the window class:

```
Ext.define('Packt.view.security.UserForm', {
    extend: 'Ext.window.Window',
    alias: 'widget.user-form',

    height: 270,
    width: 600,

    requires: [
        'Packt.util.Util',
        'Packt.util.Glyphs'
    ],

    layout: {
        type: 'fit'
    },

    bind: {
        title: '{title}' //#1
    },

    closable: false,
    modal: true,

    items: [
        {
```

```
        xtype: 'form',
        reference: 'form',
        bodyPadding: 5,
        modelValidation: true, //#2
        layout: {
            type: 'hbox',        //#3
            align: 'stretch'
        },
        items: [
            //add form items here
        ]
    }
    ]
});
```

There are three very important things that we need to notice in this class: the first one is that we are not using the autoShow attribute. And the purpose is that we can create the window, and then we display it calling the method show() manually.

The second one is the data binding in line #1. We want to use data binding to automatically set the title of the window (Add new user or Edit: name of user). This is one of the advantages of the MVVM architecture.

The third thing is the layout that we are using on the form. It is not the default layout used by the form component (which is the Anchor layout). We are going to use the hbox layout (#3) because we want to organize the form's items horizontally. And we want the items to occupy all the available vertical space, so we will use the align: 'stretch' — we do not want to set height for each form items.

And at last, we learned in *Chapter 3, The Login Page*, how to validate the form using form validations. In this chapter, we will validate the form using modelvalidations (#2).

Let's add the first item to our form. If we take a look at the window screenshot at the beginning of this topic, we will notice that we are going to use two fieldsets to organize the form items. So the first one will be a fieldset to organize all the "User Information", as follows:

```
{
    xtype: 'fieldset',
    flex: 1,                    //#4
    title: 'User Information',
    layout: 'anchor',           //#5
    defaults: {
        afterLabelTextTpl: Packt.util.Util.required, //#6
```

```
            anchor: '100%',                                  //#7
            xtype: 'textfield',
            msgTarget: 'side',
            labelWidth: 75
        },
        items: [
            //add items here
        ]
    },
```

As the form is using the `hbox` layout, we need to specify how much space this component will occupy (#4). When working with the HBox or VBox layouts, the space occupied by the child component is calculated based on the proportional space configured. If we have five items with `flex: 1` each, then the total sum will be five; each item will occupy one-fifth of the available space. Or, we can also set `width` (HBox) or `height` (VBox) for some items, and the remaining space will be divided among the items with the `flex` configuration. In this example, we will use `flex: 1` for this `fieldset`, and for the next one we are going declare, we will use a fix width, so this `fieldset` will occupy all the remaining available space.

The `fieldset` will also use the `anchor` layout (#5), which allows you to anchor the items relative to the container's dimensions. The `anchor` layout is the default layout for forms, but as we are using a fieldset, we need to specify the layout as well. For each item, we can specify the `anchor` configuration (#7). As we want the child items occupying all the available width within the fieldset, we set the `anchor` configuration to `100%`.

For all required items, we will add a red asterisk (#6). Instead of adding the HTML for each form we use, we can add this value to our `Util` class and reuse it among other forms as well. Inside the `Packt.Util.util` class, add the following code:

```
required: '<span style="color:red;font-weight:bold" data-
qtip="Required"> *</span>',
```

We are also telling the fieldset that the default `xtype` of the items will be `textfield`. If any of the declared fields does not need these default configurations, we will override them with other values. So, let's declare the fields that will be part of the `items` configuration of the "`User Information`" fieldset:

```
{
    xtype: 'hiddenfield',
    name: 'id',                    //#8
    fieldLabel: 'Label',
    bind : '{currentUser.id}' //#9
},
```

```
{
    fieldLabel: 'Username',
    name: 'userName',
    bind : '{currentUser.userName}'
},
{
    fieldLabel: 'Name',
    name: 'name',
    bind : '{currentUser.name}'
},
{
    fieldLabel: 'Email',
    name: 'email',
    bind : '{currentUser.email}'
},
{
    xtype: 'combo',
    fieldLabel: 'Group',
    displayField: 'name',    //#10
    valueField: 'id',        //#11
    queryMode: 'local',      //#12
    forceSelection: true,    //#13
    editable: false,         //#14
    name: 'groups_id',
    bind: {
        value: '{currentUser.groups_id}', //#15
        store: '{groups}',                //#16
        selection: '{currentUser.group}'  //#17
    }
},
{
    xtype: 'filefield',
    fieldLabel: 'Photo',
    name: 'picture',
    buttonText: 'Select Photo...',
    afterLabelTextTpl: '',            //#18
    listeners: {
        change: 'onFileFieldChange' //#19
    }
}
```

The id field will be hidden because we do not want the user to see it (we will use it only internally), and the userName, name, and email are simple textfields. Note that for each field, we declared a name (#8) and the bind (#9) configuration. As we are going to use a file upload capability, we will need to send the form information using the Ajax submit, and that is why we need to set a name configuration for each field. To avoid having to set the values of the form manually, we are going to use data binding from the ViewModel. We will set a variable named currentUser in the ViewModel that will refer to the current selected row of the UsersGrid.

Then, we have a combobox. When working with comboboxes, we need to set a Store to feed the information to it. In this case, we will bind (#16), the store of this combobox, with Store groups from the ViewModel. We will create the Store in a minute. The Store can represent a Model that has different fields. We can specify which field from the Model will be used as an internal value (#11) and which field will be displayed to the user (#10).

We can also specify other options such as forcing the user to select a value from the combobox (#13) and not allowing the user to write anything on it (#14) — as writing is autocomplete. As we will have the Store already loaded for this combobox, we can set the query mode to be local (#15). The default behavior is that whenever the user clicks on the combobox trigger, the Store is loaded.

Note that the binding for this field is more complex than for the other ones. We have three values bound; the store that we already mentioned (#16); the value, which refers to the groups_id foreign key (#15) of the User Model and the selection (#17), which will refer to the group object from the User Model (referring to the Group selected).

Then we have the file upload field. This field will not be mandatory, so we do not want it to display that red asterisk (#18) by overriding the defaults configuration. We also want to use a preview capability, so we are also going to add a listener declaration to this field (#19). Whenever the user selects a new picture, we will display it in the fieldset we are going to declare next (we are going to talk about the preview capability later in this chapter).

This is the first fieldset that will be displayed on the left-hand side of the form. Next, we need to declare the other fieldset that is going to wrap the Photo and will be displayed on the right-hand side of the form:

```
{
    xtype: 'fieldset',
    title: 'Photo',
    width: 170,   //#19
    items: [
```

```
            {
                xtype: 'image',
                reference: 'userPicture', //#20
                height: 150,
                width: 150,
                bind:{
                    src:
                    'resources/profileImages/{currentUser.picture}'
                    //#21
                }
            }
        ]
    }
```

In this `fieldset`, we will declare a fixed `width` (#19). As the form uses the HBox layout, when a component has a fixed `width`, the layout will respect and apply the specified `width`. Then, the first `fieldset`, which has the `flex` configuration, will occupy all the remaining horizontal space.

Inside the picture fieldset, we will use an `Ext.Image` `Component`. The `Ext.Image` (#20) class helps us to create and render images. It also creates an `<image>` tag on the DOM with `src` (#21) specified. The `src` attribute is also bound to the picture field of the `User` Model. We also declared a reference to work with the preview capability later (#20).

When we load an existing `User` and try to edit the form, we will display the user's image on this component (if any). Also, if the user uploads a new image, the preview will also be rendered in this component.

And now, the last step is to declare the bottom toolbar with the **Save** and **Cancel** buttons, as follows:

```
dockedItems: [
    {
        xtype: 'toolbar',
        dock: 'bottom',
        ui: 'footer',
        layout: {
            pack: 'end', //#22
            type: 'hbox'
        },
        items: [
            {
                xtype: 'button',
                text: 'Save',
```

```
                    glyph: Packt.util.Glyphs.getGlyph('save'),
                    listeners: {
                        click: 'onSave'
                    }
                },
                {
                    xtype: 'button',
                    text: 'Cancel',
                    glyph: Packt.util.Glyphs.getGlyph('cancel'),
                    listeners: {
                        click: 'onCancel'
                    }
                }
            ]
        }
    ]
```

As we want to align the buttons on the right-hand side of the toolbar, we will use the hbox layout as well and organize (#22) the buttons to the right toolbar. The Edit/ Add window is now ready. However, there are a few other details that we still need to take care of before implementing the Add and Edit listeners on the Controller.

Creating the Group Model

On the Group combobox, we declared a groups Store used to load all the Groups from the database. Now, we need to implement this missing Store, and the first step to do so is create the Model that is going to represent a Group record from the group table. So we are going to create a new Model named Packt.model.security.Group, as follows:

```
Ext.define('Packt.model.security.Group', {
    extend: 'Packt.model.security.Base',

    fields: [
        { name: 'name' }
    ]
});
```

As the group table is very simple, it only contains two columns, id and name; our Group Model is also simple with only these two fields. As the Group Model is extending from the Base Model we created in the beginning of this chapter, the id column will come from the Base, schema, and proxy configurations.

The Groups Store

As we already created the Group Model, now we need to create the groups Store.

 Always remember the naming convention: the Model name is the singular name of the entity you want to represent and the Store is the plural of the name of the Model/entity.

So we will create a new Store inside the UserModel class, as follows:

```
stores: {
    users: {
        model: 'Packt.model.security.User',
        autoLoad: true
    },
    groups: {
        model: 'Packt.model.security.Group',
        autoLoad: true
    }
}
```

Following the same pattern as the other stores, the groups information will be sent by the server within a data attribute in the JSON as follows:

```
{
    "success": true,
    "data": [{
        "id": "1",
        "name": "admin"
    }]
}
```

Now all the views, models, and stores needed for our user management module are created. We can focus on the ViewController to handle all the events we are interested in listening to and implementing all the magic!

 For all the server-side code of this chapter, and the group management code, please download the source code bundle of this book or go to https://github.com/loiane/masteringextjs.

Controller – listening to the Add button

The first event that we will implement for the Edit or Add Window is the Add event. When the user clicks on the **Add** button, we want to display the **Edit** user window (the `Packt.view.security.UserForm` class).

The button **Add** already has a listener. So all we need to do is add the code in the ViewController:

```
onAdd: function(button, e, options){
    this.createDialog(null);
},
```

If the user clicks on the **Add** button, we want to open a blank popup so that user can enter the new record information and save it. If the user clicks on the **Edit** button, we want to open the same popup with the data from the selected row from the Grid. So, for the **Add** button, we will open the popup passing null (no row selected). The `createDialog` method is listed in the following code:

```
createDialog: function(record){

    var me = this,
        view = me.getView();  //#1

    me.dialog = view.add({
        xtype: 'user-form',   //#2
        viewModel: {          //#3
            data: {
                title: record ? 'Edit: ' +
                record.get('name') : 'Add User' //#4
            },
            links: { //#5
                currentUser: record || { //#6
                    type: 'User',         //#7
                    create: true
                }
            }
        }
    });

    me.dialog.show(); //#7
},
```

We start getting a reference (#1) to the `User` View class reference, since the ModelView was declared inside it.

Next, we are going to create the `UserForm` window (#2) and assign it to a variable dialog that belongs to the ViewModel scope (the method add returns the instance of the component created). We are also adding the `UserForm` window to the `User` View (you might remember that we used the VBox layout instead of the Fit layout; this is the reason). When adding the `UserForm` window as an item of the `User` View, this item will also have access to the ViewModel associated to its parent. In this case, we want to add more details to the Window's ViewModel (as a child ViewModel—(#3)). We are going to add a predefined field named `title` (that we used to set the window's title—(#4)). And we are also going to create a `link` (#5). Links provide a way to assign a simple name to a more complex bind. The primary use for this is to assign names to records in the data model. If there is an existing `record` (from `Edit`—(#6)), it uses a copy of it, and if not, it creates a new phantom record (#7).

Controller – listening to the Edit button

If we want to edit an existing user, the **Edit** button will fire the click event, and the ViewController will listen to it through the following method:

```
onEdit: function(button, e, options){

    var me = this,
        records = me.getRecordsSelected(); //#1

    if(records[0]){ //#2
        me.createDialog(records[0]); //#3
    }
},
```

First, we are going to get the selected `records` from the Grid (#1). If a record (#2) was selected, we are going to create the window passing the record (#3).

The method `getRecordSelected` is listed as follows:

```
getRecordsSelected: function(){
    var grid = this.lookupReference('usersGrid'); //#4
    return grid.getSelection(); //#5
},
```

We are going to get a reference of the `UsersGrid` (#4), and by accessing its `getSelection` method, we can get the rows selected (#5).

The getSelection method returns an array of the selected records. That is why we are using records[0] to access the selected row. By default, a Grid allows you to select only one row at a time. This can be changed by setting the following configuration in the Grid:

```
selModel: {
    mode: 'MULTI'
},
```

By default, a Grid allows you to select only one row at a time; this can be changed using the selType: 'checkboxmodel' (Ext.selection.CheckboxModel).

The validation in #2 is an extra step as we are binding the **Edit** button directly to the selection configuration of the Grid, but to be careful and avoid exceptions in the code is never too much!

Controller – listening to the Cancel button

If the user decides not to save the user information, it is possible to click on the **Cancel** button that is going to fire the click event to execute the following method:

```
onCancel: function(button, e, options){
    var me = this;
    me.dialog = Ext.destroy(me.dialog);
},
```

What we want to do is very simple: if the user wants to cancel all the changes made to an existing user or wants to cancel the creation of a user, the system will destroy the window. We can use Ext.destroy to destroy it or call the method destroy as well. At the same time, me.dialog will lose the reference as well.

To learn more about JavaScript memory leaks, go to http://javascript.info/tutorial/memory-leaks. To learn more about the importance of the garbage collector (freeing up memory) go to http://goo.gl/qDdwwt.

Controller – saving a user

Now that the user is able to open the window to create or edit a User, we need to implement the **Save** button logic. No matter if the user is creating a new user or editing an existing user, we will use the same logic to save the user. We will let the server side handle this if it needs to use an UPDATE or INSERT query.

The ViewController will execute the following method to save the information:

```
onSave: function(button, e, options){

    var me = this,
        form = me.lookupReference('form'); //#1

    if (form && form.isValid()) { //#2
        form.submit({        //#3
            clientValidation: true, //#4
            url: 'php/user/save.php', //#5
            scope: me,               //#6
            success: 'onSaveSuccess',
            failure: 'onSaveFailure'
        });
    }
},
```

The first step is to get the form reference (#1). Then, we will verify that the form is valid ((#2) the user filled the form with valid values following all the rules of the model validations (#4) that we are going to implement), after which we will submit the form to the given `url` (#5).

We could use the Store features to create and edit the User (as we will see later in this book). However, we are using a different approach, which is the form submit method to directly send the values to the server, because we are also uploading a document to the server. When uploading a document to the server, it is not possible to use the Store capabilities.

Before we list the success and failure callbacks, take a look at the code again at the line `var me = this`. Whenever we have more than one reference to this or we work with callbacks, we do this assignment.

There are two reasons to use me instead of this (or you can create other variable names according to your preference (that, self)). The first one is when "this" is used a lot in a method, using "me" can save 16 bits each reference. After we do the production build, Sencha Cmd will replace me with a, b, or any other letter. The keyword this cannot be replaced with a, b, or any other value, therefore it will use four characters instead of only one.

The second reason is that we can keep a reference to this inside a scope in which this refers to something else (like a callback function, for example, the form submit — if we used this inside the submit, it would make a reference to the submit method itself and not the ViewController).

This way a callback function can refer to a function or variable that was declared in the outer function (ViewController in this example). This is called closure.

You can learn about how to handle file upload in PHP by downloading the source code from this book. If you are using another language or for some reason a form submit is not working, always inspect the request in the *Developer Tools* of the browser you are using to see what is being sent to the server. The following screenshot exemplifies what is being sent while creating a new user:

```
×  Headers  Preview  Response  Cookies  Timing
    Content-Type: multipart/form-data; boundary=-----WebKitFormBoundaryvRtzb1t4nDZGwPHP
    Cookie: ext-stateful-filter-grid=o%3Awidth%3Dn%253A700%5Eheight%3Dn%253A500%5Ecolumns%3Da%253Ao%25253Aid%25253Ds%2525253Aheader
    -201%255Eo%25253Aid%25253Ds%2525253Aheader-202%255Eo%25253Aid%25253Ds%2525253Aheader-203%255Eo%25253Aid%25253Ds%2525253Aheader-
    204%255Eo%25253Aid%25253Ds%2525253Aheader-205%255Eo%25253Aid%25253Ds%2525253Aheader-206%5EstoreState%3Do%253Asorters%253Da%2525
    3Ao%2525253Aroot%2525253Ds%252525253Adata%2525255Eproperty%2525253Ds%252525253Acompany%2525255Edirection%2525253Ds%252525253AAS
    C; ext-stateGrid=o%3Awidth%3Dn%253A750%5Eheight%3Dn%253A350%5Ecolumns%3Da%253Ao%25253Aid%25253Ds%2525253Aheader-447%255Eo%25253
    Aid%25253Ds%2525253Aheader-448%255Eo%25253Aid%25253Ds%2525253Aheader-449%255Eo%25253Aid%25253Ds%2525253Aheader-450%255Eo%25253A
    id%25253Ds%2525253Aheader-451%255Eo%25253Aid%25253Ds%2525253Aheader-452%5EstoreState%3Do%253Asorters%253Da%25253Ao%2525253Aroot
    %2525253Ds%252525253Adata%2525255Eproperty%2525253Ds%252525253Aname%2525255Edirection%2525253Ds%252525253AASC; PHPSESSID=0b2vip
    4mt4nejq1hg38pBohuu0; ext-kitchensink-viewport=o%3AhasTreeNav%3Db%253A0; ext-mainnav.east=o%3Awidth%3Dn%253A625%5Ecollapsed%3Db
    %253A0%5Eweight%3Dn%253A-20
    Host: localhost
    Origin: https://localhost
    Referer: https://localhost/masteringextjs/
    User-Agent: Mozilla/5.0 (Macintosh; Intel Mac OS X 10_9_4) AppleWebKit/537.36 (KHTML, like Gecko) Chrome/37.0.2062.124 Safari/5
    37.36
  ▼ Request Payload
    ------WebKitFormBoundaryvRtzb1t4nDZGwPHP
    Content-Disposition: form-data; name="id"
```

The next steps now are to implement the success and failure callbacks. Let's implement the success callback first:

```
onSaveSuccess: function(form, action) {
    var me = this;
    me.onCancel(); //#7
    me.refresh();  //#8
    Packt.util.Util.showToast('Success! User saved.'); //#9
},
```

If the server returns success as `true`, we will call the method `onCancel` that is responsible for closing and destroying the window (#7) that we implemented in the previous topic. As we are using a form submit to send the information to the server, we need to refresh (#8) the Store to get the new information from the server. And at last, we will display a toast (introduced in Ext JS 5) with a success message (#9) as shown by the following image:

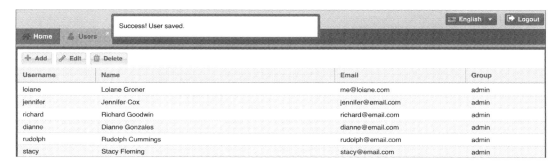

The refresh method is listed as follows:

```
refresh: function(button, e, options){
    var me = this,
        store = me.getStore('users');

    store.load();
},
```

Inside the `refresh` method, we get the reference to the `users` Store and call its method `load` to get the information from the server again.

The following is the `showToast` static method from the `Packt.util.Util` class:

```
showToast: function(text) {
    Ext.toast({
        html: text,
        closable: false,
        align: 't',
        slideInDuration: 400,
        minWidth: 400
    });
}
```

The Ext.Toast class provides lightweight, auto-dismissing pop-up notifications called toasts. We can set its content (html), a title, a **close** button, the alignment (in our example, it will be displayed at the top), how many seconds it will be displayed (4 seconds) and its width, among other options that we can check in the Ext JS documentation.

Next, let's implement the failure callback:

```
onSaveFailure: function(form, action) {
    Packt.util.Util.handleFormFailure(action);
},
```

In *Chapter 3, The Login Page*, we also handled a form failure callback. The code we are going to use here is exactly the same. As we are starting to repeat code, we can create another static function in the Util class so that we can reuse it:

```
handleFormFailure: function(action){
    var me = this,
    result =
    Packt.util.Util.decodeJSON(action.response.responseText);

    switch (action.failureType) {
        case Ext.form.action.Action.CLIENT_INVALID:
            me.showErrorMsg('Form fields may not be submitted with
            invalid values'); //#1
            break;
        case Ext.form.action.Action.CONNECT_FAILURE:
            me.showErrorMsg(action.response.responseText);
            break;
        case Ext.form.action.Action.SERVER_INVALID:
            me.showErrorMsg(result.msg);
    }
}
```

The difference is now that this code is inside the Packt.util.Util class, we can refer to it to call the showErrorMsg method (#1).

We can also go back to LoginController and replace the failure callback code with the call of the handleFormFailure function.

Our save code is now ready.

Using Model validators

As we implemented the save method, let's use the opportunity to complete the code to validate the form with Model validators.

We are going to add the following code to the `User` Model:

```
validators: {
    name: [
        { type: 'presence', message: 'This field is mandatory'},
        { type: 'length', min: 3, max: 100}
    ],
    userName: [
        { type: 'exclusion', list: ['Admin', 'Operator'] },
        { type: 'format', matcher: /([a-z]+)/i },
        { type: 'presence', message: 'This field is mandatory'},
        { type: 'length', min: 3, max: 25}
    ],
    email: [
        { type: 'presence', message: 'This field is mandatory'},
        { type: 'length', min: 5, max: 100},
        { type: 'email' }
    ],
    groups_id: 'presence'
},
```

We can have the following types of Model validators:

- `presence`: This ensures that the field has a value. Zero counts as a valid value, but empty strings do not.

- `length`: This ensures that a string is between `min` length and `max` length. Both constraints are optional.

- `format`: This ensures that a string matches a regular expression format.

- `inclusion`: This ensures that a value is within a specific set of values (for example, ensuring gender is either male or female).

- `exclusion`: This ensures that a value is not one of the specific set of values (for example, blacklisting usernames like "admin").

- `email`: This ensures that the value is a valid e-mail.

- `range`: This ensures that the value is between a `min` and a `max`. Both constraints are optional.

Each validator has a default `message` just in case the validation is not met. We can also override it.

Previewing a file before uploading

One last thing that we will implement related to the window: the file upload preview. This is something that is not that hard to implement, and it will bring a sparkle to the application user's eyes!

So what we want to do when the user selects a new file using the file upload component is read the file using the HTML5 FileReader API. Unfortunately, not every browser supports the FileReader API; only the following versions do: Chrome 6+, Firefox 4+, Safari 6+, Opera 12+, Explorer 10+, iOS Safari 6+, Android 3+, and Opera Mobile 12+. But do not worry, we will verify that the browser supports it first, and if it does not, we will not use it, which means that the file preview will not happen.

 To learn more about the FileReader API, please read its specification at http://www.w3.org/TR/file-upload/, and to learn more about this and other HTML5 features, go to http://www.html5rocks.com/.

When the user selects a new file using the Ext JS file upload component, the change event is fired, so we need to listen to it in our ViewController. The following code exemplifies what was discussed in this paragraph:

```
onFileFieldChange: function(fileField, value, options) {

    var me = this,
        file = fileField.fileInputEl.dom.files[0], //#1
        picture = this.lookupReference('userPicture'); //#2

    if (typeof FileReader !== 'undefined' &&
    (/image/i).test(file.type)) { //#3
        var reader = new FileReader();           //#4
        reader.onload = function(e){             //#5
            picture.setSrc(e.target.result); //#6
        };
        reader.readAsDataURL(file);              //#7
    } else if (!(/image/i).test(file.type)){ //#8
        Ext.Msg.alert('Warning', 'You can only upload image
        files!');
        fileField.reset();                       //#9
    }
}
```

So first, we need to get the file (#1) object that is stored inside the file input element of the Ext JS File field component (also passed as a parameter to our method). Then, we will get a reference of the Ext.Image component that is inside our form so that we can update its source to the file preview.

We will also test whether the FileReader API is available on the browser and also whether the file that the user chose is an image (#3). If positive, we will instantiate a FileReader method (#4); we will add a listener to it (#4), so when the FileReader is done reading the file, we can set its contents to the Ext.Image source (#6). And of course, to fire the onload event, the FileReader instance needs to read the contents of the file (#7). One very important note: we are displaying the contents of the file before we upload to the server. If the user saves the changes made to the form, the new user information will be sent to the server (including the file upload), and the next time we open the window, the picture will be displayed.

How do you get the full path of the file that is being uploaded? For example, the Ext JS file upload component displays C:\fakepath\nameOfTheFile.jpg, and we want to get its real path, such as C:\Program Files\nameOfTheFile.jpg. The answer is: it is not possible to do it with JavaScript (and Ext JS is a JavaScript framework).

This is not a restriction from Ext JS; if we try it with any other JavaScript framework or library, such as jQuery, it is not going to be possible because this is a browser security restriction. Imagine if it was possible. Someone could develop a malicious JavaScript file and run it while you are navigating on the web and get all the information that you have on your computer.

Another really nice thing: if the file that the user chose is not an image (#8), we will display a message saying that only images can be uploaded, and we will reset the file upload component. Unfortunately, it is not possible to filter the file types on the browse window (the one that opens so we can choose a file from the computer), and this is a wayaround, so we can do this validation on the Ext JS side and not leave it to the server.

And if the FileReader is not available, nothing is going to happen. The file preview is simply not going to work. The user will select the file and that's it.

The file size limit that you can upload depends on the upload limit that is set on the web server that you are going to deploy the Ext JS application in. For example, Apache supports a limit of 2GB. IIS has a default value of 4MB, but you can increase it to 2GB as well. Likewise for Apache Tomcat and other web servers. So the size limit is not on Ext JS; it is on the web server, and you just need to configure it.

Deleting a user

The last CRUD operation that we need to implement is the delete user. So let's add the delete listener to the ViewController, as follows:

```
onDelete: function(button, e, options){
    var me = this,
        view = me.getView(),
        records = me.getRecordsSelected(), //#1
        store = me.getStore('users');        //#2

    if (store.getCount() >= 2 && records.length){ //#3
        Ext.Msg.show({
            title:'Delete?', //#4
            msg: 'Are you sure you want to delete?',
            buttons: Ext.Msg.YESNO,
            icon: Ext.Msg.QUESTION,
            fn: function (buttonId){
                if (buttonId == 'yes'){ //#5
                    store.remove(records); //#6
                    store.sync();          //#7
                }
            }
        });
    } else if (store.getCount() === 1) { //#8
        Ext.Msg.show({
            title:'Warning',
            msg: 'You cannot delete all the users from the
            application.',
            buttons: Ext.Msg.OK,
            icon: Ext.Msg.WARNING
        });
    }
},
```

The idea of this method is to verify that the user selected any row from the grid to be deleted (record[0] exists—(#1)) and also, we will only delete a user if there are more than two users on the application (#3). If yes, we will delete the user. If not, this means there is only one user in the application (#8), and we cannot delete the only user that exists.

If it is possible to delete the user, the system will display a question asking whether we really want to delete the selected user (#4). If the answer is yes (#5), we will get the store reference (#2) and use its remove method (#6) passing the records to be deleted, and will send this request to the server (#7). The proxy will call the destroy URL when the sync method is called.

 Just remember that on the server, you can execute a DELETE query on the database, but in most cases we do a logical deletion, which means we will perform an UPDATE on a column active (in this case update the user to inactive).

Displaying the group name in the Grid

There are a few ways we can display associated data in the Grid. We will use one approach in this example, and in other chapters, we will use different ones.

The approach we are going to use is to add a hasOne association to the User Model as follows:

```
hasOne: [
    {
        model: 'Group',         //#1
        name: 'group',          //#2
        foreignKey:'groups_id', //#3
        associationKey: 'group'
    }
]
```

As we are using the same schema in the User and Group models, we can refer to the Group Model only by its entityName (#1). We can also give a name of the object that is going to come from the server with the Group information (#2). And at last, Ext JS also needs to know which field contains the foreign key to the Group Model (#3).

Then, we are going to add a new field in the user Model as well, as follows:

```
{ name:'groupName', type:'string', persist:false,
    convert:function(v, rec){
        var data = rec.data;
        if (data.group && data.group.name){
            return data.group.name;
        }
        return data.groups_id;
    }
}
```

This field will be created in runtime when a `User` Model is created. We are not going to persist this information, which means that whenever the Store sends a create, update, or destroy request to the server, this field will not be included. For this field, we are also going to declare a `convert` function, which means that the information for this field will be created from another existing field. If there is `group` information available, we will return its `name`; otherwise, we return the `groups_id` anyway.

Then, in the `UsersGrid` class, we will replace the current `dataIndex` of the `groups_id` column with the following code:

```
dataIndex: 'groupName',
```

And the Grid will display the name of the group instead of its ID.

We can refresh the application and test all functionalities from this chapter!

Summary

In this chapter, we covered how to create, update, delete, and list all the users from our application.

While we developed this module, we covered some important Ext JS concepts and some features introduced in Ext JS 5. We developed this module using MVVM, and we covered some other ModelView capabilities, such as data binding. We learned how to use a schema in the Model and validate a form using Model validation. We also explored a new HTML5 feature for the file upload preview capability, which is another example of how we can use other technologies along with Ext JS.

In this next chapter, we will implement the MySQL table management module, which means we will implement a screen very similar to the **Edit** table data screen that we find in the MySQL Workbench application.

7
Static Data Management

So far, we have implemented capabilities related to basic features of the application. From now on, we will start implementing the application's core features, starting with static data management. What exactly is this? Every application has information that is not directly related to the core business, but this information is used by the core business logic somehow.

There are two types of data in every application: static data and dynamic data. For example, the types of categories, languages, cities, and countries can exist independently of the core business and can be used by the core business information as well; this is what we call static data because it does not change very often. And there is the dynamic data, which is the information that changes in the application, what we call core business data. Clients, orders, and sales would be examples of dynamic or core business data.

We can treat this static information as though they are independent MySQL tables (since we are using MySQL as the database server), and we can perform all the actions we can do on a MySQL table. So in this chapter, we will cover:

- Creating a new system module called static data
- Listing all information as a MySQL table
- Creating new records on the tables
- Live search on the table
- Filtering information
- Editing and deleting a record
- Creating an abstract component for reuse in all tables

Presenting the tables

If we open and analyze the **Entity Relationship** (**ER**) diagram that comes with the Sakila installation, we will notice the following tables:

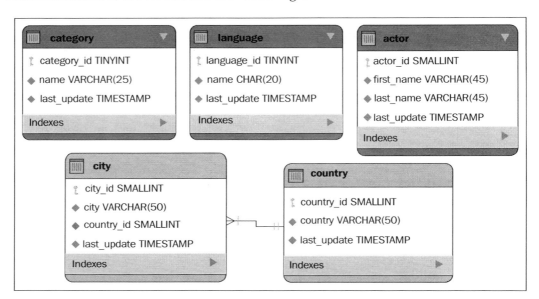

As a reminder, the Sakila database can be downloaded at `http://dev.mysql.com/doc/index-other.html`, and its documentation with installation instructions can be found at `http://dev.mysql.com/doc/sakila/en/`.

These tables can exist independently of the other tables, and we are going to work with them in this chapter.

When we open SQL editor in MySQL Workbench (version 6) (`http://dev.mysql.com/downloads/workbench/`), we can select a table, right-click on it, and select **Select Rows – Limit 1000**. When we choose this option, a new tab will be opened, and it looks as follows:

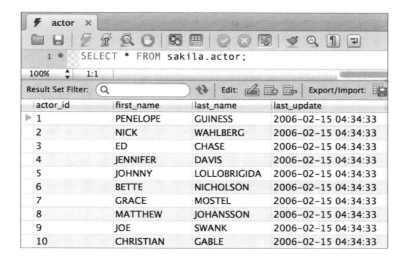

The table shown previously is the `actor` table. The idea is to implement screens that look similar to the preceding screenshot for each of the tables that we selected: **Actors, Categories, Languages, Cities,** and **Countries** as displayed in the following screenshot (which is the final result of the code that we will be implementing in this chapter):

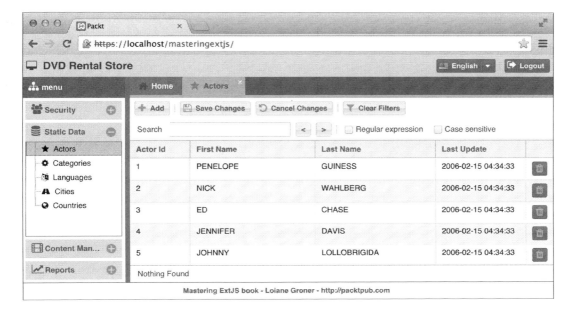

Our goal in this chapter is to minimize the amount of code to implement these five screens. This means we want to create the most generic code as possible and will facilitate future code fixes and enhancements and also make it easier to create new screens with these same features if needed.

So let's go ahead and start the development.

Creating a Model

As usual, we are going to start by creating the models. First, let's list the tables we will be working with and their columns:

- Actor: `actor_id`, `first_name`, `last_name`, `last_update`
- Category: `category_id`, `name`, `last_update`
- Language: `language_id`, `name`, `last_update`
- City: `city_id`, `city`, `country_id`, `last_update`
- Country: `country_id`, `country`, `last_update`

We could create one Model for each of these entities with no problem at all; however, we want to reuse as much code as possible. Take another look at the list of tables and their columns. Notice that all tables have one column in common — the `last_update` column.

All the previous tables have the `last_update` column in common. That being said, we can create a super model that contains this field. When we implement the `actor` and `category` models, we can extend the super Model, in which case we do not need to declare the column. Don't you think?

Abstract Model

In OOP, there is a concept called inheritance, which is a way to reuse the code of existing objects. Ext JS uses an OOP approach, so we can apply the same concept in Ext JS applications. If you take a look back at the code we already implemented, you will notice that we are already applying inheritance in most of our classes (with the exception of the `util` package), but we are creating classes that inherit from Ext JS classes. Now, we will start creating our own super classes.

As all the models that we will be working with have the `last_update` column in common (if you take a look, all the Sakila tables have this column), we can create a super Model with this field. So, we will create a new file under `app/model/staticData` named `Base.js`:

```
Ext.define('Packt.model.staticData.Base', {
    extend: 'Packt.model.Base', //#1

    fields: [
        {
            name: 'last_update',
            type: 'date',
            dateFormat: 'Y-m-j H:i:s'
        }
    ]
});
```

This Model has only one column, that is, `last_update`. On the tables, the `last_update` column has the type `timestamp`, so the `type` of the field needs to be `date`, and we will also apply `date format: 'Y-m-j H:i:s'`, which is years, months, days, hours, minutes, and seconds, following the same format as we have in the database (`2006-02-15 04:34:33`).

When we can create each Model representing the tables, we will not need to declare the `last_update` field again.

Look again at the code at line #1. We are not extending the default `Ext.data.Model` class, but another `Base` class. Remember the `security.Base` Model we created in the preceding chapter? We are going to move its code to the model package and make some changes.

Adapting the Base Model schema

Create a file named `Base.js` inside the `app/model` folder with the following content in it:

```
Ext.define('Packt.model.Base', {
    extend: 'Ext.data.Model',

    requires: [
        'Packt.util.Util'
    ],
```

```
schema: {
    namespace: 'Packt.model', //#1
    urlPrefix: 'php',
    proxy: {
        type: 'ajax',
        api :{
            read : '{prefix}/{entityName:lowercase}/list.php',
            create:
                '{prefix}/{entityName:lowercase}/create.php',
            update:
                '{prefix}/{entityName:lowercase}/update.php',
            destroy:
                '{prefix}/{entityName:lowercase}/destroy.php'
        },
        reader: {
            type: 'json',
            rootProperty: 'data'
        },
        writer: {
            type: 'json',
            writeAllFields: true,
            encode: true,
            rootProperty: 'data',
            allowSingle: false
        },
        listeners: {
            exception: function(proxy, response, operation){
          Packt.util.Util.showErrorMsg(response.responseText);
            }
        }
    }
}
});
```

The only difference between this code and the code we implemented in the preceding chapter is namespace (#1). Instead of using Packt.model.security, we are going to use only Packt.model.

The Packt.model.security.Base class we created in the preceding chapter will look simpler now as follows:

```
Ext.define('Packt.model.security.Base', {
    extend: 'Packt.model.Base',

    idProperty: 'id',
```

```
    fields: [
        { name: 'id', type: 'int' }
    ]
});
```

It is very similar to the `staticData.Base` Model we are creating for this chapter. The difference is in the field that is common for the `staticData` package (`last_update`) and `security` package (`id`).

Having a single schema for the application now means `entityName` of the models will be created based on their name after `'Packt.model'`. This means that the `User` and `Group` models we created in the preceding chapter will have `entityName` `security.User`, and `security.Group` respectively. However, we do not want to break the code we have implemented already, and for this reason we want the `User` and `Group` Model classes to have the entity name as `User` and `Group`. We can do this by adding `entityName: 'User'` to the `User` Model and `entityName: 'Group'` to the `Group` Model. We will do the same for the specific models we will be creating next.

Having a super `Base` Model for all models within the application means our models will follow a pattern. The proxy template is also common for all models, and this means our server-side code will also follow a pattern. This is good to organize the application and for future maintenance.

Specific models

Now we can create all the models representing each table. Let's start with the Actor Model. We will create a new class named `Packt.model.staticData.Actor`; therefore, we need to create a new file name `Actor.js` under `app/model/staticData`, as follows:

```
Ext.define('Packt.model.staticData.Actor', {
    extend: 'Packt.model.staticData.Base', //#1

    entityName: 'Actor', //#2

    idProperty: 'actor_id', //#3

    fields: [
        { name: 'actor_id' },
        { name: 'first_name'},
        { name: 'last_name'}
    ]
});
```

There are three important things we need to note in the preceding code:

- This Model is extending (#1) from the `Packt.model.staticData.Base` class, which extends from the `Packt.model.Base` class, which in turn extends from the `Ext.data.Model` class. This means this Model inherits all the attributes and behavior from the classes `Packt.model.staticData.Base`, `Packt.model.Base`, and `Ext.data.Model`.

- As we created a super Model with the schema `Packt.model`, the default `entityName` created for this Model would be `staticData.Actor`. We are using `entityName` to help the proxy compile the `url` template with `entityName`. To make our life easier we are going to overwrite `entityName` as well (#2).

- The third point is `idProperty` (#3). By default, `idProperty` has the value `"id"`. This means that when we declare a Model with a field named `"id"`, Ext JS already knows that this is the unique field of this Model. When it is different from `"id"`, we need to specify it using the `idProperty` configuration. As all Sakila tables do not have a unique field called `"id"` — it is always the *name of the entity* + `"_id"` — we will need to declare this configuration in all models.

Now we can do the same for the other models. We need to create four more classes:

- `Packt.model.staticData.Category`
- `Packt.model.staticData.Language`
- `Packt.model.staticData.City`
- `Packt.model.staticData.Country`

At the end, we will have six Model classes (one super Model and five specific models) created inside the `app/model/staticData` package. If we create a UML-class diagram for the Model classes, we will have the following diagram:

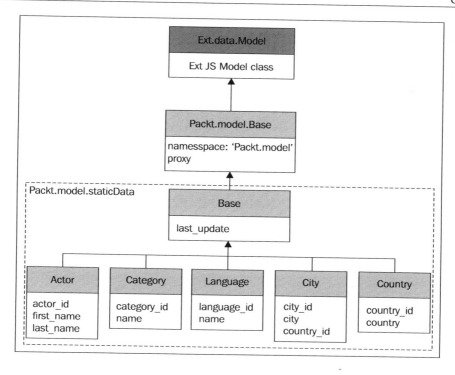

The **Actor**, **Category**, **Language**, **City**, and **Country** models extend the `Packt.model.staticData` Base Model, which extends from `Packt.model.Base`, which in turn extends the `Ext.data.Model` class.

Creating a Store

The next step is to create the stores for each Model. As we did with the Model, we will try to create a generic Store as well (in this chapter, will create a generic code for all screens, so creating a super Model, Store, and View is part of the capability). Although the common configurations are not in the Store, but in the Proxy (which we declared inside the schema in the `Packt.model.Base` class), having a super Store class can help us to listen to events that are common for all the static data stores.

We will create a super Store named `Packt.store.staticData.Base`.

As we need a Store for each Model, we will create the following stores:

- `Packt.store.staticData.Actors`
- `Packt.store.staticData.Categories`

- `Packt.store.staticData.Languages`
- `Packt.store.staticData.Cities`
- `Packt.store.staticData.Countries`

At the end of this topic, we will have created all the previous classes. If we create a UML diagram for them, we will have something like the following diagram:

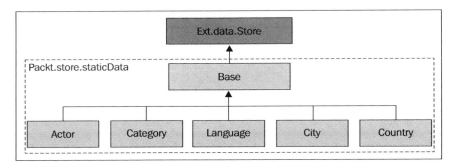

All the Store classes extend from the `Base` Store.

Now that we know what we need to create, let's get our hands dirty!

Abstract Store

The first class we need to create is the `Packt.store.staticData.Base` class. Inside this class, we will only declare `autoLoad` as `true` so that all the subclasses of this Store can be loaded when the application launches:

```
Ext.define('Packt.store.staticData.Base', {
    extend: 'Ext.data.Store',

    autoLoad: true
});
```

All the specific stores that we will create will extend this Store. Creating a super Store like this can feel pointless; however, we do not know that during future maintenance, we will need to add some common Store configuration.

As we will use MVC for this module, another reason is that inside the Controller, we can also listen to Store events (available since Ext JS 4.2). If we want to listen to the same event of a set of stores and we execute exactly the same method, having a super Store will save us some lines of code.

Specific Store

Our next step is to implement the Actors, Categories, Languages, Cities, and Countries stores.

So let's start with the Actors Store:

```
Ext.define('Packt.store.staticData.Actors', {
    extend: 'Packt.store.staticData.Base', //#1

    model: 'Packt.model.staticData.Actor' //#2
});
```

After the definition of the Store, we need to extend from the Ext JS Store class. As we are using a super Store, we can extend directly from the super Store (#1), which means extending from the Packt.store.staticData.Base class.

Next, we need to declare the fields or the model that this Store is going to represent. In our case, we always declare the Model (#2).

> Using a model inside the Store is good for reuse purposes. The fields configuration is recommended just in case we need to create a very specific Store with specific data that we are not planning to reuse throughout the application, as in a chart or a report.

For the other stores, the only thing that is going to be different is the name of the Store and the Model.

> As models and stores are very similar, we are not going to list their code in this chapter. However, if you need the code to compare with yours or simply want to get the complete source code, you can download the code bundle from this book or get it at https://github.com/loiane/masteringextjs.

Creating an abstract GridPanel for reuse

Now is the time to implement the views. We have to implement five views: one to perform the CRUD operations for Actor, one for Category, one for Language, one for City, and one for Country.

The following screenshot represents the final result we want to achieve after implementing the **Actors** screen:

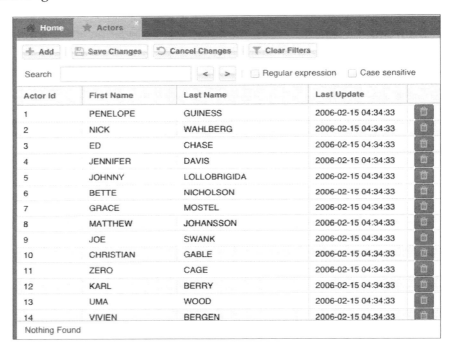

And the following screenshot represents the final result we want to achieve after implementing the **Categories** screen:

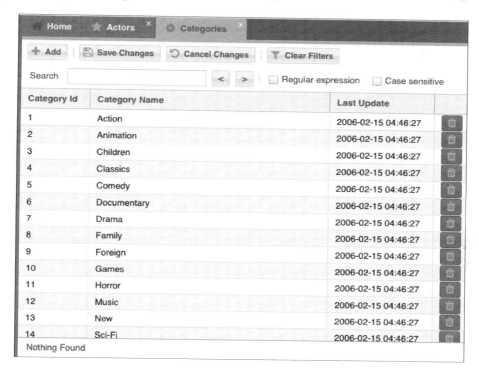

Did you notice anything similar between these two screens? Let's take a look again:

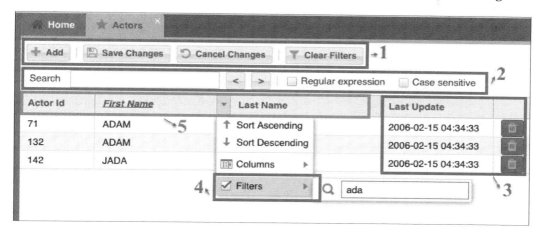

The top toolbar is the same (**1**); there is a Live Search capability (**2**); there is a filter plugin (**4**), and the **Last Update** and widget columns are also common (**3**). Going a little bit further, both GridPanels can be edited using a cell editor (similar to MS Excel capabilities, where you can edit a single cell by clicking on it). The only things different between these two screens are the columns that are specific to each screen (**5**). Does this mean we can reuse a good part of the code if we use inheritance by creating a super GridPanel with all these common capabilities? Yes!

So this is what we are going to do. So let's create a new class named `Packt.view.staticData.BaseGrid`, as follows:

```
Ext.define('Packt.view.staticData.BaseGrid', {
    extend: 'Ext.ux.LiveSearchGridPanel', //#1
    xtype: 'staticdatagrid',

    requires: [
        'Packt.util.Glyphs' //#2
    ],

    columnLines: true,      //#3
    viewConfig: {
        stripeRows: true //#4
    },

    //more code here
});
```

We will extend the `Ext.ux.LiveSearchGridPanel` class instead of `Ext.grid.Panel`. The `Ext.ux.LiveSearchGridPanel` class already extends the `Ext.grid.Panel` class and also adds the Live Search toolbar (**2**). The `LiveSearchGridPanel` class is a plugin that is distributed with the Ext JS SDK. So, we do not need to worry about adding it manually to our project (you will learn how to add third-party plugins to the project later in this book).

As we will also add a toolbar with the **Add**, **Save Changes**, **Cancel Changes** buttons, we need to require the `util.Glyphs` class we created (#2).

The configurations #3 and #4 show the border of each cell of the grid and to alternate between a white background and a light gray background.

Likewise, any other component that is responsible for displaying information in Ext JS, such as the "Panel" piece is only the shell. The View is responsible for displaying the columns in a GridPanel. We can customize it using the `viewConfig` (#4).

The next step is to create an `initComponent` method.

To initComponent or not?

While browsing other developers' code, we might see some using the
initComponent when declaring an Ext JS class and some who do not (as we have
done until now). So what is the difference between using it and not using it?

When declaring an Ext JS class, we usually configure it according to the application
needs. They might become either a parent class for other classes or not. If they
become a parent class, some of the configurations will be overridden, while some
will not. Usually, we declare the ones that we expect to override in the class as
configurations. We declare inside the initComponent method the ones we do not
want to be overridden.

As there are a few configurations we do not want to be overridden, we will declare
them inside the initComponent, as follows:

```
initComponent: function() {
    var me = this;

    me.selModel = {
        selType: 'cellmodel' //#5
    };

    me.plugins = [
        {
            ptype: 'cellediting',  //#6
            clicksToEdit: 1,
            pluginId: 'cellplugin'
        },
        {
            ptype: 'gridfilters'  //#7
        }
    ];

    //docked items

    //columns

    me.callParent(arguments); //#8
}
```

We can define how the user can select information from the GridPanel: the default configuration is the `Selection RowModel` class. As we want the user to be able to edit cell by cell, we will use the `Selection CellModel` class (#5) and also the `CellEditing` plugin (#6), which is part of the Ext JS SDK. For the `CellEditing` plugin, we configure the cell to be available to edit when the user clicks on the cell (if we need the user to double-click, we can change to `clicksToEdit: 2`). To help us later in the Controller, we also assign an ID to this plugin.

To be able to filter the information (the Live Search will only highlight the matching records), we will use the **Filters** plugin (#7). The **Filters** plugin is also part of the Ext JS SDK.

The `callParent` method (#8) will call `initConfig` from the superclass `Ext.ux.LiveSearchGridPanel` passing the arguments we defined.

 It is a common mistake to forget to include the `callParent` call when overriding the `initComponent` method. If the component does not work, make sure you are calling the `callParent` method!

Next, we are going to declare `dockedItems`. As all GridPanels will have the same toolbar, we can declare `dockedItems` in the super class we are creating, as follows:

```
me.dockedItems = [
    {
        xtype: 'toolbar',
        dock: 'top',
        itemId: 'topToolbar', //#9
        items: [
            {
                xtype: 'button',
                itemId: 'add', //#10
                text: 'Add',
                glyph: Packt.util.Glyphs.getGlyph('add')
            },
            {
                xtype: 'tbseparator'
            },
            {
                xtype: 'button',
                itemId: 'save',
                text: 'Save Changes',
                glyph: Packt.util.Glyphs.getGlyph('saveAll')
            },
```

```
            {
                xtype: 'button',
                itemId: 'cancel',
                text: 'Cancel Changes',
                glyph: Packt.util.Glyphs.getGlyph('cancel')
            },
            {
                xtype: 'tbseparator'
            },
            {
                xtype: 'button',
                itemId: 'clearFilter',
                text: 'Clear Filters',
                glyph: Packt.util.Glyphs.getGlyph('clearFilter')
            }
        ]
    }
];
```

We will have **Add, Save Changes, Cancel Changes**, and **Clear Filters** buttons. Note that the toolbar (#9) and each of the buttons (#10) has `itemId` declared. As we are going to use the MVC approach in this example, we will declare a Controller. The `itemId` configuration has a responsibility similar to the reference that we declare when working with a ViewController. We will discuss the importance of `itemId` more when we declare the Controller later in this chapter.

 When declaring buttons inside a toolbar, we can omit the `xtype: 'button'` configuration since the button is the default component for toolbars.

Inside the `Glyphs` class, we need to add the following attributes inside its `config`:

```
saveAll: 'xf0c7',
clearFilter: 'xf0b0'
```

And finally, we will add the two columns that are common for all the screens (`Last Update` column and Widget Column `delete` (#13)) along with the columns already declared in each specific GridPanel:

```
me.columns = Ext.Array.merge(  //#11
    me.columns,                //#12
    [{
        xtype    : 'datecolumn',
        text     : 'Last Update',
        width    : 150,
```

```
                dataIndex: 'last_update',
                format: 'Y-m-j H:i:s',
                filter: true
        },
        {
                xtype: 'widgetcolumn',  //#13
                width: 45,
                sortable: false,        //#14
                menuDisabled: true,     //#15
                itemId: 'delete',
                widget: {
                        xtype: 'button',    //#16
                        glyph: Packt.util.Glyphs.getGlyph('destroy'),
                        tooltip: 'Delete',
                        scope: me,                  //#17
                        handler: function(btn) {    //#18
                                me.fireEvent('widgetclick', me, btn);
                        }
                }
        }]
);
```

In the preceding code we merge (#11) me.columns (#12) with two other columns and assign this value to me.columns again. We want all child grids to have these two columns plus the specific columns for each child grid. If the columns configuration from the BaseGrid class were outside initConfig, then when a child class declared its own columns configuration the value would be overridden. If we declare the columns configuration inside initComponent, a child class would not be able to add its own columns configuration, so we need to merge these two configurations (the columns from the child class #12 with the two columns we want each child class to have).

For the delete button, we are going to use a Widget Column (#13) (introduced in Ext JS 5). Until Ext JS 4, the only way to have a button inside a Grid Column was using an Action Column. We are going to use a button (#16) to represent a Widget Column. Because it is a Widget Column, there is no reason to make this column sortable (#14), and we can also disable its menu (#15).

We are going to discuss lines #17 and #18 in the next section.

Handling the Widget Column in the MVC architecture

Let's take a look again at the Widget Column declared in the super GridPanel, especially in the `handler` configuration:

```
scope: me,                    //#17
handler: function(btn) {  //#18
    me.fireEvent('widgetclick', me, btn);
}
```

Even though the Widget Column is a widget and contains `xtype`, it is not possible to listen to its events in the MVC Controller, so we need a workaround to make it work in the MVC architecture. The reason is that the items that can be declared inside a Widget Column are subclasses of the `Ext.Widget` class, which is a subclass of the `Ext.Evented` class. MVC Controllers can only listen to events fired by a component subclass (panel, button, grid, tree, chart, and so on).

That is why we are firing a custom event (#18) passing the parameters we need, so we can catch this event in this Controller and handle the programming logic needed to delete a record.

In this example, we are setting `scope` of the handler as `me` (#17), which refers to `this` of the GridPanel. This means it will be the GridPanel that will be firing the `widgetclick` event, passing the grid itself and the widget button. The `btn` parameter contains a method named `getWidgetRecord`, which is used to retrieve the Model represented by the GridPanel row where the user clicked on the **Delete** button.

If we were using an Action Column (a very popular choice until Ext JS 4) we would handle it in the MVC architecture in the same way (firing a custom event). An example can be found at: `http://goo.gl/pxdU4i`.

> Handling Widget Column handlers in the MVVM approach is easier. Instead of firing a custom event, we can simply refer to the method used in the ViewController as follows: `handler: 'onWidgetClick'`.

Live Search plugin versus Filter plugin

Both plugins have the objective of helping the user to search for information quickly. In our project, we are using both.

The Live Search plugin will search for any matching result in all the columns of the GridPanel. The search is also performed locally, which means that if we use the paging toolbar, this plugin will not work as expected. When using the paging toolbar, the grid only displays one page at a time, which means it is a limited number of rows. The remaining information is not kept locally, the paging toolbar only fetches the requested information, and this is the reason the search will not work when using paging. In our case, we display all the records from the database at once, so the plugin works as expected. For example, if we search for "ada", we will get the following output:

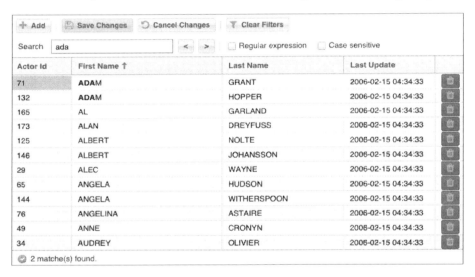

And the Filter plugin will apply the filters on the Store as well, so it will only display to the user the matching results, as follows:

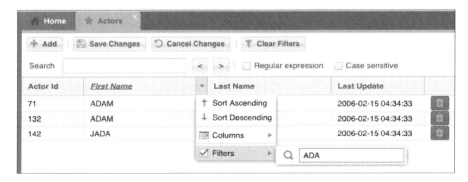

Specific GridPanels for each table

Our last stop before we implement the Controller is the specific GridPanels. We have already created the super GridPanel that contains most of the capabilities that we need. Now we just need to declare the specific configurations for each GridPanel.

We will create five GridPanels that will extend from the `Packt.view.staticData.BaseGrid` class, as follows:

- `Packt.view.staticData.Actors`
- `Packt.view.staticData.Categories`
- `Packt.view.staticData.Languages`
- `Packt.view.staticData.Cities`
- `Packt.view.staticData.Countries`

Let's start with the `Actors` GridPanel, as follows:

```
Ext.define('Packt.view.staticData.Actors', {
    extend: 'Packt.view.staticData.BaseGrid',
    xtype: 'actorsgrid',          //#1

    store: 'staticData.Actors', //#2

    columns: [
        {
            text: 'Actor Id',
            width: 100,
            dataIndex: 'actor_id',
            filter: {
                type: 'numeric'    //#3
            }
        },
        {
            text: 'First Name',
            flex: 1,
            dataIndex: 'first_name',
            editor: {
                allowBlank: false, //#4
                maxLength: 45        //#5
            },
            filter: {
                type: 'string'       //#6
            }
        },
```

```
        {
            text: 'Last Name',
            width: 200,
            dataIndex: 'last_name',
            editor: {
                allowBlank: false, //#7
                maxLength: 45      //#8
            },
            filter: {
                type: 'string'     //#9
            }
        }
    ]
});
```

Each specific class has its own xtype (#1). We also need to execute an UPDATE query in the database to update the menu table with the new xtypes we are creating:

```
UPDATE `sakila`.`menu` SET `className`='actorsgrid' WHERE
`id`='5';
UPDATE `sakila`.`menu` SET `className`='categoriesgrid' WHERE
`id`='6';
UPDATE `sakila`.`menu` SET `className`='languagesgrid' WHERE
`id`='7';
UPDATE `sakila`.`menu` SET `className`='citiesgrid' WHERE
`id`='8';
UPDATE `sakila`.`menu` SET `className`='countriesgrid' WHERE
`id`='9';
```

The first declaration that is specific to the Actors GridPanel is the Store (#2). We are going to use the Actors Store. Because the Actors Store is inside the staticData folder (store/staticData), we also need to pass the name of the subfolder; otherwise, Ext JS will think that this Store file is inside the app/store folder, which is not true.

Then we need to declare the columns specific to the Actors GridPanel (we do not need to declare the Last Update and the Delete Action Column because they are already in the super GridPanel).

What you need to pay attention to now are the editor and filter configurations for each column. The editor is for editing (cellediting plugin). We will only apply this configuration to the columns we want the user to be able to edit, and the filter (filters plugin) is the configuration that we will apply to the columns we want the user to be able to filter information from.

For example, for the id column, we do not want the user to be able to edit it as it is a sequence provided by the MySQL database auto increment, so we will not apply the editor configuration to it. However, the user can filter the information based on the ID, so we will apply the filter configuration (#3).

We want the user to be able to edit the other two columns: first_name and last_name, so we will add the editor configuration. We can perform client validations as we can do on a field of a form too. For example, we want both fields to be mandatory (#4 and #7) and the maximum number of characters the user can enter is 45 (#5 and #8).

And at last, as both columns are rendering text values (string), we will also apply filter (#6 and #9).

For other filter types, please refer to the Ext JS documentation as shown in the following screenshot. The documentation provides an example and more configuration options that we can use:

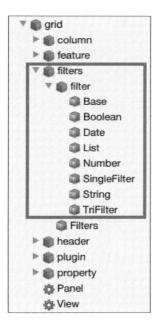

And that is it! The super GridPanel will provide all the other capabilities.

Adding the Live Search CSS

When we navigate to the Live Search Grid example (`http://dev.sencha.com/ext/5.0.1/examples/grid/live-search-grid.html`) and we go through its source code, we can see that the example imports two CSS files: the `LiveSearchGridPanel.css` and `statusbar.css` (because the Live Search plugin has a dependency on the `statusbar` plugin). We also need to add this CSS to our application.

We are going to copy these two CSS files and rename the extension to `scss`. The Live Search CSS can be copied from `ext/src/ux/css`, and the `statusbar` CSS can be copied from `ext/src/ux/statusbar`. We need to place these two files inside our application custom CSS, which is located in the `sass/etc` directory. Create a new folder named `ux` and paste these files. Inside `all.scss`, we are going to import these two Sass files:

```
@import "ux/statusbar";
@import "ux/LiveSearchGridPanel";
```

The `statusbar` plugin displays an icon, and we need to fix the path to the `statusbar` images as well. Inside the `statusbar.scss` file, replace all matches `"../images"` by `"images/statusbar"`. Go to `ext/src/ux/statusbar`, copy the `images` folder, and paste it inside `resources/images`. Rename `resources/images/images` to `resources/images/statusbar`. If you have `Sencha app watch` being executed in the terminal, Sencha Cmd will rebuild the app CSS file and the plugin will work 100 percent.

Generic Controller for all tables

Now it is time to implement the last piece of the static data module. The goal is to implement a Controller that has the most generic code that will provide the functionalities for all the screens, without us having to create any specific method for any screens.

So let's start with the base of the Controller. We are going to create a new class named `Packt.controller.StaticData`, as follows:

```
Ext.define('Packt.controller.StaticData', {
    extend: 'Ext.app.Controller',

    requires: [
        'Packt.util.Util', //#1
        'Packt.util.Glyphs'
    ],
```

```
    stores: [  //#2
        'staticData.Actors',
        'staticData.Categories',
        'staticData.Cities',
        'staticData.Countries',
        'staticData.Languages'
    ],

    views: [  //#3
        'staticData.BaseGrid',
        'staticData.Actors',
        'staticData.Categories',
        'staticData.Cities',
        'staticData.Countries',
        'staticData.Languages'
    ],

    init: function(application) {
        var me = this;
        me.control({
            //event listeners here
        });
    }
});
```

For now, we are going to declare the `requires` ((#1)—we are going to use the `Util` class in some methods and also the `Glyphs` class), the `stores` ((#2)—where we can list all the stores of this module), and also the `views` ((#3)—where we can list all views of this module).

As we are instantiating the views by their `xtype`, we need to declare them somewhere (#2). This can be inside the `requires` configuration in the `Application.js` file or inside a Controller. This is needed because Ext JS does not know the xtypes we are creating, so the names of the classes need to be listed somewhere.

The `stores` declaration (#2) that we are listing in this Controller will be instantiated when the Controller is instantiated as well. As this is a Controller from the MVC architecture, its scope is global, and it will be created when the application launches. Using the MVC approach for this case is interesting; after all, we are constructing the static data module that refers to common data used by other entities of the application. In this case, this information will be live throughout the life cycle of the application. This is unlike the Views, ViewModels, ViewControllers, and stores declared inside ViewModels, which are alive as long as the View is alive (tab opened). As we set `autoLoad:true` in the `Base` Store, when the application launches, the stores listed in this Controller will be instantiated and loaded.

We also have the `init` function and `this.control` where we are going to listen to all the events that we are interested in.

Finding the correct selector

On the toolbar from each static data grid panel, we have a button with the text **Add**. When we click on this button, we want to add a new Model entry to the Store (and consequently, add a new record on the GridPanel) and enable editing so that the user can fill in the values to save them later (when they click on the **Save Changes** button).

When listening to an event in a Controller, first we need to pass the selector that is going to be used by the `Ext.ComponentQuery` class to find the component. Then we need to list the event that we want to listen to. And then, we need to declare the function that is going to be executed when the event we are listening to is fired, or declare the name of the Controller method that is going to be executed when the event is fired. In our case, we are going to declare the method only for code organization purposes.

Now let's focus on finding the correct selector for the **Add** button (the other buttons will be similar as well). According to the `Ext.ComponentQuery` API documentation, we can retrieve components by using their `xtype` (if you are already familiar with JQuery, you will notice that `Ext.ComponentQuery` selector behavior is very similar to JQuery selector behavior). Well, we are trying to retrieve two buttons, and their `xtype` is `button`. We can then try the selector `'button'`. But before we start coding, let's make sure that this is the correct selector to avoid changing the code all the time trying to figure out the correct selector. There is one very useful tip we can try: open the browser console—Command Editor—and type the following command and click on Run:

```
Ext.ComponentQuery.query('button');
```

As we can see in the following screenshot, it returned an array of the buttons that were found by the selector we used, and the array contains several buttons! Too many buttons is not what we want. We want to narrow down to the **Add** button from the **Actors** screen, as shown in the following screenshot:

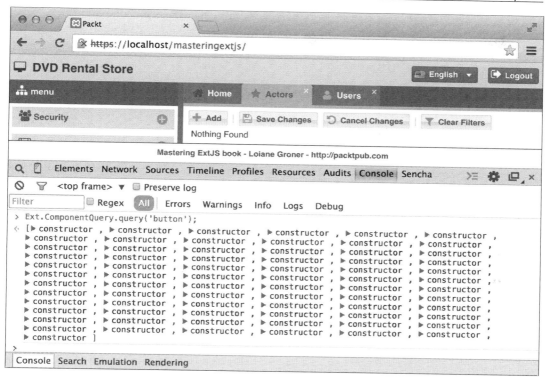

Let's try to draw a path of the **Actors** screen using the components xtype we used. We have the **Actors** screen (xtype: actorsgrid); inside the screen, we have a toolbar (xtype: toolbar); and inside the toolbar, we have some buttons (xtype: button). Therefore, we have actorsgrid | toolbar | button. So we can try the following command:

```
Ext.ComponentQuery.query('actorsgrid toolbar button');
```

So let's try this last selector on the **Console**, as follows:

Now the result is an array of six buttons, and these are the buttons that we are looking for! There is still one detail missing: if we use the `'actorsgrid toolbar button'` selector, it will listen to the click event (which is the event we want to listen to) of all the six buttons.

However, when we click on the **Cancel** button, an action should happen; when we click on the **Save** button, a different action should happen because it is a different button. So we still want to narrow down the selector even more until it returns the **Add** button that we are looking for.

Going back to the Base Grid panel code, notice that we declared a configuration named `itemId` for all buttons. We can use these `itemId` configurations to identify the buttons in a unique way. And according to the `Ext.ComponentQuery` API documentation, we can use # as a prefix of `itemId`. So let's try the following command on the **Console** to get the **Add** button reference:

```
Ext.ComponentQuery.query('actorsgrid toolbar button#add');
```

And the output will be only one button as we expect:

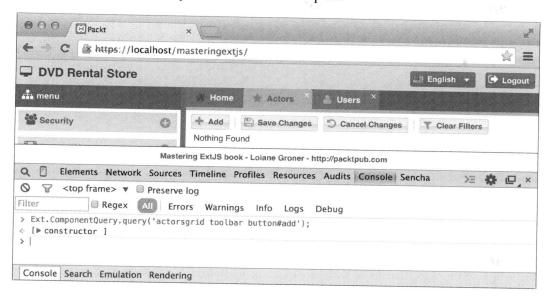

So now we have the selectors that we were looking for! Using the **Console** is a great tool and can save us a lot of time when trying to find the exact selector that we want instead of coding, testing, not getting the selector we want, coding again, testing again, and so on.

> Could we use only `button#add` as selector? Yes, we could use a shorter selector. However, it would work perfectly for now. As the application grows and we declare more classes and more buttons, the event would be fired for all buttons that have the `itemId` with `add` value, and this could lead to an error of the application. We always need to remember that `itemId` is scoped locally to its container. Using the `actorsgrid toolbar button` or `actorsgrid button` as selector, we make sure that the event will come from the button from the **Actors** screen.

Now's the time for one last detail. The selector we found is specific to the **Actors** screen. We want some generic code—code that can be used for all screens from the static data module. The good news is that we created a super class (`Packt.view.staticData.BaseGrid`) with `xtype staticdatagrid`.

Using itemId versus id – Ext.Cmp is bad!

Whenever we can, we will always try to use the `itemId` configuration instead of `id` to uniquely identify a component. And here comes the question: Why?

When using `id`, we need to make sure that `id` is unique and none of all the other components of the application can have the same `id` property. Now, imagine the situation where you are working with other developers on the same team and it is a big application. How can you make sure that `id` is going to be unique? It will be pretty difficult. Don't you think? And this can be a hard task to achieve.

Components created with `id` can be accessed globally using `Ext.getCmp`, which is shorthand for `Ext.ComponentManager.get`.

Just to mention one example, when using `Ext.getCmp` to retrieve a component by its `id`, it is going to return the last component declared with the given `id`. And if `id` is not unique, it can return the component that you are not expecting, and this can lead to an error in the application, as shown in the following figure:

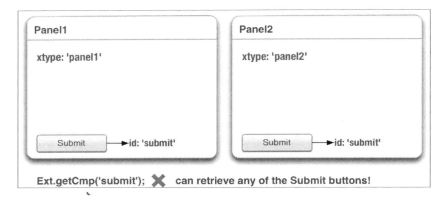

Do not panic! There is an elegant solution: using `itemId` instead of `id`.

The `itemId` can be used as an alternative way to get a reference of a component. The `itemId` is an index to the container's internal `MixedCollection`, and that is why `itemId` is scoped locally to the container. This is the biggest advantage of `itemId`.

For example, we can have a class named `MyWindow1` extending from `Window`, and inside this class, we can have a button with `itemId` containing the `submit` value. Then, we can have another class named `MyWindow2`, also extending from `Window`, and inside the class, we can also have a button with the `itemId` as `submit`.

Having two `itemIds` with the same value is not an issue. We only need to be careful when we use `Ext.ComponentQuery` to retrieve the component we want. For example, if we have a **Login** window whose alias is `login` and another screen called **Registration** window whose alias is `registration` and both windows have a button **Save**, whose `itemId` is `save`, if we simply use `Ext.ComponentQuery.query('button#save')`, the result will be an array with two results. However, if we narrow down the selector even more—let's say we want the **Login Save** button, and not the **Registration Save** button, we need to use `Ext.ComponentQuery.query('login button#save')`, and the result will be only one, which is exactly what we expect. The contents of this paragraph are aptly encapsulated in the following image:

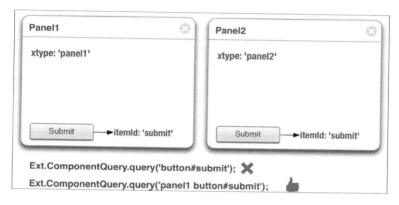

You will notice that we will not use `Ext.getCmp` in the code of our project as it is not a good practice because of the reasons listed previously. Until Ext JS 3, this was the way that we had to use to retrieve components. But from Ext JS 4 onwards, and with the introduction of the MVC architecture and MVVM, this is not needed anymore.

Adding a new record on the GridPanel

Now that we know how to find the correct selector to use in the Controller, let's go ahead and declare the selector for the **Add** button:

```
'staticdatagrid button#add': {
    click: me.onButtonClickAdd
}
```

Then, we need to implement the method `onButtonClickAdd`:

```
onButtonClickAdd: function (button, e, options) {
    var grid = button.up('staticdatagrid'),    //#1
        store = grid.getStore(),                //#2
        modelName = store.getModel().getName(), //#3
        cellEditing = grid.getPlugin('cellplugin');  //#4

    store.insert(0, Ext.create(modelName, {  //#5
        last_update: new Date()               //#6
    }));

    cellEditing.startEditByPosition({row: 0, column: 1}); //#7
}
```

From the parameters, we only have the `button` reference. We need to get the GridPanel reference. So, we are going to use the `up` method to get it (#1). Again, we are going to use the super GridPanel `xtype` as selector (`staticdatagrid`), because this way we have the most generic code possible.

All components in Ext JS have methods to query other components. They are listed as follows:

- `up`: This navigates up the ownership hierarchy searching for an ancestor container that matches any passed selector or component
- `down`: This retrieves the first descendant of this container that matches the passed selector
- `query`: This retrieves all descendant components that match the passed selector

The method query also has some alternatives, such as `queryBy(function)` and `queryById`.

Once we have the GridPanel reference, we can get the Store reference using the `getStore` method (#2).

We need to have the Model name to instantiate it (#5) so that we can insert on the first position of the Store (this way it will be the first line of the GridPanel). So, still targeting generic code, we can get the `modelName` from the `store` (#3).

We can pass some configurations to the Model when we instantiate it. We want the `Last Update` column to be updated as well; we will only pass it as configuration with the most current *Date* and *Time*.

And at last, we also want to focus on a cell of the row so that the user can be aware that the cell can be edited, so we will focus on the second column of the grid (the first one is the id, which is not editable) of the first row (#7). But to do so, we need a reference to the celleditor plugin; we can get it by using the getPlugin method, passing pluginId as the parameter (#4).

Just to remember, we declared the pluginId for the cellediting plugin of the Packt.view.staticData.BaseGrid class, as shown in the following code snippet:

```
{
    ptype: 'cellediting',
    clicksToEdit: 1,
    pluginId: 'cellplugin'
}
```

> Note that with only one method, we can program the necessary logic. The code is generic and provides the same capability to all static data grid panels.

Editing an existing record

The editing of a cell will be done automatically by the cellediting plugin. However, when the user clicks on a cell to edit and finishes the editing, we need to update the **Last Update** value to the current *Date* and *Time*.

The cellediting plugin has an event named edit that allows us to listen to the event we want. Unfortunately, the Controller is not able to listen to plugin events. Lucky for us, the GridPanel class also fires this event (the cellediting plugin forwards the event to the GridPanel internally), so we can listen to it. So we are going to add the following code to the Controller init control:

```
"staticdatagrid": {
    edit: me.onEdit
}
```

Next, we need to implement the onEdit method, as follows:

```
onEdit: function(editor, context, options) {
    context.record.set('last_update', new Date());
}
```

The second parameter is the event (context). From this parameter, we can get the **Model** instance (record) that the user edited and then set the last_update field to the current *Date* and *Time*.

Deleting the handling Widget Column in the Controller

Well, the read, create, and update actions have already been implemented. Now, we need to implement the delete action. We do not have a button for the delete action, but we do have an `item` of an Action Column.

In the topic *Handling the Widget Column in the MVC architecture,* you learned how to fire the event from the item of the Action Column so that we could handle it on the Controller. We cannot listen to the event fired by the Action Column itself; however, we can listen to the event fired by the Action Column that we created:

```
"staticdatagrid actioncolumn": {
    itemclick: this.handleActionColumn
}
```

Now, let's see how you can implement the `handleActionColumn` method:

```
handleActionColumn: function(column, action, view, rowIndex,
colIndex, item, e) {
        var store = view.up('staticdatagrid').getStore(),
        rec = store.getAt(rowIndex);

        if (action == 'delete'){
            store.remove(rec);
            Ext.Msg.alert('Delete', 'Save the changes to persist
            the removed record.');
        }
    }
```

As this is a custom event, we need to get the parameters that were passed by the item of the Action Column.

So first, we need to get the Store and also the `record` that the user clicked to delete. Then, using the second parameter, which is the name of the `action` of the Action Column item, we have a way to know which item fired the event. So if the `action` value is `delete`, we are going to remove the `record` from the Store and ask the user to commit the changes by pressing the button **Save Changes**, which is going to synchronize the models from the Store with the information we have on the server.

Saving the changes

After the user performs an update, delete, or create action, the cells that were updated will have a mark (the dirty mark so that the Store knows what models were modified) as shown in the following screenshot:

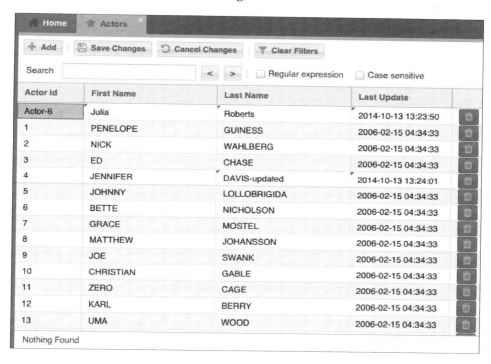

In the same way that we can perform changes on the MySQL table, we need to save the changes (commit). That is why we created the **Save Changes** button; this way, we will synchronize all the changes at once to the server.

So first, we need to add a listener to `me.control`, as follows:

```
'staticdatagrid button#save': {
    click: me.onButtonClickSave
}
```

Then, we need to implement the `onButtonClickSave` method:

```
onButtonClickSave: function (button, e, options) {
    var grid = button.up('staticdatagrid'),    //#1
        store = grid.getStore(),                //#2
        errors = grid.validate();               //#3
```

```
if (errors === undefined){    //#4
    store.sync();             //#5
} else {
    Ext.Msg.alert(errors);    //#6
}
}
```

The implementation of the method is pretty straightforward: we simply need to get the Store (#2) from the GridPanel (#1) and call the method sync (#5).

However, we are going to validate that the information entered in the cells of the Grid contain valid information. To do so, we are going to call the method validate from the grid (#3) and get the errors. If no errors were found (#4), then we sync the Store with the server (#5); otherwise, we display the errors (#6).

The Grid Panel does not have a validate method by default. We are going to add this method to the Base Grid Panel.

Validating cellediting in GridPanel

Going back to the class Packt.view.staticData.BaseGrid, we are going to add the logic to validate a row from the grid and also the entire grid before saving. In this example, you will learn that we can also add useful methods to the classes we create; we do not need to develop all the code inside the Controller.

The first method we are going to implement is validateRow. Given a record, we are going to validate it using Model validators, and if there are any errors, we will add the same form icon that Ext JS displays in the forms in case of validation errors in the cell that contains the error, and we will also add a tooltip in this cell (similar behavior from the form validation). The code for the method is as follows (we need to add it inside the initComponent method):

```
me.validateRow = function(record, rowIndex){

    var me = this,
        view = me.getView(),
        errors = record.validate(); //#1

    if (errors.isValid()) {         //#2
        return true;
    }

    var columnIndexes = me.getColumnIndexes(); //#3
```

```
Ext.each(columnIndexes, function (columnIndex, col) { //#4
    var cellErrors, cell, messages;

    cellErrors = errors.getByField(columnIndex);          //#5
    if (!Ext.isEmpty(cellErrors)) {
        cell = view.getCellByPosition({
        row: rowIndex, column: col
});

        messages = [];
        Ext.each(cellErrors, function (cellError) { //#6
            messages.push(cellError.message);
        });

        cell.addCls('x-form-error-msg x-form-invalid-icon x-
        form-invalid-icon-default'); //#7

        cell.set({ //#8
            'data-errorqtip': Ext.String.format('<ul><li
            class="last">{0}</li></ul>',
                messages.join('<br/>'))
        });
    }
});

    return false;
};
```

Given a `record` Model (#1), we are going to use its method `validate`. This method verifies that the information contained in the Model is valid according to the Model validators (we need to go back to the models we defined for this chapter and add the validators). This method returns an object with all the errors found in the record.

Using the `isValid` method (#2), we can easily find out whether the Model is valid or not. If it is valid, we return `true` (we will use this information later).

The `columnIndexes` (#3) is in an array that contains `dataIndex` of each column of the grid. This method was present in the grid panel class back in Ext JS 4.1, but in Ext JS 4.2, it was removed, and it is not present in Ext JS 5. We are going to implement this method as well, but with the difference being that in this case, we are only interested in the columns that have the editor enabled (since we want to validate it).

Then, for each `column` of the grid that has the editor enabled (#4), we are going to retrieve the `errors` specific for that column from the Model (#5). We are going to add each error `message` (#6) to an array of messages. After that, we are going to add the same error icon from an invalid form field to the grid cell (#7). And, at last, we are also going to add a tooltip to the cell with error (#8).

Next, we are going to implement the `getColumnIndexes` function, as follows:

```
me.getColumnIndexes = function() {
    var me = this,
        columnIndexes = [];

    Ext.Array.each(me.columns, function (column) { //#9
        if (Ext.isDefined(column.getEditor())) {    //#10
            columnIndexes.push(column.dataIndex);  //#11
        } else {
            columnIndexes.push(undefined);
        }
    });

    return columnIndexes; //#12
};
```

For each column of the grid (#9), we are going to verify that the editor is enabled (#10), and if yes, we are going to add `dataIndex` to the `columnIndexes` array (#11). In the end, we return this array (#12).

The `validateRow` method will only work for a single row. When we click on the **Save Changes** button, we want to validate the entire grid. To do so, we are going to implement one more method inside the `initComponent`, which is called `validate` (the method we called in the Controller):

```
me.validate = function(){

    var me = this,
        isValid = true,
        view = me.getView(),
        error,
        record;

    Ext.each(view.getNodes(), function (row, col) { //#13
        record = view.getRecord(row);

        isValid = (me.validateRow(record, col) && isValid); //#14
    });
```

```
error = isValid ? undefined : { //#15
    title: "Invalid Records",
    message: "Please fix errors before saving."
};


return error; //#16
};
```

For the `validate` method, we are going to retrieve all the rows from the grid, and for each one (#13), we are going to call the `validateRow` method (#14). In line #14, we are also keeping track of whether any previous row `is valid` or not.

In the end, we return (#16) `undefined` if no error was found or we return an object with a title and message (#15) that we can use in the Controller to display an alert.

If we add an empty row or edit a cell with invalid information, the grid will display an error icon on the cell and also a tooltip when we mouse over it. The output will be similar to the following screenshot:

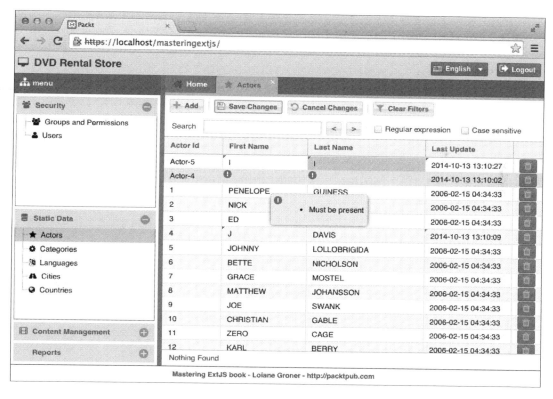

Model validators

To make this code work, we need to add the Model validators to `staticData` model. For example, for the `Actors` model, we can add the following code based on the database validations for the `actor` table:

```
validators: {
        first_name: [
            { type: 'presence', message: 'This field is
            mandatory'},
            { type: 'length', min: 2, max: 45}
        ],
        last_name: [
            { type: 'presence', message: 'This field is
            mandatory'},
            { type: 'length', min: 2, max: 45}
        ]
    }
```

And in the `Packt.model.staticData.Base` class, we can add the `last_update` validator that is going to be common to all `staticData` models:

```
validators: {
    last_update: 'presence'
}
```

The autoSync configuration

The Store has a configuration named `autoSync`. The default value is `false`, but if we set it to `true`, the Store will automatically synchronize with the server whenever a change is detected. This can be good, but it also can be bad — it depends on how we are going to use it.

For example, if we did not have the validations, the user could create an empty row and try to send it to the server. The server code would fail (some columns cannot be `null`), and this would be bad for the application. With `autoSync` set to `false`, the user can also choose when to save the information and the information can be sent in bulk instead of sending one request per action (create, update, or destroy) — `allowSingle` has to be set to `false` in the proxy writer as well.

Canceling the changes

As the user can save the changes (commit), the user can also cancel them (rollback). All you have to do is to reload the Store so that you get the most updated information from the server, and the changes made by the user will be lost.

So we need to listen to the event, as follows:

```
staticdatagrid button#cancel"' {
    click: this.onButtonClickCancel
}
```

And we need to implement the method:

```
onButtonClickCancel: function (button, e, options) {
button.up('staticdatagrid').getStore().reload();
}
```

If you want, you can add a message asking whether the user really wants to roll back the changes. Calling the `reload` method from the Store is what we need to do to make it work.

 As an alternative to the `reload` method of the Store, we could also call the method `rejectChanges` instead; however, the `reload` method is more failsafe, since we are getting the information from the server again.

Clearing the filter

When using the `filter` plugin on the GridPanel, it will do everything that we need (when used locally). But there is one thing that it doesn't provide to the user: the option to clear all the filters at once. So that is why we implemented a **Clear Filters** button.

So first, let's listen to the event:

```
'staticdatagrid button#clearFilter {
    click: this.onButtonClickClearFilter
}
```

And then we can implement the method:

```
onButtonClickClearFilter: function (button, e, options) {
button.up('staticdatagrid').filters.clearFilters();
}
```

When using the `filter` plugin, we are able to get a property named `filters` from the GridPanel. Then, all we need to do it is to call the `clearFilters` method. This will clear the filter values from each column that was filtered and will also clear the filters from the Store.

Listening to Store events in the Controller

And the last event we will be listening to is the `write` event from the Store. We already added an `exception` listener to the Proxy (in Ext JS 3, the Store had an exception listener, while in Ext JS 4 and 5 this listener was moved to the Proxy). Now we need to add a listener in case of success.

The first step is to listen to the event from the Store in the Controller. This feature was introduced in Ext JS 4.2.x.

Inside the `init` function of the Controller, we will add the following code:

```
me.listen({
    store: {
        '#staticData.Actors': {
            write: this.onStoreSync
        }
    }
});
```

We can listen to Store events inside the store option. The previous code will work for the **Actors** screen. If we want to do the same for the other screen, we need to add the same code as the preceding one. For example, the following code needs to be added for the **Categories** screen:

```
'#staticData.Categories': {
    write: this.onStoreSync
}
```

We cannot use the Base Store `storeId` here because each child Store will have its own `storeId`.

The write event is fired whenever the Store receives the response from the server. So let's implement the method:

```
onStoreSync: function(store, operation, options){
Packt.util.Util.showToast('Success! Your changes have been
saved.');
}
```

We will simply display a message saying the changes have been saved. Notice that the message is also generic; this way we can use it for all the static data modules. A screenshot of the output is as follows:

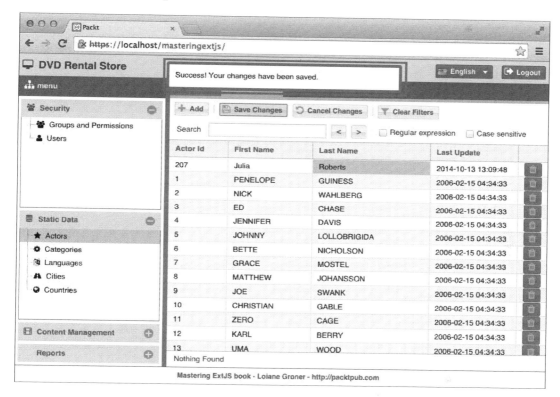

Debug tip – Sencha extension for Chrome

Sometimes we need to inspect a particular Ext JS component we have instantiated for debugging purposes. Finding which methods are available and the current attributes and configurations that are set in the object can be a little tricky. When working in MVC, we might need to find the Store ID created and the stores that are alive in the application. Using `console.log` to output a particular object to inspect it is a lot of work!

The Sencha Labs team released a free extension for Chrome called **Sencha App Inspector**. When working with Ext JS (or Sencha Touch), it is recommended that you use this extension to help debug the application. In the following screenshot, we can see the extension in action—stores that have been instantiated by the application and the data that has been loaded into it:

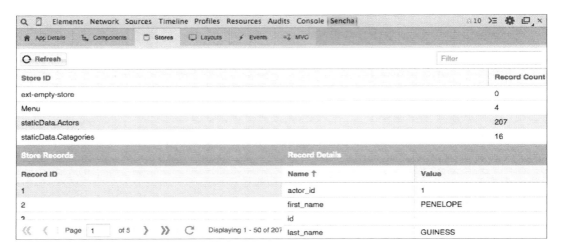

 For more information about Sencha App Inspector and the download link please visit `https://github.com/senchalabs/AppInspector/`.

Firefox extension – Illuminations for Developers

If your favorite browser for development is not Chrome, there is also a Sencha extension for Firefox (which can be used within Firebug) called Illuminations for Developers.

It is not a free extension (but it is possible to try it for free for a limited period of time), and its cost has a good cost-benefit.

In the following screenshot, we can see the extension in action (stores that have been instantiated by the application and its properties):

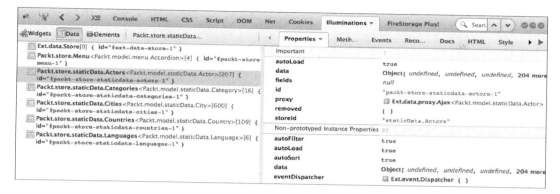

For more information about Illuminations for Developers and the download link, please visit `http://www.illuminations-for-developers.com/`.

Summary

In this chapter, we covered how to implement screens that look very similar to the MySQL Table Editor. The most important concept we covered in this chapter is implementing abstract classes, using the inheritance concept from OOP. We are used to using these concepts on server-side languages, such as PHP, Java, .NET, and so on. This chapter demonstrated that it is also important to use these concepts on the Ext JS side; this way, we can reuse a lot of code and also implement generic code that provides the same capability for more than one screen.

We created a Base Model, Store, View and a Controller. We used the following plugins: `celleditor` for the GridPanel and Live Search grid and `filter` plugin for the GridPanel as well. You learned how to perform CRUD operations using the Store capabilities. You also learned how to create custom events and handle Widget Column events on the Controller. We also explored many of the MVC Controller capabilities in this chapter.

Reminder: you can get the complete source code for this chapter (with extra capabilities and server-side code) by downloading the code bundle from this book or from the GitHub repository `https://github.com/loiane/masteringextjs`.

In the next chapter, you will learn how to implement the Content Management module, which goes further than just managing one single table as we did on this chapter. We will manage information from other tables (related to the business of the application) and all its relations within the database.

8
Content Management

In the preceding chapter, we developed the static data module that consisted of emulating the edition of a table from a database. Basically, it was a **Create, Read, Update, Delete (CRUD)** of a single table with some extra capabilities. In this chapter, we are going further in the complexity of managing information from a table. Usually, in real-world applications, the tables, the information of which we want to manage have relationships with other tables, and we have to manage the relationships as well. And this is what this chapter is all about. How can we build screens and manage complex information in Ext JS?

So in this chapter, we will cover:

- Managing complex information with Ext JS
- How to handle many-to-many associations
- Forms with associations
- Reusing components

Managing information – films

The Sakila database has four major modules within it: **Inventory**, which consists of the films' information, along with the inventory information (how many movies we have in each store available for rental); customer data, which consists of customer information; business, which consists of the stores, staff and also rental and payment information (this depends on inventory and customer data to feed some information); and views, which consists of data we can use for reports and charts.

For now, we are only interested in **Inventory**, customer data, and business, which contains the core business information of the application. Let's take a look at **Inventory**, which has more tables than the other two:

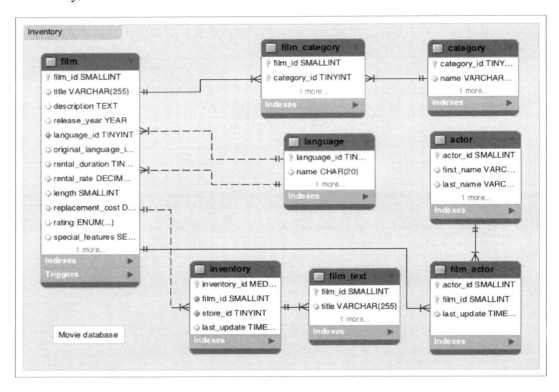

According to the Sakila documentation:

> The film *table is a list of all films potentially in stock in the stores. The actual in-stock copies of each film are represented in the* inventory *table.*

> The film *table refers to the* language *table and is referred to by the* film_category, film_actor, *and* inventory *tables.*

The film table has a many-to-many relationship with the category and actor tables. It has two many-to-one relationships with the language table. In the last chapter, we have already developed code to manage the category, actor, and language tables. Now, we need to manage the relationships between the film table and these other tables.

Ext JS 5 has really nice capabilities to manage associated entities similar to the `film` table. We will dive into them in this chapter.

So let's take a brief look at the screens that we are going to develop in this chapter.

First, we need a screen to list the films we have, which is as follows:

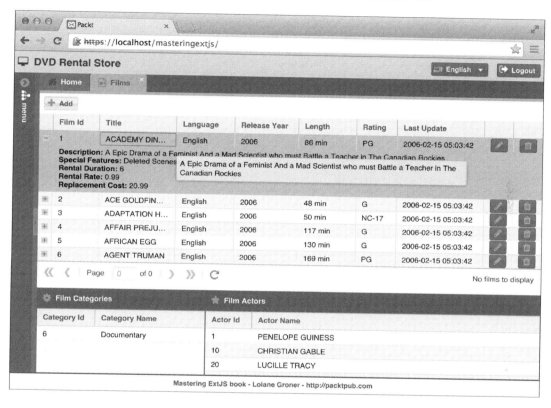

This screen displays three data grids. The first one is the `film` table, which is going to display the list of all **Films**. The second one is the **Film Categories**, which represents the many-to-many relationship between the `film` and `category` tables. And the third one is the **Film Actors**, which represents the many-to-many relationship between the `film` and `actor` tables.

Then, if we want to create or edit a film, we will create a FormPanel within a window so that we can edit its information, as follows:

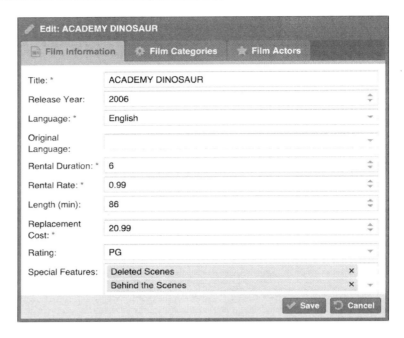

As the `film` table has a many-to-many association with the `categories` table, we also need to handle it within the FormPanel using a different tab. If we want to add more categories associated with the film, we can **Search** and add, as follows:

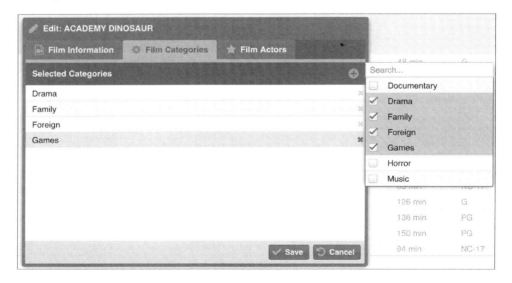

Likewise, the `film` table has also a many-to-many association with the `actor` table, so we also need to handle it within the FormPanel. The following screenshot exemplifies this:

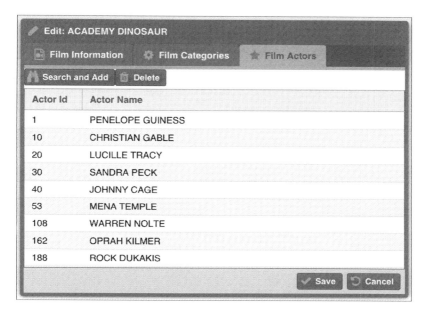

If we want to add more actors associated to the film, we can use **Search and Add Actor**, as follows:

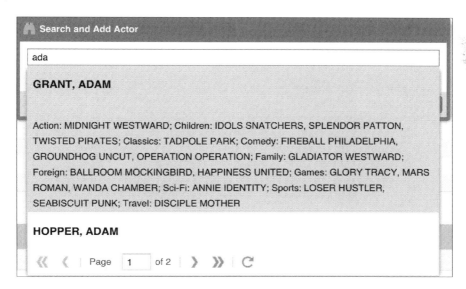

Notice that we are taking a different approach for each screen. This way we can learn more ways of handling these scenarios in Ext JS. By the end of this chapter, we will learn to create this complex form and save associated data as well.

So now that we have an idea of what we will implement throughout this chapter, let's have some fun and get our hands dirty!

Displaying the Film data grid

First, let's start with the basics. Whenever we need to implement a complex screen, we need to start with the simplest component we can develop. When this component is working, we can start incrementing it and add more complex capabilities. So first, we need to create a Model to represent the `film` table. In this chapter, we are going to use the MVVM approach, so we can dive into capabilities we have not covered in previous chapters. Once we have this part of the code working, we can work with the relationships between the `category`, `language`, and `actor` tables.

The Film Model

First, we are going to create the Model to represent the `film` table. Let's not worry about the relationships this table has for now.

We need to create a new class named `Packt.view.film.FilmsGrid`, as follows:

```
Ext.define('Packt.model.film.Film', {
    extend: 'Packt.model.staticData.Base', //#1

    entityName: 'Film',

    idProperty: 'film_id',

    fields: [
        { name: 'film_id' },
        { name: 'title'},
        { name: 'description'},
        { name: 'release_year', type: 'int'},
        { name: 'language_id'},
        { name: 'original_language_id'},
        { name: 'rental_duration', type: 'int'},
        { name: 'rental_rate', type: 'float'},
        { name: 'length', type: 'int'},
        { name: 'replacement_cost', type: 'float'},
        { name: 'rating'},
        { name: 'special_features'}
    ]
});
```

As all Sakila tables have the `last_update` column, we will extend `Packt.model.staticData.Base` to avoid declaring this field in every single Model we create that represents a Sakila table. The `staticData.Base` class also extends `Packt.model.Base`, which contains the `schema` and `proxy` details for our models.

For the fields, we will have the same ones we have in the `film` table.

Films ModelView

Our next step is to create a ModelView that will contain a Store that will load the collection of films. Let's create a Store named `films` (remember that the Store name is always the plural of the name of the Model—if you want to follow the Sencha naming convention) inside the ViewModel, as follows:

```
Ext.define('Packt.view.film.FilmsModel', {
    extend: 'Ext.app.ViewModel',

    alias: 'viewmodel.films',

    stores: {
        films: {
            model: 'Packt.model.film.Film', //#1
            pageSize: 15,    //#2
            autoLoad: true, //#3
            session: true    //#4
        }
    }
});
```

We need to create a file named `FilmsModel.js` inside the `app/view/film` folder and put the preceding code inside the file.

In the `films` Store, we are declaring the `model` as usual (#1), and we are also declaring `pageSize` as 15 (#2), meaning we will use the PagingToolbar in the Films data grid, and we will retrieve sets of 15 films per unit time to display in the GridPanel.

The `autoLoad` configuration is also set to `true` (#3). As the ViewModel is created once the View is instantiated, the Store will be loaded once the View is created as well.

At last, we have a `session` configuration (#4). We have not worked with sessions so far in this book. When we worked with CRUD in the preceding chapter, we used the Store to save the data. In this chapter, we are going to work with associated data, and a session can be really helpful when we need to save data from different models. The session will be created in the View. Having `session: true` declared inside a Store inside the ViewModel links the Store with the session of the View. We will discuss how this works later on in this chapter.

Film data grid (with paging)

Now that we have the Model and the ViewModel with the Store, we need to create `FilmsGrid`, which we can do as follows:

```
Ext.define('Packt.view.film.FilmsGrid', {
    extend: 'Packt.view.base.Grid', //#1
    xtype: 'films-grid',

    bind : '{films}',   //#2

    reference: 'filmsGrid', //#3

    columns: [{
        text: 'Film Id',
        width: 80,
        dataIndex: 'film_id'
    },{
        text: 'Title',
        flex: 1,
        dataIndex: 'title',
     renderer: function(value, metaData, record ){   //#4
            metaData['tdAttr'] = 'data-qtip="' +
                    record.get('description') + '"'; //#5
            return value;
        }
    },{
        text: 'Language',
        width: 100,
        dataIndex: 'language_id'
    },{
        text: 'Release Year',
        width: 110,
        dataIndex: 'release_year'
    },{
```

```
        text: 'Length',
        width: 100,
        dataIndex: 'length',
        renderer: function(value, metaData, record ){ //#6
            return value + ' min';
        }
    },{
        text: 'Rating',
        width: 70,
        dataIndex: 'rating'
    }]
});
```

As our application starts to grow, we notice that we use some of the configurations in different components. For example, for most of the GridPanels, we use a toolbar with the **Add**, **Edit** and **Delete** buttons, or we can use a toolbar with the **Add** button and have the **Edit** and **Delete** buttons inside the grid as Widget Columns (or Action Columns). As all tables from the Sakila database have the Last Update column, this column is also common to all the GridPanels we use to list information from Sakila tables. For this reason, we can create a super GridPanel (as we did specifically for the static data module). So, for the Films GridPanel, we will extend from base.Grid (#1) that we will create next.

Having declared the ViewModel already, we can bind the films Store in this grid as well (#2). To make our job easier later, we will also declare reference for this grid (#3).

Then, we have the columns mapping dataIndex with the field of the Film Model. When we want to manipulate the information that is going to be displayed in the grid, we can use the renderer function. For the length column, we want to display the length and 'min' because the length of a film is based in minutes. So, we can return the value itself (length) concatenated to the string we want (#6).

Inside the renderer function, we can also use other fields to manipulate the information by retrieving the desired field from record. For example, inside the renderer function (#4) of the title column, we want to display a tooltip with the film's description (#5) when the user does a mouse over on the title column. But we are not changing the value that is going to be displayed, which is title (value parameter of the renderer function) itself.

Creating the Base Grid

To create the base `Grid` class, we are going to create a new base folder named `base` inside `app/view` so that we can place all our `base` classes. Then we are going to create a new file named `Grid.js` with the following content:

```
Ext.define('Packt.view.base.Grid', {
    extend: 'Ext.grid.Panel',

    requires: [
        'Packt.util.Glyphs'
    ],

    columnLines: true,
    viewConfig: {
        stripeRows: true
    },

    initComponent: function() {
        var me = this;

        me.columns = Ext.Array.merge(
            me.columns,
            [{
                xtype    : 'datecolumn',
                text     : 'Last Update',
                width    : 150,
                dataIndex: 'last_update',
                format: 'Y-m-j H:i:s',
                filter: true
            },{
                xtype: 'widgetcolumn',
                width: 50,
                sortable: false,
                menuDisabled: true,
                widget: {
                    xtype: 'button',
                    glyph: Packt.util.Glyphs.getGlyph('edit'),
                    tooltip: 'Edit',
                    handler: 'onEdit'    //#1
                }
            },{
                xtype: 'widgetcolumn',
                width: 50,
```

```
                    sortable: false,
                    menuDisabled: true,
                    widget: {
                        xtype: 'button',
                        glyph: Packt.util.Glyphs.getGlyph('destroy'),
                        tooltip: 'Delete',
                        handler: 'onDelete'   //#2
                    }
                }]
        );

        me.callParent(arguments);
    }
});
```

We have created a similar class to this one in *Chapter 7, Static Data Management*. However, this class has something different. In lines #1 and #2 we are declaring a handler that is going to be handled in the ViewController. Working with MVVM and Widget Columns is much simpler than working using the MVC approach because we do not need to fire a custom event; we can simply declare the onEdit and onDelete methods inside the ViewController.

Adding the RowExpander plugin

Let's go back to the FilmsGrid class and add the RowExpander plugin. The film table has more columns than the ones we are displaying inside the FilmsGrid class. We can use the RowExpander plugin to display other information.

We are going to add the following code inside the FilmsGrid class, as follows:

```
plugins: [{
    ptype: 'rowexpander',
    rowBodyTpl: [
        '<b>Description:</b> {description}</br>',
        '<b>Special Features:</b> {special_features}</br>',
        '<b>Rental Duration:</b> {rental_duration}</br>',
        '<b>Rental Rate:</b> {rental_rate}</br>',
        '<b>Replacement Cost:</b> {replacement_cost}</br>'
    ]
}]
```

We need to configure a template to display the extra information we want. In this case, we are displaying the description of the film and some other information that could not fit on the columns, such as the rental information.

For more information about the template, you can visit `http://docs.sencha.com/extjs/5.0/5.0.0-apidocs/#!/api/Ext.Template` and `http://docs.sencha.com/extjs/5.0/5.0.0-apidocs/#!/api/Ext.XTemplate`.

Unfortunately, it is not possible to use the `RowExpander` plugin with the associated models. If we want to display associated data, we can use the `SubTable` plugin. It is also not possible to use the `RowExpander` and `SubTable` plugins at the same time.

With the preceding code, a new column will be added in the Grid so that we can see this extra information:

	Film Id	Title	Language	Release Year	Length	Rating	Last Update
⊟	1	ACADEMY DINOSAUR	English	2006	86 min	PG	2006-02-15 05:03:42
	Description: A Epic Drama of a Feminist And a Mad Scientist who must Battle a Teacher in The Canadian Rockies **Special Features:** Deleted Scenes,Behind the Scenes **Rental Duration:** 6 **Rental Rate:** 0.99 **Replacement Cost:** 20.99						
⊞	2	ACE GOLDFINGER	English	2006	48 min	G	2006-02-15 05:03:42
⊞	3	ADAPTATION HOLES	English	2006	50 min	NC-17	2006-02-15 05:03:42
⊞	4	AFFAIR PREJUDICE	English	2006	117 min	G	2006-02-15 05:03:42

Actor-Language – handling a hasOne association

In *Chapter 6, User Management*, we handled the relationship between the `User` and `Group` models using a `hasOne` association by adding a new field in the `User` Model (creating a `User` Model section). We will learn a different way to display a `hasOne` association in the grid in this chapter.

A film has a `hasOne` association with language (language has a `hasMany` association with film). We will display the language `name` instead of `language_id` using a `renderer` function as demonstrated in the following code:

```
dataIndex: 'language_id',
renderer: function(value, metaData, record ){
    var languagesStore = Ext.getStore('staticData.Languages'); //#1
    var lang = languagesStore.findRecord('language_id', value);//#2
    return lang != null ? lang.get('name') : value;            //#3
}
```

We will take advantage of the fact that the Languages Store was created within the global scope of the application (which we created in *Chapter 7, Static Data Management*) and use this. This way, we do not need to load the language name from the server again. So, we are going to retrieve the Store (#1) using the store manager and search for the Language Model that has language_id, which we are looking for (#2). If the value exists, then we display it; otherwise, we display the language_id parameter anyway (#3).

Even though Ext JS has the capability to load the information from the server and parse using the association capability, is it worth using it in this scenario since we already have a Store with the values we need loaded? If we do use association, it means that more data will be loaded from the server, and some of them can be duplicated for a different Model (in this case, all films have language_id as 1, which is English). So the same language Model would be loaded several times, and the JSON we would load from the server would be larger.

Adding the PagingToolbar

Next, we are going to declare a PagingToolbar. Inside the FilmsGrid class, we are going to add the following code:

```
dockedItems: [{
    dock: 'bottom',
    xtype: 'pagingtoolbar',
    bind : {
        store: '{films}' //#1
    },
    displayInfo: true,
    displayMsg: 'Displaying films {0} - {1} of {2}',
    emptyMsg: "No films to display"
}]
```

The PagingToolbar is a special toolbar that is bound to a Store. For this reason, we need to specify the Store (#1). In this case, it will be the same Store we declared in FilmsGrid.

Handling paging on the server side

Since we are using the PagingToolbar, it is important to remember a few things. Ext JS provides tools to help us to page the content, but let's emphasize the word "provide". Ext JS will not do the paging for us if we retrieve all the records from the database at once.

If we want to page data that is already loaded, we can use PagingMemoryProxy (Ext.ux.data.PagingMemoryProxy) provided within the Ext JS SDK.

If we take a look at the request Ext JS sends to the server, we will find that it sends three extra parameters when we use the PagingToolbar. These parameters are **start**, **limit**, and **page**. For example, as we can see, when we load the GridPanel information for the first time, **start** is **0**, **limit** is the pageSize configuration we set on the Store (in this case, **15**), and **page** is **1**. The following figure exemplifies this:

When we click on the next page of the GridPanel, **start** will be **15** (0 + **limit** (15) = 15), **limit** will have the value **15** (this value does not change unless we change pageSize dynamically), and **page** will be **2**. This is demonstrated by the following figure:

 There is a third-party plugin that can change pageSize dynamically according to the user's selection at https://github.com/loiane/extjs4-ux-paging-toolbar-resizer.

These parameters help us to page the information on the database as well. For example, for MySQL, we only need `start` and `limit`, so we need to get them from the request, as follows:

```
$start = $_REQUEST['start'];
$limit = $_REQUEST['limit'];
```

Then, when we execute the SELECT query, we need to add LIMIT $start, $limit at the end (after the WHERE, ORDER BY, GROUP BY clauses, if any):

```
$sql = "SELECT * FROM film LIMIT $start,  $limit";
```

This will bring the information we need from the database.

Another very important detail is that the PagingToolbar displays the total number of records we have on the database:

```
$sql = "SELECT count(*) as num FROM film";
```

So, we also need to return a `total` property on the JSON with the count of the table:

```
echo json_encode(array(
  "success" => $mysqli->connect_errno == 0,
  "data" => $result,
  "total" => $total
));
```

Then Ext JS will receive all the information required to make the paging work as expected.

Paging queries on MySQL, Oracle, and Microsoft SQL Server

We need to be careful because if we use a different database, the query to page the information directly from the database is different.

If we were using the Oracle database, the SELECT query with paging would be as follows:

```
SELECT * FROM
  (select rownum as rn, f.* from
    (select * from film order by film_id) as f
  ) WHERE rn > $start  and rn <= ($start + $limit)
```

This would be much more complicated than MySQL. Now let's see Microsoft SQL Server (SQL Server 2012):

```
SELECT   *
FROM ( SELECT ROW_NUMBER() OVER ( ORDER BY film_id ) AS RowNum, *
         FROM films
       ) AS RowConstrainedResult
WHERE    RowNum > $start
   AND RowNum <= ($start + $limit)
ORDER BY RowNum
```

In SQL Server 2012, it is simpler:

```
SELECT * FROM film
ORDER BY film_id
OFFSET $start ROWS
FETCH NEXT $limit ROWS ONLY
```

In Firebird, it is also simpler than MySQL:

```
SELECT FIRST $limit SKIP $start * FROM film
```

So be careful with the SQL syntax if you are using a different database than MySQL.

Creating the films container

The next step is creating the **Films** screen that we presented at the beginning of this chapter. It consists of a toolbar with a button (**Add**), the Films grid, and two associated grids (Categories and Actors). We are going to create this View in the Films.js file, as follows:

```
Ext.define('Packt.view.film.Films', {
    extend: 'Ext.panel.Panel',
    xtype: 'films',

    requires: [
        'Packt.view.base.TopToolBar',
        'Packt.view.film.FilmsGrid',
        'Packt.view.film.FilmActorsGrid',
        'Packt.view.film.FilmCategoriesGrid',
        'Packt.view.film.FilmsModel',
        'Packt.view.film.FilmsController'
    ],
```

```
    controller: 'films', //#1
    viewModel: {
        type: 'films'     //#2
    },

    session: true,        //#3

    layout: {
        type: 'vbox',
        align: 'stretch'
    },

    items: [{
        xtype: 'films-grid',  //#4
        flex: 1
    },{
        xtype: 'container',
        split: true,
        layout: {
            type: 'hbox',
            align: 'stretch'
        },
        height: 150,
        items: [{
            xtype: 'film-categories', //#5
            flex: 1
        },{
            xtype: 'film-actors',     //#6
            flex: 2
        }]
    }],

    dockedItems: [{
        xtype: 'top-tool-bar'     //#7
    }]
});
```

In this class, we declared a ViewController (#1) and also the ViewModel (#2). The ViewModel was already created, so we need to create the ViewController.

Next, we have `session` (#3). If provided, this creates a new session instance for this component. As this class is a container for other classes, the session will then be inherited by all child components. We will dive into the session when we work in the ViewController.

In line #4, we have the `FilmsGrid` class we created. And in lines #5 and #6 ,we have the `categories` and `actors` grid that we will use to display the many-to-many association.

We also have `TopToolBar` declared in line #7. This toolbar was created separately, so we can reuse it, as follows:

```
Ext.define('Packt.view.base.TopToolBar', {
    extend: 'Ext.toolbar.Toolbar',
    xtype: 'top-tool-bar',

    requires: [
        'Packt.util.Glyphs'
    ],

    dock: 'top',
    items: [
        {
            xtype: 'button',
            text: 'Add',
            itemId: 'add',
            glyph: Packt.util.Glyphs.getGlyph('add'),
            listeners: {
                click: 'onAdd'
            }
        }
    ]
});
```

We cannot forget to update the menu table to reflect the films `xtype`:

```
UPDATE `sakila`.`menu` SET `className`='films' WHERE `id`='11';
```

We will be adding more buttons to this toolbar in the next chapter.

Handling many-to-many associations

The `film` and `category` tables are associated by a many-to-many relationship. When this happens, a matrix table is created with two columns to hold the IDs of a pair of related entities. There is a matrix table representing the many-to-many relationship between the `film` and `category` tables, called `film_category` and a table called `film_actor` representing the many-to-many relationship between `film` and `actor`.

To represent a many-to-many relationship in Ext JS, we will add the following code to the `Film` Model:

```
manyToMany: {
    FilmCategories: {              //#1
        type: 'Category',         //#2
        role: 'categories',       //#3
        field: 'category_id',  //#4
        right: {
            field: 'film_id', //#5
            role: 'films'         //#6
        }
    },
    FilmActors: {
        type: 'Actor',
        role: 'actors',
        field: 'actor_id',
        right: {
            field: 'film_id',
            role: 'films'
        }
    }
}
```

For each many-to-many relationship, we need to define a `name` (#1). The name must be unique within the schema. We also need to define a `type` (#2). The `type` is the name of the `model` of the association—we can use `entityName` to define the associated Model. We can also define `role` (#3), which will be the name of the method generated to retrieve the associated data. We also need to specify the foreign key (#4) used to identify the association. As the many-to-many relationship is created between two tables, we can also specify the information that links this Model to the matrix table, which is the `field` (foreign key—#5) and also the `role` of the association in the `Category` and `Actor` models (#6).

In the `Category` Model, we will also declare the many-to-many association:

```
manyToMany: {
    CategoryFilms: {
        type: 'Film',
        role: 'films',
        field: 'film_id',
        right: {
            field: 'category_id',
            role: 'categories'
        }
    }
}
```

And we will do this inside the `Actor` Model as well:

```
manyToMany: {
    ActorFilms: {
        type: 'Film',
        role: 'films',
        field: 'film_id',
        right: {
            field: 'actor_id',
            role: 'actors'
        }
    }
}
```

Loading nested JSON from the server

In the server-side code, we need to retrieve the film information and its categories and actors as well. The JSON that the server will return to Ext JS will have the following format:

```
{
    "success":true,
    "data":[
        {
            "film_id":"1",
            "title":"ACADEMY DINOSAUR",
            "description":"A Epic Drama of a Feminist And a Mad
            Scientist who must Battle a Teacher in The Canadian
            Rockies",
            "release_year":"2006",
            "language_id":"1",
            "original_language_id":null,
            "rental_duration":"6",
            "rental_rate":"0.99",
            "length":"86",
            "replacement_cost":"20.99",
            "rating":"PG",
            "special_features":"Deleted Scenes,Behind the Scenes",
            "last_update":"2006-02-15 05:03:42",
            "categories":[
                {
                    "category_id":"6",
                    "name":"Documentary",
                    "last_update":"2006-02-15 04:46:27"
                }
```

```
        ],
        "actors":[
            {
                "actor_id":"1",
                "first_name":"PENELOPE",
                "last_name":"GUINESS",
                "last_update":"2006-02-15 04:34:33"
            },
            {

                "actor_id":"10",
                "first_name":"CHRISTIAN",
                "last_name":"GABLE",
                "last_update":"2006-02-15 04:34:33"
            }
        ]
    }
    ],
    "total":"1000"
}
```

 The server-side code is included within the source code of this book.

If we inspect a `Film` Model instance of the `films` Store, we will see that a function/method is created for each of the associations, as follows:

```
▼ constructor {data: Object, session: constructor, internalId: 967, id: "1", _categories: constructor…}
    Ext.data.Model#persistenceProperty: (...)
  ▶ _actors: constructor
  ▶ _categories: constructor
  ▶ data: Object
    id: "1"
    internalId: 967
  ▶ joined: Array[3]
  ▶ raw: Object
```

 When accessing `model.actors()` or `model.categories()`, the methods will return a Store for each association and not an array of the `Actor` or `Category` Model.

Changing the ViewModel – chained stores

Ext JS will understand the association and will be able to create the methods and associated stores, but we need to add the stores to the session as well by adding the `actors` and `categories` Store in the same ViewModel, as follows:

```
categories: {
    source: 'staticData.Categories',
    autoLoad: true,
    session: true
},
actors: {
    source: 'staticData.Actors',
    autoLoad: true,
    session: true
}
```

Note the highlighted code. The stores we are creating use existing stores (which we created in the preceding chapter, and which are available in the global scope of the application through their `storeId`) through a `source` configuration. This capability was also introduced in Ext JS 5, and it is called a chained store (`Ext.data.ChainedStore`). A chained store is a store that is a view of an existing store. The data comes from the `source`; however, this view of the store can be sorted and filtered independently without having any impact on the source store. This is very useful when we want to have two different stores with synchronized data, but independent instances.

Film-Actor – handling many-to-many associations

Now that we have the many-to-many association in place, we can create the `FilmActorsGrid` class. This class will have the following content:

```
Ext.define('Packt.view.film.FilmActorsGrid', {
    extend: 'Ext.grid.Panel',
    xtype: 'film-actors',

    requires: [
        'Packt.util.Glyphs'
    ],

    bind : '{filmsGrid.selection.actors}', //#1
    border: true,

    title: 'Film Actors',
    glyph: Packt.util.Glyphs.getGlyph('actor'),
```

```
    columns: [
        {
            text: 'Actor Id',
            width: 80,
            dataIndex: 'actor_id'
        },
        {
            xtype: 'templatecolumn',
            text: 'Actor Name',
            flex: 1,
            tpl: '{first_name} {last_name}' //#2
        }
    ]
});
```

This grid contains a column we have not used so far, which is the Template Column. When using this column, you can create a template to display more than one field (#2) instead of using a `renderer` function to do so.

The preceding code presents how to display associated data in a detail grid. When we select a film from the `FilmsGrid`, the Actors grid will automatically display the associated data by binding the `actors` (role of the association) with the Actors grid (#1).

Film-Category – handling many-to-many associations

We will use the same approach used for the Film-Actor many-to-many associations for the Film-Category many-to-many associations. We will create a class named `FilmCategoriesGrid`. This class will have the following content:

```
Ext.define('Packt.view.film.FilmCategoriesGrid', {
    extend: 'Ext.grid.Panel',
    xtype: 'film-categories',

    requires: [
        'Packt.util.Glyphs'
    ],

    bind : '{filmsGrid.selection.categories}', //#1
    border: true,

    title: 'Film Categories',
    glyph: Packt.util.Glyphs.getGlyph('category'),
```

```
        columns: [
            {
                text: 'Category Id',
                width: 100,
                dataIndex: 'category_id'
            },
            {
                text: 'Category Name',
                flex: 1,
                dataIndex: 'name'
            }
        ]
    });
```

We will also `bind` the Store of this grid to the data loaded from the association (#1).

Creating the ViewController

The missing piece now is the ViewController, which will handle all the handlers and listeners declared in our code. We will split the code into two classes: the `base.ViewController` that contains generic code and can be reused, and the `film.FilmsController` that contains the code to handle specific details of the `Films` View.

The base ViewController

Inside this class, we will put all the generic code that can be reused by other views that have the same behavior as the `Films` View. For example, editing or deleting a record by clicking on a button of a Widget Column opens the pop-up window. If the user clicks on the **Add** button, then close the pop-up window that is used to create or edit information.

The code for this class is presented as follows:

```
Ext.define('Packt.view.base.ViewController', {
    extend: 'Ext.app.ViewController',

    requires: [
        'Packt.util.Util',
        'Packt.util.Glyphs'
    ],
```

```
onAdd: function(button, e, options){ //#1
    this.createDialog(null);
},

onEdit: function(button){ //#2
    this.createDialog(button.getWidgetRecord());
},

onCancel: function(button, e, options){ //#3
    var me = this;
    me.dialog = Ext.destroy(me.dialog);
},

onDelete: function(button, e, options){ //#4
    var record = button.getWidgetRecord();
    Ext.Msg.show({
        title:'Delete?',
        msg: 'Are you sure you want to delete?',
        buttons: Ext.Msg.YESNO,
        icon: Ext.Msg.QUESTION,
        fn: function (buttonId){
            if (buttonId == 'yes'){
                record.drop();
            }
        }
    });
}
});
```

In the preceding chapter, you learned that it is possible to create a generic Controller in MVC to handle events from multiple screens. It was implemented using a generic selector from the components we created. In MVVM, it is also possible to create a generic ViewController, but not using a generic selector (because we do not work with selectors in MVVM). This is possible if we set a pattern of listeners (the components will have the same `handler` name), and declare a generic ViewController. However, we also need to specify a specific ViewController for the View, and this ViewContoller is going to extend our base ViewController. Generic code in ViewController is handled by inheritance.

In the `FilmsGrid`, class we have two handlers: one for the **Edit** Widget Button and one for the **Delete** Widget Button.

For the **Delete** button (#4), all we have to do is ask whether the user is certain that they want to delete the `record`, and then if we receive a positive response, we use the `record.drop()` method to do it. The `drop` method marks the record as dropped and waiting to be deleted on the server. When a record is dropped, it is automatically removed from all association stores, and any child record associated with this record is also dropped (a cascade delete) depending on the cascade parameter. As the View and the Store are associated with a session, when we call the method `drop`, the session records that this record and its associated data need to be deleted, and the Store is also notified. We could also use the remove method from the Store; it would have the same output.

For the **Add** (#1) and **Edit** (#2) handlers, we want to open the **Edit** window so that we can modify or create a new film. We are going to use the same approach we used in *Chapter 6, User Management*, when we handled `Users` and `Groups`. The `createDialog` method will be created in the specific ViewController, which is the `FilmsController` class we will create next. This way we can have a generic code, but the details will be implemented in the specific ViewController.

A detail for the `edit` and `delete` handlers is that we can easily use the method `getWidgetRecord` from the button (Widget Column) to retrieve the `record` from the grid. This approach is very different from the approach we used in the preceding chapter (where we created a custom event to be handled in the MVC Controller).

Just as we did in *Chapter 6, User Management*, we will create the **Edit** window, and it will have a **Cancel** button. When the user clicks on this button, we will destroy the window (#3).

 We can go back to *Chapter 6, User Management*, and modify the code to use this ViewController as well.

Creating the FilmsController

Now we are going to implement the ViewController for the `Films` View. Its initial code is presented here; in the subsequent topics, we will add more code to it:

```
Ext.define('Packt.view.film.FilmsController', {
    extend: 'Packt.view.base.ViewController',

    alias: 'controller.films'
});
```

Adding or editing a film

Now that `FilmsGrid` is already being rendered and loaded and the `add` and `edit` handlers are in place in the ViewController, we need to create the `createDialog` method. But first, we need to create the `Edit` window class.

As we could see in the screenshots at the beginning of this chapter, the **Edit** window has three tabs: one for editing the film details, another one to edit the categories related to the film, and the third one to edit the actors related to the film. For now, we are going to deal with the film details only.

So, inside `app/view/film`, we are going to create a new view named `Packt.view.film.FilmWindow`. This class will be a window that has a form with a TabPanel as an `item`. Inside each of the tabs, we will place the film's details, the categories, and the actors, as follows:

```
Ext.define('Packt.view.film.FilmWindow', {
    extend: 'Packt.view.base.WindowForm', //#1
    xtype: 'film-window',                 //#2

    requires: [
        'Packt.view.film.FilmFormContainer',
        'Packt.view.film.FilmActorsGrid',
        'Packt.view.film.FilmFormCategories'
    ],

    width: 537,

    items: [
        {
            xtype: 'form',
            reference: 'filmForm',  //#3
            layout: {
                type: 'fit'
            },
            items: [{
                xtype: 'tabpanel', //#4
                activeTab: 0,
                items: [{
                    xtype: 'film-form-container', //#5
                    glyph: Packt.util.Glyphs.getGlyph('film')
                },{
                    xtype: 'film-categories-form', //#6
                    glyph: Packt.util.Glyphs.getGlyph('category')
                }
```

```
                              //film actors here
                    ]
                }
            ]
    });
```

This window extends from a custom class (#1) that we are going to create. As for the creation and editing of grid rows, we always use a window, so we can create a super window class with the common configuration and use it throughout our application. We will create this new class in a minute; let's finish overviewing this class first. We cannot forget to declare an xtype configuration (#2); we will use this xtype configuration in the ViewController later.

Inside this window, we have a form (#3), to which we need to declare a reference to easily retrieve in the ViewController. Inside the form we have a TabPanel (#4), which contains a tab with the film information (#5) — we are going to create a separate class for it, and the categories (#6), for which we are also going to create a separate class.

The last piece of this class is the actors details that are presented in the following code:

```
{
    xtype: 'film-actors',    //#7
    reference: 'actorsGrid', //#8
    dockedItems: [{
        dock: 'top',
        items: [
            {
                xtype: 'button',
                text: 'Search and Add',
                glyph: Packt.util.Glyphs.getGlyph('searchAndAdd'),
                listeners: {
                    click: 'onAddActor' //#9
                }
            },
            {
                xtype: 'button',
                text: 'Delete',
                glyph: Packt.util.Glyphs.getGlyph('destroy'),
                listeners: {
                    click: 'onDeleteActor' //#10
                }
            }
        ]
    }]
}
```

For the actors details, we are going to reuse the `Actors` grid (#7) displayed in the `Films` View. We are going to add a reference as well (#8), because it is going to be useful when we work on the **Search and Add** screen to handle the `onAddActor` (#9) listener. And at last, we also need a listener for the delete button (#10).

The **Add** and **Delete** actor buttons are going to add and delete entries of the `film_actor` table.

Packt.view.base.WindowForm

All the **Edit** windows we have already implemented are a window with Fit layout and usually have a FormPanel inside it. The window also has a **Cancel** and a **Save** button. As all these configurations are default for our components, we can create a super window for them:

```
Ext.define('Packt.view.base.WindowForm', {
    extend: 'Ext.window.Window',
    alias: 'widget.windowform',

    requires: [
        'Packt.util.Util',
        'Packt.util.Glyphs',
        'Packt.view.base.CancelSaveToolbar'
    ],

    height: 400,
    width: 550,
    autoScroll: true,
    layout: {
        type: 'fit'
    },
    modal: true,
    closable: false,

    bind: {
        title: '{title}', //#1
        glyph: '{glyph}'  //#2
    },

    dockedItems: [{
        xtype: 'cancel-save-toolbar'
    }]
});
```

Note that we are not declaring a configuration inside the `initConfig` method (which is not present in this class). This means this class is a base, and anything can be overridden in a child class.

An important detail here is that the `title` (#1) and the `glyph` (#2) configurations used in this window can be bound to the information from the ViewModel. We will handle these details in the `createDialog` method.

This window class uses `CancelSaveToolbar`. The code for this toolbar is as follows:

```
Ext.define('Packt.view.base.CancelSaveToolbar', {
    extend: 'Ext.toolbar.Toolbar',
    xtype: 'cancel-save-toolbar',

    requires: [
        'Packt.util.Glyphs'
    ],

    dock: 'bottom',
    ui: 'footer',
    layout: {
        pack: 'end',
        type: 'hbox'
    },
    items: [
        {
            xtype: 'button',
            text: 'Save',
            glyph: Packt.util.Glyphs.getGlyph('save'),
            listeners: {
                click: 'onSave' //#3
            }
        },
        {
            xtype: 'button',
            text: 'Cancel',
            glyph: Packt.util.Glyphs.getGlyph('cancel'),
            listeners: {
                click: 'onCancel' //#4
            }
        }
    ]
});
```

Inside the preceding class there are `listeners` for the **Save** button (#3), which we are going to handle inside the `FilmsController` class and for the **Cancel** button (#4), which is handled by the base ViewController class.

> We can go back to the code we implemented in *Chapter 6, User Management*, and *Chapter 7, Static Data Management*, and refactor to use the base classes and toolbar classes. This is what is nice about Ext JS and its object-oriented approach: it allows you to reuse code, and you can refactor it as you can do in any other object-oriented language, and there are no headaches involved.

The films form

The first item of the TabPanel (#3) is the `film-form-container`. Inside this class, we are going to declare all the fields that represent the columns of the `film` table.

Let's go back to the Sakila documentation and take a look at the fields of the `film` table (`http://dev.mysql.com/doc/sakila/en/sakila-structure-tables-film.html`). You can also refer to the first image of this chapter:

- `film_id`: This is the primary key of the table and has a unique value. So, for this field, we can use a hidden field to control this.

- `title`: This is the title of the film. So, we can use a text field for it. The maximum length on the database is 255, so we also need to add validation.

- `description`: This is a short description or plot summary of the film. As the description can be 5,000 characters in length, we can use a text area to represent it.

- `release_year`: This is the year in which the movie was released. This can be a numeric field, with a minimum value of 1950 until the current year + 1 (let's say we want to add a film that is going to be released next year).

- `language_id`: This is a foreign key pointing at the language table. It identifies the language of the film. This can be a combobox with the language Store (already populated when we load the application).

- `original_language_id`: This is a foreign key pointing at the language table that identifies the original language of the film. This is used when a film has been dubbed in a new language. Also, this can be a combobox with the language Store (already populated when we load the application).

- `rental_duration`: This is the length of the rental period in days. This can be a number field, with a minimum value of 1 and maximum value of 10 (let's give a limit to the maximum value).

- `rental_rate`: This is the cost to rent the film for the period specified in the `rental_duration` column. This can also be a number field. The minimum value is 0 and the maximum value is 5, and we need to allow decimal values as well.

- `length`: This is the duration of the film in minutes. The `length` column can also be a number field between 1 and 999.

- `replacement_cost`: This is the amount charged to the customer if the film is not returned or is returned in a damaged state. This is also a numeric field. Let's give a minimum value of 0 and maximum value of 100.

- `rating`: This is the rating assigned to the film. It can be one of G, PG, PG-13, R, or NC-17. As these have fixed values, we can represent them on a radio button group or a Combobox. We are going to use a Combobox.

- `special_features`: This lists which common special features are included on the DVD. It can be zero or more of trailers, commentaries, deleted scenes, and behind the scenes. As this can be one or more, we can use the TagField introduced in Ext JS 5. We can also use checkboxes or a combobox allowing multiple selection.

Let's declare the class structure first, as follows:

```
Ext.define('Packt.view.film.FilmFormContainer', {
    extend: 'Ext.panel.Panel',
    xtype: 'film-form-container',

    requires: [
        'Packt.util.Util',
        'Packt.util.Glyphs'
    ],

    bodyPadding: 10,
    layout: {
        type: 'anchor'
    },
    title: 'Film Information',
    defaults: {
        anchor: '100%',
        msgTarget: 'side',
        labelWidth: 105
    },

    items: [
        //fields
    ]
});
```

The fields will be inside a panel (which will become a tab) that uses the Anchor layout, and each field will occupy all available horizontal space (`anchor: 100%`). The labels are `105` pixels wide, and any error messages will be displayed on the `side` of the field. There has been no news for us so far.

Let's declare the first two fields—`title` and `release_year`:

```
{
    xtype: 'textfield',
    fieldLabel: 'Title',
    afterLabelTextTpl: Packt.util.Util.required,
    bind : '{currentFilm.title}' //#1
},
{
    xtype: 'numberfield',
    fieldLabel: 'Release Year',
    allowDecimals: false,               //#2
    bind : '{currentFilm.release_year}' //#3
},
```

Both values are bound (#1 and #3) to the fields of a record called `currentFilm` (that we will create in `FilmsController` later). `Release Year` is a numeric field, and as we want the value to be an integer, we will not allow the user to enter decimal numbers (#2).

> For more information about forms and field validation, please refer to http://docs.sencha.com/extjs/5.0/components/forms.html.

Next, we have the language fields, which are as follows:

```
{
    xtype: 'combobox',
    fieldLabel: 'Language',
    displayField: 'name',
    valueField: 'language_id',
    queryMode: 'local',
    store: 'staticData.Languages', //#4
    afterLabelTextTpl: Packt.util.Util.required,
    bind : '{currentFilm.language_id}' //#5
},
{
    xtype: 'combobox',
    fieldLabel: 'Original Language',
```

```
        displayField: 'name',
        valueField: 'language_id',
        queryMode: 'local',
        store: 'staticData.Languages',
        bind : '{currentFilm.original_language_id}' //#6
    },
```

As both comboboxes represent language, their configuration is going to be exactly the same except for `fieldLabel` and `bind` (#5 and #6).

Note that we are using the same Store for both fields (#4) and we want them to have the same values, which means that if the user goes to the language GridPanel on static data and add or change a language, we want these changes to be applied to these stores at the same time, and that is why we are using the same Store as used by static data module.

Then we have four numeric fields: `rental_duration`, `rental_rate`, `length`, and `replacement_cost`:

```
    {
        xtype: 'numberfield',
        fieldLabel: 'Rental Duration',
        allowDecimals: false,
        afterLabelTextTpl: Packt.util.Util.required,
        bind : '{currentFilm.rental_duration}'
    },
    {
        xtype: 'numberfield',
        fieldLabel: 'Rental Rate',
        step: 0.1,
        afterLabelTextTpl: Packt.util.Util.required,
        bind : '{currentFilm.rental_rate}'
    },
    {
        xtype: 'numberfield',
        fieldLabel: 'Length (min)',
        allowDecimals: false,
        bind : '{currentFilm.length}'

    },
    {

        xtype: 'numberfield',
        name: 'replacement_cost',
        fieldLabel: 'Replacement Cost',
```

```
        step: 0.1,
        afterLabelTextTpl: Packt.util.Util.required,
        bind : '{currentFilm.replacement_cost}'
    },
```

One thing is very important: whenever we have numeric fields and we want to load them from a Model, we need the field from the Model to be numeric as well (`int` or `float`); otherwise, the form will not load the values properly.

Then we have the rating combobox with its `store`, as follows:

```
    {
        xtype: 'combobox',
        fieldLabel: 'Rating',
        displayField: 'text',
        valueField: 'text',
        queryMode: 'local',
        bind: {
            value: '{currentFilm.rating}', //#6
            store: '{ratings}'            //#7
        }
    },
```

We have the combobox `value` (#6) and a `store` (#7) bound to this `combobox`. We are going to create this Store in `FilmsModel`.

And at last, we have `tagfield` and `textareafield`:

```
    {
        xtype: 'tagfield',
        fieldLabel: 'Special Features',
        displayField: 'text',
        valueField: 'text',
        filterPickList: true,
        queryMode: 'local',
        publishes: 'value',
        stacked: true,
        bind: {
            value: '{specialFeatures}', //#8
            store: '{special_features}' //#9
        }
    },
    {
        xtype: 'textareafield',
        fieldLabel: 'Description',
        bind : '{currentFilm.description}'
    }
```

Tag field was introduced in Ext JS 5, and its behavior is very similar to that of a combobox that allows you to select multiple values. To set the selected values, we need to pass an array (#8). In the `Film` Model, `special_features` is a string. For this reason, we will handle these values in the ViewModel as well using a formula. We are also going to create a `store` configuration (#9) in the ViewModel to represent this static Store.

Film categories

Now that we have the film details part covered, we can handle the most complex part, which is the association with the `category` and `actor` tables. The `category` and `actor` tables have a many-to-many association with the `film` table.

As declared inside the films form, we are going to declare a new class to represent this tab:

```
Ext.define('Packt.view.film.FilmFormCategories', {
    extend: 'Ext.container.Container',

    xtype: 'film-categories-form',

    requires: [
        'Ext.view.MultiSelector'
    ],

    title: 'Film Categories',

    layout: 'fit',

    items: [{
        xtype: 'multiselector',
        title: 'Selected Categories',
        reference: 'categoriesMultiSelector',

        fieldName: 'name',

        viewConfig: {
            deferEmptyText: false,
            emptyText: 'No categories selected'
        },

        bind: '{currentFilm.categories}', //#1
```

```
        search: {
            field: 'name',
            store: {
                type: 'categories', //#2
                autoLoad: true
            }
        }
    }]
});
```

This class contains a `multiselector`, which is a new component introduced in Ext JS 5. It created a grid to render the selected values, and it is also going to display a red cross sign to remove unwanted values. We can set any selected values in its Store (#1). This component also allows you to add values using the plus sign that is configured by the `search` configuration. We also need to set a `store` (#2) to feed the options the user can select.

Film Actors

The actor relationship with the film is very similar to the relationship between `category` and `film` tables, meaning it is also a many-to-many relationship. We will handle the `actor` tables' many-to-many relationship in a way that is different from how we handled `film_categories`. As the available options for categories are limited, we could use a `multiselector` component to represent it. We do not know how many actors we can have in our database, so it is a little bit more complicated. The approach we are going to use here is to display a grid to render the selected actors and have an **Add** button so that the user can search for and add desired values.

We have declared the grid inside the `FilmWindow` class already. What is pending is the class that will display a pop up so that we can search for available Actors.

Search Actors – Live Search combobox

The idea of the Live Search combobox is to display the **Search** screen for the user and a combobox field, where the user can enter a few characters and then the system will do a live search, displaying the actors that match the search made by the user. All the actors that match the search will be displayed as items of the combobox, and the combobox will also have paging. When the user selects the actor, we will display its `last_name` and `first_name`. Along with the actor name, we will also display a list of films this actor has acted in.

Model

First, we need a Model to represent the information we want to retrieve from the
server. We will retrieve the actors information plus the film the actor already made.
So, we can create a Model extending from the `Actor` Model, and in the `SearchActor`
Model, we only need to declare the missing field:

```
Ext.define('Packt.model.film.SearchActor', {
    extend: 'Packt.model.staticData.Actor',

    fields: [
        { name: 'film_info' }
    ]
});
```

Store

Next, we need a Store to load the `SearchActor` Model collection, as follows:

```
Ext.define('Packt.store.film.SearchActors', {
    extend: 'Ext.data.Store',

    requires: [
        'Packt.model.film.SearchActor'
    ],

    alias: 'store.search-actors',

    model: 'Packt.model.film.SearchActor',

    pageSize: 2,

    proxy: {
        type: 'ajax',
        url: 'php/actor/searchActors.php',

        reader: {
            type: 'json',
            rootProperty: 'data'
        }
    }
});
```

On the server, we will use the `actor_info` view to retrieve the information. However, the combobox also passes three extra parameters: `start` and `limit` for the paging and a parameter named `query` with the text the user entered to do the live search.

Our SELECT query will be something like the following:

```
$start = $_REQUEST['start'];
$limit = $_REQUEST['limit'];
$query = $_REQUEST['query'];

//select the information
$sql = "SELECT * FROM actor_info ";
$sql .= "WHERE first_name LIKE '%" . $query . "%' OR ";
$sql .= "last_name LIKE '%" . $query . "%' ";
$sql .= "LIMIT $start,  $limit";
```

And as we are working with paging, we cannot forget to COUNT how many records we have that match the search and return the result inside the `total` attribute of the JSON:

```
$sql = "SELECT count(*) as num FROM actor_info ";
$sql .= "WHERE first_name LIKE '%" . $query . "%' OR ";
$sql .= "last_name LIKE '%" . $query . "%' ";
```

And now, we are able to retrieve the information according to the search text entered by the user.

Live Search combobox

Our next step now is to implement the view that is going to provide the tools for searching. So, we are going to create a class that extends from `Ext.window.Window`, and inside this class, we will have a combobox that will provide all the features to do the Live Search. The code is presented as follows:

```
Ext.define('Packt.view.film.FilmSearchActor', {
    extend: 'Ext.window.Window',
    xtype: 'search-actor',

    requires: [
        'Packt.store.film.SearchActors'
    ],

    width: 600,
    bodyPadding: 10,
    layout: {
```

```
            type: 'anchor'
    },
    title: 'Search and Add Actor',
    autoShow: true,
    closable: false,
    glyph: Packt.util.Glyphs.getGlyph('searchAndAdd'),
    reference: 'search-actor',

    items: [
        {
            //combobox // #1
        }, {
            xtype: 'component',
            style: 'margin-top:10px',
            html: 'Live search requires a minimum of 2
            characters.'
        }
    ]
});
```

At the bottom, there's only a comment for the user to know that they are required to enter at least two characters so that the Live Search can work, as shown in the following screenshot:

Now, let's see the code for the combobox that goes where #1 is in the previous code:

```
xtype: 'combo',
reference: 'comboActors',      //#2
displayField: 'first_name',   //#3
valueField: 'actor_id',       //#4
typeAhead: false,
hideLabel: true,
hideTrigger:true,             //#5
anchor: '100%',
minChars: 2,                  //#6
pageSize: 2,                  //#7
```

```
store: {
    type: 'search-actors'    //#8
},

displayTpl: new Ext.XTemplate( //#9
        '<tpl for=".">' +
        '{[typeof values === "string" ? values :
        values["last_name"]]}, ' +
        '{[typeof values === "string" ? values :
        values["first_name"]]}' +
        '</tpl>'
),

listConfig: {                    //#10
    loadingText: 'Searching...',
    emptyText: 'No matching posts found.',

    // Custom rendering template for each item
    getInnerTpl: function() {
        return '<h3><span>{last_name},
        {first_name}</span></h3></br>' +
            '{film_info}';
    }
}
}
```

To get started, we are going to declare `reference` so that we can easily retrieve this component in the ViewController later (#2). As always, we need a `store` declaration (#8) to populate the combobox. In this example, we are instantiating the Store by its type. For this reason, we need to declare the full name of the Store in the `requires` of this class.

Then we need `displayField` (#3). The `displayField` will only show the `first_name` of the actor when an actor is selected from the Live Search. However, we want to display `last_name` and `first_name`. So to be able to do it, we need to overwrite the `displayTpl` template (#9). This is the result we will get:

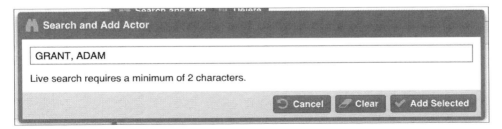

Next, we have `valueField` (#4), which is the ID of the selected actor; we are going to hide the down arrow (called `trigger` — #5) to make the Live Search work. The user needs to enter at least two characters (#6), and the combobox will display only two actors per page (#7).

Then, we have `listConfig` (#10), where we can configure the loading text and the empty text, and also the template to display the actor's information. Basically, we are displaying `last_name`, `first_name` at the top and in bold, and on the next line, we are displaying all the films already made by this actor.

Complementing the ViewModel

There are two pending things we need to do in the ViewModel: add the `ratings` and `special_features` stores and also implement the `specialFeatures` formula that we used to `bind` in the film details form.

So let's begin declaring the stores to our ViewModel, as follows:

```
ratings: {
    model: 'Packt.model.TextCombo',
    data : [ // ENUM('G','PG','PG-13','R','NC-17')
        ['G'],
        ['PG'],
        ['PG-13'],
        ['R'],
        ['NC-17']
    ],
    session: true
},
special_features: {
    model: 'Packt.model.TextCombo',
    data : [
        ['Trailers'],
        ['Commentaries'],
        ['Deleted Scenes'],
        ['Behind the Scenes']
    ],
    session: true
}
```

Both stores have predefined `data`, meaning they are an instance of the ArrayStore. This kind of Store is very useful in situations like this. The Model both stores are using is listed as follows:

```
Ext.define('Packt.model.TextCombo', {
    extend: 'Ext.data.Model',

    idProperty: 'text',

    fields: [
        { name: 'text' }
    ]
});
```

The Model is very simple, with a single field. We can reuse this Model for any Store we create to be used in comboboxes.

Working with formulas and two-way data binding

We created a tag field to declare the special features of a film. This field requires an array of values to be set and also an array of values to be returned as field values. The out field `special_features` in the Model is a string, which clearly is not an array! Until Ext JS 4, we had to encode and decode the values manually in a Controller (or somewhere else in the code, but preferably in a Controller). With Ext JS 5 and the introduction of the ViewModel we can use a capability called formulas.

It is possible to create simple formulas similar to the extra `fields` we can declare in a Model (we declare `groupName` in the `User` Model), and it is also possible to declare more complex `formulas`. In the Ext JS examples, we can find some examples of how to use simple `formulas`.

Let's take a look at the formula named `specialFeatures` that we bound to `tagfield` in the `FilmFormContainer` class:

```
formulas: {
    specialFeatures : { //#1

        bind: {
            bindTo: '{currentFilm.special_features}', //#2
            deep: true                                //#3
        },

        get: function(value){ //#4
            var values = value ? value.split(',') : [],
                texts = [];
```

```
            values.forEach(function(item){
                texts.push(Ext.create('Packt.model.TextCombo',{
                    text: item
                }));
            });
            return texts;
        },

        set: function(value){ //#5
            if (value){
                this.get('currentFilm').set('special_features',
                value.join());
            }
        }
    }
}
```

The first thing we need to do is give a name to our `formulas` declaration (#1). We can `bind` our formula to an existing value (such as selection). In our case, we are binding to the `special_features` attribute of `currentFilm` ((#2) — which we will pass to the **Edit** window later in the ViewController). We are also specifying that this is a `deep` data binding (#3), which means any change that happens in `currentFilm.special_features` will update the formula, or any update that happens in the formula through its methods will update `currentFilm.special_features` as well.

We can also define a getter and a setter method to a formula. First, we are defining a `get` method (#4). This method receives the `value` from `currentFilm.special_features`, splits the string, and transforms it into an array, and will be used by the tag field. Likewise, we have a `set` method (#5), which will receive the `value` set in the tag field, transform it into a string, and update `currentFilm.special_features`. Just keep in mind that `currentFilm` is an instance of the `Film` Model.

The Films ViewController

In past chapters, we have already covered some examples of how to save data. We used the form `submit`, an Ajax `request`, and also the writing resource from the Store. In this chapter, let's focus on functionalities we have not implemented yet. Do not worry. The complete implementation is available within the source code distributed with this book.

The createDialog method

We created all the views for our application. In the base **ViewController**, we created the handlers for the Add and Edit buttons, and both call the `createDialog` method, which we are going to develop now.

The idea is to display a blank **Edit** window in case the user clicks on the **Add** button, and to display the selected film in case the user clicks on the **Edit** button. The source code for this method is as follows:

```
createDialog: function(record){

    var me = this,
        view = me.getView(),          //#1
        glyphs = Packt.util.Glyphs;

    me.isEdit = !!record;             //#2
    me.dialog = view.add({            //#3
        xtype: 'film-window',
        viewModel: {                  //#4
            data: {                   //#5
                title: record ? 'Edit: ' + record.get('title') :
                'Add Film',
                glyph: record ? glyphs.getGlyph('edit') :
                glyphs.getGlyph('add')
            },
            links: {                          //#6
                currentFilm: record || { //#7
                    type: 'Film',
                    create: true
                }
            }
        },
        session: true //#8
    });

    me.dialog.show(); //#9
}
```

The first thing we are going to do is get the reference of the View, which is the `Films` class (#1). Next, we are also going to create an `isEdit` flag (#2) and assign it to the ViewController so that we can access other methods later (such as the `save` method).

Then, we are going to instantiate the **Edit** window, adding it to the View (#3). When we add a child to the main View, it inherits the ViewModel and the ViewController as well. However, in this case, we are setting specific configurations to the **Edit** window ViewModel as well (#4), meaning it will have access to whatever configuration is already there plus the ones we are setting, such as `title` and `glyph`, which is predefined `data` (#5) to this ViewModel.

Next, we will create a link (#6) to a record called `currentFilm` ((#7), which we used in the bind configurations in the **Edit** window). If it is an `edit`, it will link to the selected row in the grid; otherwise, we create a new `Film` Model instance.

We are also going to create a child `session` (#8) for this View. We are going to discuss `session` when we discuss the `save` method.

Finally, we display the **Edit** window pop up (#9).

Getting the selected actor from Live Search

When a user searches for an actor and clicks on `Add Selected`, we will have to handle the event in the ViewController in the `onSaveActors` methods. The logic for this method is that we need to get the actor ID selected in the combobox and search for its value in the `actors` Store. Once we have the `Actor` Model instance, we can add it to the `actorsGrid` store. The code is as follows:

```
onSaveActors: function(button, e, options){
    var me = this,
        value = me.lookupReference('comboActors').getValue(),  //#1
        store = me.getStore('actors'),                          //#2
        model = store.findRecord('actor_id', value),            //#3
        actorsGrid = me.lookupReference('actorsGrid'),          //#4
        actorsStore = actorsGrid.getStore();                    //#5

    if (model){
        actorsStore.add(model); //#6
    }

    me.onCancelActors(); //#7
}
```

First, we get the reference of the combobox (#1) and get its `value`, which will return the ID of the selected actor. Next, we will get the reference of the `actors` Store declared in the `FilmsModel` (#2). We will search for the actor selected in the Store (#3); it will return the `Actor` Model reference or null if the actor does not exist. Then we get the `actorsGrid` reference ((#4)—the one inside the films form), and we also get its Store (#5).

If an actor is found, we add to the `actorsGrid` Store (#6). This grid is bound to the selected film actors association, so if an actor is added or deleted from the grid Store, it is also added or deleted from the association. This is another example of two-way data binding in Ext JS 5.

And at last, we close the Live Search pop up (#7) with the following method:

```
onCancelActors: function(button, e, options){
    var me = this;
    me.searchActors = Ext.destroy(me.searchActors);
}
```

Saving the form and working with sessions

Now it is time to save any data updated, deleted, or created. Any changes we make in the form will be saved to the session (`Ext.data.Session`). Sessions were introduced in Ext JS 5 and are great for when we are working with associations. We added a session to our films View by adding the configuration `session: true` in it. Then, all the stores from the ViewModel are also bound to the session, meaning any change made in the stores or in the session will be synchronized.

Let's take a look at the `onSave` method:

```
onSave: function(button, e, options){
    var me = this,
        dialog = me.dialog,
        form = me.lookupReference('filmForm'),
        isEdit = me.isEdit,
        session = me.getSession(), //#1
        id;

    if (form.isValid()) {
        if (!isEdit) {
            id = dialog.getViewModel().get('currentFilm').id; //#2
        }
        dialog.getSession().save(); //#3
        if (!isEdit) {
            me.getStore('films').add(session.getRecord('Film',
                id)); //#4
        }
        me.onCancel();
    }
}
```

```
        var batch = session.getSaveBatch(); //#5
        if (batch){
            batch.start();                    //#6
        }
    }
```

We are going to get the pending information to be saved from the session and save it in the server. First, we need to get the `session` (#1). Then, we are going to get the film's `id` if it is a new film ((#2)—a random temporary ID is created for every Model in Ext JS, usually with the name of the entity and a sequential number). This `id` will be overwritten after we save it in the database and use the database table sequential ID.

Remember that when we created the dialog, we assigned a child session to the **Edit** window? This allows us to work with the data without committing to it, meaning we can roll back the changes easily by destroying the **Edit** window. When we want to save the data from the child session into the `Films` session officially, we can call the `getSession` method from the **Edit** window and save it (#3). This will save the child session data in the `Film` session.

Next, if it is a new film, we also want to add the record to the `films` Store (so it can be displayed in the `FilmsGrid` as well—(#4)).

There are two different ways to save information from a session. The first way is using `batch` (`Ext.data.Batch`) that can be retrieved from the session (#5), and the second way is executing its method `start` (#6). This will trigger the CRUD operations and will use the `proxy` details to connect to the server of the pending models of the session to be saved.

Custom Writer – saving associated data

However, the session does not save associated data. If we create a Film, Category, and Actor, the create operation from each respective Model will be triggered, but the data to be saved in the many-to-many matrix tables will not be sent to the server.

We can create a custom `writer` class that will send any associated data to the server as well in a single batch. Then, we need to handle the proper CRUD operations of the associated data on the server as well. The code is as follows:

```
Ext.define('Packt.ux.data.writer.AssociatedWriter', {
    extend: 'Ext.data.writer.Json',
    alias: 'writer.associatedjson',

    constructor: function(config) {
        this.callParent(arguments);
    },
```

```
getRecordData: function (record, operation) {
    record.data = this.callParent(arguments);
    Ext.apply(record.data, record.getAssociatedData());
    return record.data;
}
});
```

Then, we need to go back to the `Packt.model.Base` class, add this `writer` class to the `requires` declaration, and change the writer type as follows:

```
writer: {
    type: 'associatedjson',
    //...
},
```

All associated data will be sent to the server; in the same way, we are receiving a nested JSON from the server when we read information from it.

Saving session data manually

A second option to save the session data to the server is doing it manually. If we use the `getChanges` method of the session, it will return an object with all the pending information to be saved in the server, including associated data.

For example, if we try to edit a Film, add some Actor information and Category information, and call `JSON.stringify(session. getChanges(), null, 4)`, we will have an output similar to the following:

```
{
    "Film": {
        "U": [
            {
                "title": "ACADEMY DINOSAUR - edit",
                "language_id": "2",
                "original_language_id": "3",
                "film_id": "1",
                "id": null
            }
        ],
        "categories": {
            "D": {
                "1": [
                    "6"
                ]
            },
```

```
        "C": {
            "1": [
                "7",
                "8",
                "9"
            ]
        }
    },
    "actors": {
        "D": {
            "1": [
                "1"
            ]
        },
        "C": {
            "1": [
                "71"
            ]
        }
    }
}
}
```

This means we are updating (U) some fields of the Film with ID of 1, deleting (D) the category with ID of 6 from the Film 1 and adding (C) the categories 7, 8, and 9 to the Film 1 as well. We are also deleting (D) the Actor 1 from Film 1 and adding (C) the Actor 71 to the Film 1 as well. Note that the categories and actors are the names of the many-to-many associations we created for Film Model.

We can also use this object to save the data manually in the server.

Summary

In this chapter, you learned how to implement a more complex screen to manage the inventory information from the database. You learned to handle a many-to-many association as well. You learned how to use some different form fields and how to do a Live Search. You also learned how to save data from a session.

In the next chapter, we will learn how to add some extra capabilities that are not native to the Ext JS API to the screens we have already developed so far, such as print, export to Excel, and export to PDF, the contents of a GridPanel. Also, we will learn how to implement charts and export them to images and PDFs.

Adding Extra Capabilities

We are almost on the final stage of our application. Ext JS provides great capabilities, but there are some capabilities that we need to code by ourselves with the help of other technologies. Despite possessing a GridPanel with paging, sorting, and filter capabilities, sometimes the user is going to expect more from the application. Adding features such as printing, the ability to export to Excel and PDF, and the ability to export charts to images and PDF can add great value to the application and please the final user.

So, in this chapter, we will cover:

- Printing records of a GridPanel
- Exporting GridPanel information to PDF and Excel
- Creating charts
- Exporting charts to PDF and images
- Using third-party plugins

Exporting a GridPanel to PDF and Excel

The first capability we are going to implement is exporting the contents of a GridPanel to PDF and Excel. We will implement these features for the Films GridPanel we implemented in the preceding chapter. However, the logic is the same for any GridPanel you might have in an Ext JS application.

The first thing we are going to do is add the export buttons to the GridPanel toolbar. We will add three buttons: one to **Print** the contents of the GridPanel (we will develop this feature later, but let's add this button right now), one button for **Export to PDF**, and one button for **Export to Excel**:

Remember that in the preceding chapter, we created a toolbar, Packt.view.base. TopToolBar. We are going to add these three buttons on this toolbar:

```
items: [
    //Add Button
    {
        xtype: 'tbseparator'
    },
    {
        xtype: 'button',
        text: 'Print',
        glyph: Packt.util.Glyphs.getGlyph('print'),
        listeners: {
            click: 'onPrint'
        }
    },
    {
        xtype: 'button',
        text: 'Export to PDF',
        glyph: Packt.util.Glyphs.getGlyph('pdf'),
        listeners: {
            click: 'onExportPDF'
        }
    },
    {
        xtype: 'button',
        text: 'Export to Excel',
        glyph: Packt.util.Glyphs.getGlyph('excel'),
        listeners: {
            click: 'onExportExcel'
        }
    }
]
```

All buttons have `listeners` that we will handle in the ViewController. In this case, buttons will be in the `FilmsController` class.

Inside the `Glyphs` class, we are also going to add the following attributes to represent the icons:

```
print: 'xf02f',
pdf: 'xf1c1',
excel: 'xf1c3'
```

Exporting to PDF

Now that the buttons are being displayed on the `Films` GridPanel, it is time to go back to `FilmsController` and add these capabilities.

The first button we are going to listen to is the **Export to PDF** `click` event. When the user clicks on this button, we will execute the following method:

```
onExportPDF: function(button, e, options) {
    var mainPanel = Ext.ComponentQuery.query('mainpanel')[0]; //#1

    var newTab = mainPanel.add({
        xtype: 'panel',
        closable: true,
        glyph: Packt.util.Glyphs.getGlyph('pdf'),
        title: 'Films PDF',
        layout: 'fit',
        html: 'loading PDF...',
        items: [{
            xtype: 'uxiframe',                    //#2
            src: 'php/pdf/exportFilmsPdf.php' //#3
        }]
    });

    mainPanel.setActiveTab(newTab); //#4
}
```

What we want to implement is that when the user clicks on the **Export to PDF** button, a new tab (#4) will be opened with the PDF file in it. This means we need to get that **Main Panel** class (xtype `mainpanel`) we declared as the center item of the Viewport of the application (#1), add a new tab to it, and as the PDF file will be inside it, we can implement it as **iFrame**. To implement iFrame in Ext JS, we can use the iFrame plugin (#2) that is distributed within the SDK.

Inside the ViewController, we have access to the `Films` View, but we need to access `mainpanel`. We can get the `Films` View using the `getView` method and then use the `up` method to get `mainpanel`, or we can use `Ext.ComponentQuery` to query `mainpanel`. Remember that `Ext.ComponentQuery` returns an array of all matching results, but as we know, there is only one `mainPanel` in the application, so we can retrieve the first position.

Now comes the most important part: Ext JS does not provide the **Export to PDF** capability natively. If we want the application to have it, we need to implement it using a different technology. In this case, the PDF will be generated on the server side (#3), and we will only display its output inside the iFrame.

When we execute the code, we will get the following output:

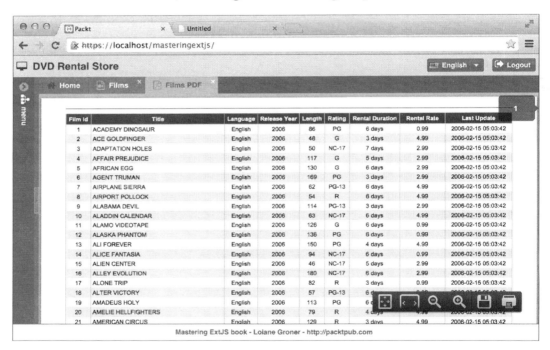

Generating the PDF file on the server – PHP

As we need to generate the file on the server side, we can use any framework or library that is available for the language we are using on the server. We can use *TCPDF* (`http://www.tcpdf.org/`). There are other libraries as well, and you can use the one you are most familiar with.

If you are using Java, you can use *iText* (`http://itextpdf.com/`), and if you are using .NET, you can use *excellibrary* (`https://code.google.com/p/excellibrary/`).

Generating and viewing the PDF file with JavaScript – HTML5

Thanks to HTML5, it is also possible to generate a PDF file using the HTML5 API. There are a few solutions that we can use to generate the file without using any server-side code and only using JavaScript. One of them is using jsPDF (`https://github.com/MrRio/jsPDF`).

By default, the browser is going to use whatever PDF viewer software the user has installed on the computer to view the PDF file. It is also possible to use a PDF viewer developed with JavaScript called `pdf.js`. This solution is implemented and maintained by Mozilla (`https://github.com/mozilla/pdf.js/`). There is also an Ext JS plugin developed on `pdf.js` (`https://market.sencha.com/extensions/pdf-panel-without-plugin-needed`).

Exporting to Excel

To export the GridPanel to Excel, we will also use a server-side technology to help us.

On the Ext JS side, the only thing we need to do is to call the URL that will generate the Excel file as follows:

```
onExportExcel: function(button, e, options) {
    window.open('php/pdf/exportFilmsExcel.php');
}
```

On the server side, we will use the *PHPExcel* (`http://phpexcel.codeplex.com/`) library to help us generate the Excel file.

 If you are using Java, you can use the Apache POI library (`http://poi.apache.org/`), and if you are using .NET, you can use *excellibrary* (`https://code.google.com/p/excellibrary/`).

If you want to export the GridPanel of any other content from an Ext JS component to Excel, PDF, .txt, or a Word document, you can use the same approach.

 There is also an Ext JS plugin that exports a grid to an Excel file: `http://goo.gl/E7jif4`.

Printing GridPanel content with the GridPrinter plugin

The next functionality we will implement is printing the contents of the GridPanel. When the user clicks on the **Print** button, the application will open a new browser window and display the contents of the grid in this new window.

To do this, we will use a plugin named `Ext.ux.grid.Printer`, which receives the GridPanel reference to be printed, gets the information that is on the Store, generates HTML from this content, and displays the information in a new window.

 The GridPrinter plugin is a third-party plugin available at `https://github.com/loiane/extjs4-ux-gridprinter`. This plugin will only print the information that is available on the GridPanel Store, meaning if you are using the PagingToolbar, the plugin will only generate the HTML of the current page. The plugin also supports the RowExpander plugin. Please feel free to contribute to this plugin (or any other Ext JS plugin), and this way, we can help in growing the Ext JS community! It works with Ext JS 4 and 5.

To install the plugin, we are going to get the contents of the ux folder and place it inside the `app/ux` folder. As Ext JS also ships some plugins within the native SDK with the namespace `Ext.ux`, we are going to rename the plugin from `Ext.ux.grid.Printer` to `Packt.ux.grid.Printer` to avoid conflict (you can search for the occurrences inside the `Printer.js` file and replace it). This way, the plugin will be part of the application. The following screenshot demonstrates how the project structure will look after installing the plugin:

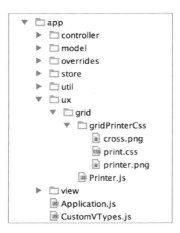

After installing the plugin, we simply need to add it to the `requires` declaration of
`FilmsController`:

```
requires: [
    // other requires here
    Packt.ux.grid.Printer'
]
```

When the user clicks on the **Print** button, the controller will execute the
following method:

```
onPrint: function(button, e, options) {
    var printer = Packt.ux.grid.Printer;
    printer.printAutomatically = false;
    printer.print(this.lookupReference('filmsGrid'));
},
```

The `printAutomatically` property means you want the print window to be displayed
automatically. If set to `false`, the plugin will display the print window, and then, if the
user wants to print it, they need to go to the browser's menu and select **Print** (*Ctrl + P*).

To make the plugin work, we need to pass the GridPanel reference to the `print`
method. In this case, we can get the `Films` GridPanel reference.

When we execute the code, we will get the following output:

Creating a Sales by Film Category chart

Ext JS provides a great set of visual charts we can implement, and users love things like this. For this reason, we will implement a chart using three different series (pie, column, and bar) where the user can see the **Sales by Film Category**.

The following is a screenshot of the final result we will have at the end of this topic. As we can see in the following screenshot, we have the chart. Above it, we have a toolbar with two buttons: **Change Chart Type**, where the user will be able to change the chart series from **Pie** to **Column** or **Bar**, and the **Download Chart** button, where the user will be able to download the chart in the following formats: **Download as Image** or **Download as PDF**. Here's the screenshot we are discussing:

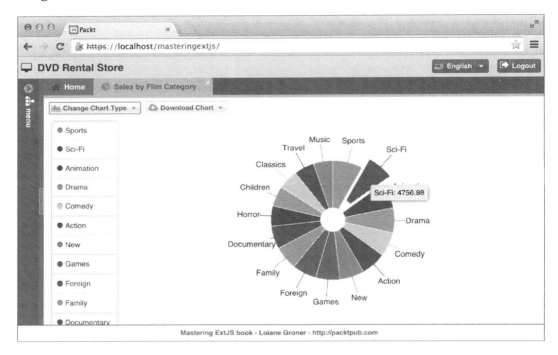

Ext JS 5 charts and terminology

Before we start coding, let's understand a little bit about how Ext JS charts work. Ext JS 4 introduced great charting capabilities by leveraging the HTML5 canvas and SVG features. However, in Ext JS 5, the charts introduced in Ext JS 4 became deprecated. Ext JS 5 introduces a new Sencha Charts package that comes from Sencha Touch, with built-in support for touch, which means we can use touch gestures to interact with the charts.

You might ask, but why am I interested in touch support in the charts? There are many companies that want to use the same application in tablets without developing a new application with the same capabilities for touch devices. Ext JS 5 offers this capability. We will discuss more about touch support later.

Sencha Charts supports three types of charts:

- **Cartesian chart**: This represents a chart that uses cartesian coordinates. A cartesian chart has two directions, the x direction and y direction. The series and axes are coordinated along these directions. By default, the x direction is horizontal and the y direction is vertical (the directions can be flipped as well).

- **Polar chart**: This represents a chart that uses polar coordinates. A polar chart has two axes: an angular axis (which is a circle) and a radial axis (a straight line from the center to the edge of the circle). The angular axis is usually a category axis while the radial axis is typically numerical.

- **Space Filling chart**: This creates a chart that fills the entire area of the chart, for example, a gauge or a treemap chart.

A chart consists of a **Legend**, **Axis**, **Series**, **Interaction**, and **Theme** and can load data from a Store as displayed in the following image:

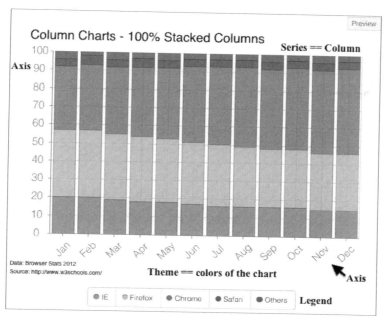

The **Series** contains the logic about how the data will be rendered in the chart. The series can be **Pie**, **Line**, **Bar**, **Column**, and so on.

The **Axis** is responsible for rendering the chart axis based on the type of data. There are three types of axes: `numeric`, `category`, and `time`. The `numeric` type is used to render numeric values, `category` is used to render data that is a finite set (for example, the names of the months of the year), and `time` is used to render data that represents time.

The **Legend** is responsible for displaying the legend box of the chart.

Sencha Charts also supports interactions. The available interactions are presented as follows:

- **Crosshair**: This allows the user to get precise values for a specific point on the chart. The values are obtained by single-touch dragging on the chart.

- **CrossZoom**: This allows the user to zoom in on a selected area of the chart.

- **Item Highlight**: This allows the user to highlight series items in the chart.

- **Item Info**: This allows displaying detailed information about a series data point in a popup panel.

- **Pan/Zoom**: This allows the user to navigate the data for one or more chart axes by panning or zooming.

- **Rotate**: This allows the user to rotate a polar chart about its central point. There is also a special rotate interaction for 3D pie charts.

 More information about charts can be obtained by diving into the *Charts Kitchen Sink* example (`http://dev.sencha.com/ext/5.1.0/examples/kitchensink/?charts=true`) and also into the `charts` package (`http://docs.sencha.com/extjs/5.0/5.0.0-apidocs/#!/api/Ext.chart.AbstractChart`) in the documentation.

Adding Sencha Charts to the project

A very important detail: Sencha Charts is available for use in Ext JS 5 applications via a package, meaning the source code of the charts is not available automatically to an application like the grids, forms, and other components. Packages in Sencha applications have a similar concept as gems in Ruby or JARs in Java.

To add Sencha Charts to our project, we need to open the `app.json` file located in the root folder of the application. Around line 34, we should find the `requires` declaration. We need to add `sencha-charts` to `requires`. It is going to look like the following:

```
"requires": [
    "sencha-charts"
],
```

After this change, if we start using charts in the project, our code should work.

 We cannot forget to have `sencha app watch` executed in a terminal application as well.

Also, here's the last update we are going to do in the `menu` table to be able to see the report option in the application menu:

```
UPDATE `sakila`.`menu` SET `className`='salesfilmcategory' WHERE `id`='13';
```

Creating the Store inside the ViewModel

Let's go back to our code and start implementing some charts. The Store is going to provide the charts with the data. No matter whether we want to create a pie chart or column chart or bar chart, we need a Store to provide the information we want to display.

As we are going to create charts, we need to create a Store that is going to hold the collection of data especially for the chart, which means it is not going to be used anywhere else in the application. For this reason, we can create it directly inside the ViewModel. So we are going to create a new package named `reports` inside the `app/view` folder, where we are going to place the files from this topic. We are going to start creating the ViewModel this time, as follows:

```
Ext.define('Packt.view.reports.SalesFilmCategoryModel', {
    extend: 'Ext.app.ViewModel',

    alias: 'viewmodel.sales-film-category',

    stores: {
        salesFilmCategory: {
            fields: [                      // #1
                {name: 'category'},
                {name: 'total_sales'}
            ],
```

```
            autoLoad: true,
            proxy: {                        // #2
                type: 'ajax',
                url: 'php/reports/salesFilmCategory.php',
                reader: {
                    type: 'json',
                    rootProperty: 'data'
                }
            }
        }
    }
}
});
```

For this Store, we will not declare a Model; we are going to declare its `fields` (#1) directly on it. As this Store is going to be used exclusively by the chart, there is no need to create a specific Model for it, as we do not intend to reuse it later.

We are also going to declare `proxy` (#2) with the `ajax`, `url`, and `reader` details on it. Most of the models we created in the previous chapters were part of a `schema` that contained a `proxy`. This time, we do not have this information available, so we need to declare it.

On the server side, we can query the data that will feed the chart from the `sales_by_ film_category` view from the Sakila database as follows:

```
SELECT * FROM sales_by_film_category
```

Pie chart

Now that we are able to retrieve the information we need from the server, let's work on the implementation of the chart. First, we will develop the pie chart, as follows:

```
Ext.define('Packt.view.reports.SalesFilmCategoryPie', {
    extend: 'Ext.chart.PolarChart',      //#1
    alias: 'widget.salesfilmcategorypie',

    legend: {
        docked: 'left'    //#2
    },
    interactions: ['rotate', 'itemhighlight'], //#3

    bind: '{salesFilmCategory}', //#4
    insetPadding: 40,
    innerPadding: 20,
    series: {
```

```
        type: 'pie',          //#5
        highlight: true,
        donut: 20,            //#6
        distortion: 0.6,
        style: {              //#7
            strokeStyle: 'white',
            opacity: 0.90
        },
        label: {
            field: 'category',    //#8
            display: 'rotate'
        },
        tooltip: {                //#9
            trackMouse: true,
            renderer: function(storeItem, item) {
                this.setHtml(storeItem.get('category') + ': '
                    + storeItem.get('total_sales'));
            }
        },
        xField: 'total_sales'  //#10
    }
});
```

Let's go through the most important parts of the preceding code; first, we need to extend the `PolarChart` class (#1) because we want to implement a chart with a pie series (#5).

Next, we are going to add `legend` to this chart, and we are going to dock it on the `left` (#2). We are also going to add some interactions to this chart (#3). The user is going to be able to rotate and highlight the slices of `pie`. We are going to bind the Store (#4) we declared in the ViewModel as well.

Next, there is the `series` configuration that defines what `type` of chart we are implementing (#5), which is the `pie` chart in this case. The `pie` chart needs a field that is going to be used to do the sum and then calculate the fraction of each piece. We only have two fields, and `total_sales` (#10) is the numeric one, so we will use this field. The `donut` configuration (#6) sets the radius of the donut. This chart is actually a donut chart (because of the hole in the middle of the pie).

We can also style our chart (#7). The style in this example will add some white lines separating each slice of the chart.

Inside each slice, we also want to display its film category so that we can easily identify it. We can do this by adding the `label` configuration (#8) to `series`.

On the `tooltip` configuration, we can define whether we want to display a quick tip or not (#9). In this case, we want Ext JS to track the movements of the mouse, and if the user does a mouseover over any item of the chart, Ext JS will display a tip with the name of `category` and the `total_sales` number.

 It is also possible to define `theme` in the chart. We can do so by adding the configuration `theme` in this class. The possible values we can set are: `'green'`, `'sky'`, `'red'`, `'purple'`, `'blue'`, `'yellow'` — `'category1'` to `'category6'` — and the mentioned theme names with the `'-gradients'` suffix (`'green-gradients'` and so on).

3D column chart

As we can change the chart `type`, we will also implement a column chart that looks like the following screenshot:

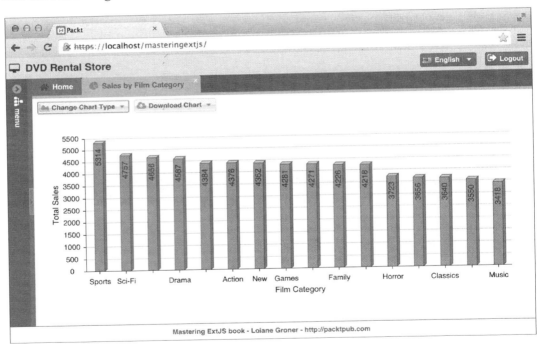

So let's get our hands on the code, which is as follows:

```
Ext.define('Packt.view.reports.SalesFilmCategoryColumn', {
    extend: 'Ext.chart.CartesianChart',   //#1
    alias: 'widget.salesfilmcategorycol',

    bind: '{salesFilmCategory}', //#2

    insetPadding: {
        top: 40,
        bottom: 40,
        left: 20,
        right: 40
    },
    interactions: 'itemhighlight', //#3

    //axes
    //series
});
```

The column chart extends from the CartesianChart class (#1) because we want to display a chart with *x* and *y* axes. We will also use the same Store we used in the pie chart (#2), and the user will also be able to highlight (#3) the columns in this chart.

Let's take a look at the axes declaration in the following code:

```
axes: [{
    type: 'numeric',    //#4
    position: 'left',
    fields: ['total_sales'],
    label: {
        renderer: Ext.util.Format.numberRenderer('0,0')
    },
    titleMargin: 20,
    title: {
        text: 'Total Sales',
        fontSize: 14
    },
    grid: true,
    minimum: 0
}, {
    type: 'category', //#5
    position: 'bottom',
    fields: ['category'],
```

```
        titleMargin: 20,
        title: {
            text: 'Film Category',
            fontSize: 14
        }
    }],
```

We have two `axes` in a column chart. The *x* axis is going to display `category` (#5), which is going to be placed at the `bottom`, and the *y* axis is going to display the `numeric` (#4) data that is going to be displayed in the `right` or `left` (in this example, we chose `left`). In the case of a bar chart, all we have to do is swap the axes. The `category` value becomes the *y* axis and the `numeric` values become the *x* axis.

Let's take a look at the `series` configuration to finish configuring our chart:

```
series: [{
    type: 'bar3d', //#6
    highlight: true,
    style: {
        minGapWidth: 20
    },
    label: {
        display: 'insideEnd',
        'text-anchor': 'middle',
        field: 'total_sales',        //#7
        renderer: Ext.util.Format.numberRenderer('0'),
        orientation: 'vertical',
        color: '#333'
    },
    xField: 'category',    //#8
    yField: 'total_sales' //#9
}]
```

In this example, we are implementing a 3D column chart (#6) that can also be used as a 3D bar chart. If we want to implement the normal chart, the series type would be `'bar'`. As mentioned before, column and bar charts are very similar; only the configuration of the *x* and *y* axes are swapped. If we want to display a `label` (#7), we can also configure one.

It is important to note that `xField` (#8) matches the `Category` axis (#5), and `yField` (#9) matches the `Numeric` axis (vertical/`left` position−(#4)).

The bar chart code is exactly the same as the column chart code with a small change. We need to invert `Axis` (Category will be `left` and Numeric will be `bottom`), `xField` (which will be `total_sales` instead of `category`), and `yField` (which will be `category` instead of `total_sales`).

The bar chart is going to look as follows:

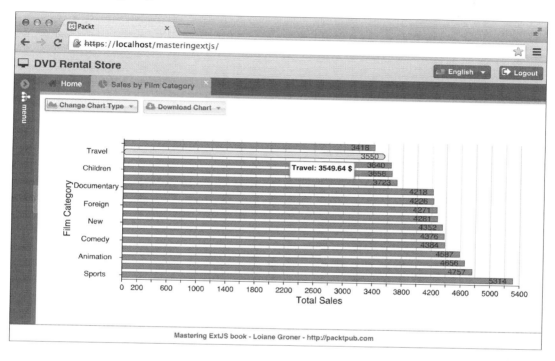

The Chart panel

As we want to display a panel and offer the user the possibility to change the chart type, we will create a panel and use the Card layout. To refresh our memory, the Card layout is mostly used for wizards and also when we have several items but want to display only one at a time. And the item that is currently being displayed uses the FitLayout.

So let's create a Chart panel, as follows:

```
Ext.define('Packt.view.reports.SalesFilmCategory', {
    extend: 'Ext.panel.Panel',
    alias: 'widget.salesfilmcategory',
```

```
    requires: [
        'Packt.view.reports.SalesFilmCategoryModel',
        'Packt.view.reports.SalesFilmCategoryController',
        'Packt.view.reports.SalesFilmCategoryPie',
        'Packt.view.reports.SalesFilmCategoryColumn',
        'Packt.view.reports.SalesFilmCategoryBar',
        'Packt.util.Glyphs'
    ],

    controller: 'sales-film-category', //#1
    viewModel: {
        type: 'sales-film-category'    //#2
    },

    layout: 'card',
    activeItem: 0,

    items: [{
        xtype: 'salesfilmcategorypie' //#3
    },{
        xtype: 'salesfilmcategorycol' //#4
    },{
        xtype: 'salesfilmcategorybar' //#5
    }],

    dockedItems: [{
        xtype: 'toolbar',
        flex: 1,
        dock: 'top',
        items: [
            //items of toolbar here #6
        ]
    }]
});
```

So we need to declare `panel` and declare each chart we created as an item. So we can declare the pie chart (#3), the column chart (#4), and the bar chart (#5) as items of a **Sales by Film Category** panel. By default, the item 0 (which is the first item — pie chart) is going to be the default item to be displayed when the Chart panel is rendered.

We also cannot forget to declare the ViewModel (#2) and the ViewController (#1), which we are going to create next.

All the classes we mention are `xtype` of which(#1 to #5) are inside `requires` declaration.

Next, we can declare the toolbar that will contain the button with the menu so that the user can choose `Chart Type` and `Download Type`. We will add the following code in the place where we have the comment in the preceding code (#6):

```
{
    text: 'Change Chart Type',
    glyph: Packt.util.Glyphs.getGlyph('menuReports'),
    menu: {
        xtype: 'menu',
        defaults: {
            listeners: {
                click: 'onChangeChart' //#7
            }
        },
        items: [
            {
                xtype: 'menuitem',
                text: 'Pie',
                itemId: 'pie',   //#8
                glyph: Packt.util.Glyphs.getGlyph('chartPie')
            },
            {
                xtype: 'menuitem',
                text: 'Column',
                itemId: 'column',   //#9
                glyph: Packt.util.Glyphs.getGlyph('chartBar')
            },
            {
                xtype: 'menuitem',
                text: 'Bar',
                itemId: 'bar',   //#10
                glyph: Packt.util.Glyphs.getGlyph('chartColumn')
            }
        ]
    }
},
```

For the preceding menu, all menu items have the same `listener` declaration (#7). Instead of having the same code declare three times, we will have it declare only once in the ViewController. To help us identify which menu item fired the event, we are also going to declare `itemId` for each menu item on lines #8, #9, and #10. The output of the preceding code is displayed in the following screenshot:

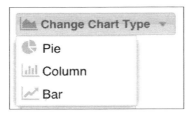

As the second `item` of the toolbar, we have the **Download Chart** button. Following the same behavior as the **Change Chart Type** button, the **Download Chart** button also has a menu with two menu items in it, one for each download type, as follows:

```
{
    text: 'Download Chart',
    glyph: Packt.util.Glyphs.getGlyph('download'),
    menu: {
        xtype: 'menu',
        defaults: {
            listeners: {
                click: 'onChartDownload' //#11
            }
        },
        items: [
            {
                xtype: 'menuitem',
                text: 'Download as Image',
                itemId: 'png',
                glyph: Packt.util.Glyphs.getGlyph('image')
            },
            {
                xtype: 'menuitem',
                text: 'Download as PDF',
                itemId: 'pdf',
                glyph: Packt.util.Glyphs.getGlyph('pdf')
            }
        ]
    }
}
```

We will have `listener` (#11) for this menu in the ViewController. The output for the preceding code will be the following:

The ViewController

Before we develop the two methods we need to implement to close this chapter, let's declare the structure of the `ViewController` for the `reports` module:

```
Ext.define('Packt.view.reports.SalesFilmCategoryController', {
    extend: 'Ext.app.ViewController',

    alias: 'controller.sales-film-category',

    //methods here
});
```

Next, we will see how to develop the `onChangeChart` and `onChartDownload` methods.

Changing the chart type

As the user has the capability to change the chart type by choosing an option from the menu, we will develop the following method:

```
onChangeChart: function(item, e, options) {
    var panel = this.getView(); // #1

    if (item.itemId == 'pie'){
        panel.getLayout().setActiveItem(0); // #2
    } else if (item.itemId == 'column'){
        panel.getLayout().setActiveItem(1); // #3
    } else if (item.itemId == 'bar'){
        panel.getLayout().setActiveItem(2); // #4
    }
}
```

First, we need to get the Chart panel. We can simply retrieve it by calling the `getView` method from the ViewController (#1).

As the menu item that was clicked on fired the event click, the first parameter this method receives is the item itself. We can get its `itemId` property to compare which `itemId` the user clicked on, and we set `ActiveItem` accordingly (#2, #3, and #4) to the option the user chose.

The `setActiveItem` method is from the Card layout. From the View, we can get the layout, which will return an instance of the Card layout, and the method will be available.

Exporting charts to images (PNG or JPEG)

On the `onChartDownload` method, we will follow the same logic as we did for the **Change Chart Type** menu items. But in this case, we want to save the chart as an image (PNG) or PDF file. Here's how we go about the task:

```
onChartDownload: function(item, e, options) {
    var panel = this.getView();
    var chart = panel.getLayout().getActiveItem(); //#1

    if (item.itemId == 'png'){
        Ext.MessageBox.confirm('Confirm Download',
            'Would you like to download the chart as Image?',
            function(choice){
            if(choice == 'yes'){
                chart.download({    //#2
                    format: 'png',
                    filename: 'SalesXFilmCategory'
                });
            }
        });
    } else if (item.itemId == 'pdf'){
        Ext.MessageBox.confirm('Confirm Download',
            'Would you like to download the chart as PDF?',
            function(choice){
            if(choice == 'yes'){
                chart.download({  //#3
                    format: 'pdf',
                    filename: 'SalesXFilmCategory',
                    pdf: {
                        format: 'A4',
                        orientation: 'landscape',
                        border: '1cm'
                    }
                });
```

```
            }
        });
    }
}
```

The Chart class already has a method named download, which we can use to download the chart in different formats. This is a native feature from Ext JS.

So first, we need to get a reference of the Chart class, which we can get through ActiveItem of the Chart panel (#1).

Then, depending on the user's choice, we will first ask whether the user really wants to download the chart in the specific format, and if yes, we will ask Ext JS to generate the file. So, if the user chooses to download in PNG (#2) or PDF (#3), we simply need to call the method download from the chart reference, passing the specific type selected by the user. In this case, the application will send a request to http://svg.sencha.io and the download will start.

According to the documentation, we can pass an object configuration to the download method with some options:

- url: This is the URL to post the data to. This defaults to the Sencha IO.

- format: This is the format of the image to export. This defaults to 'png'. The possible values are png, pdf, jpeg, and gif.

- width: This is a width value to send to the server to configure the image width. This defaults to the natural image width on the Sencha IO server.

- height: This is a height value to send to the server to configure the image height. This defaults to the natural image height on the Sencha IO server.

- filename: This is the filename of the downloaded image. This defaults to 'chart' on the Sencha IO server. The config.format is used as a filename extension.

- pdf: This is a PDF-specific option. This configuration is only used if config.format is set to 'pdf'. Check the documentation for more details.

- jpeg: This is a JPEG-specific option. This configuration is only used if config.format is set to 'jpeg'. Check the documentation for more details.

 If you are planning to have the application running in a device with touch support, it is recommended that you use the method preview instead of download. The preview method opens a popup with the chart image, and in this case, the user can use the native capability of the device to save the image.

The following screenshot is from an image that was generated by choosing to save the chart as PNG:

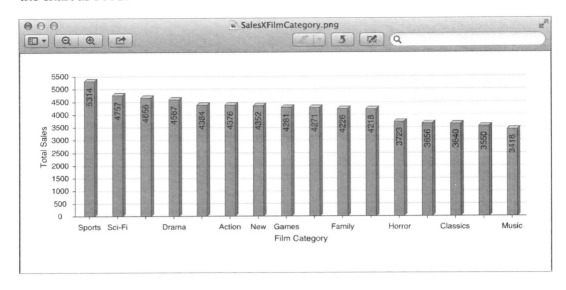

If you want to generate the image or the PDF in your own server, you can specify the `url` where the data is going to be posted. In the server, you can retrieve a POST variable named `data`. The variable has the following content (it is a *Base64* image) that can be manipulated in the server to return an image or PDF or other required format:

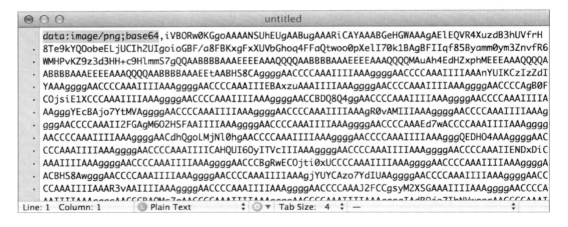

Summary

In this chapter, we learned how to export the content of a GridPanel to PDF, Excel, and also a page that is printer-friendly.

We have also learned how to create different types of charts, use only one component and change its active item, and export a chart to an image or PDF using Ext JS native features.

In the next chapter, we will learn how to test the application, how to enable touch support (so that we can execute the application from a tablet or smartphone), and also how to enable routing.

10
Routing, Touch Support, and Debugging

In this chapter, we will perform the last steps before we customize the theme and create the production build of our application. We will cover some different topics, such as enabling routing in our application, a quick overview about responsive design and Ext JS, touch support, debugging Ext JS apps, and a quick overview about testing.

So, in this chapter we will cover:

- Ext JS routing
- Responsive design and touch support
- Transforming Ext JS projects into mobile apps
- Debugging Ext JS applications
- Tools for testing Ext JS applications
- Helpful tools
- Where to find extra and open source plugins

Ext JS routing

Routing is a capability introduced in Ext JS 5 that makes the process of handling history using the `Ext.util.History` class in the application easier.

On a normal website, a user navigates to and from different pages as they click links or fill out forms. However, in a single-page application, a user's interaction doesn't load a new page. Instead, it is handled within a single page and components react to that interaction. So how do we still allow users to use the browser's forward and back buttons? Using routes allows the user to use this capability by mapping hash tokens to controller methods.

For example, we have a screen to manage the Films information. Using routing, we can allow the user to access this screen (if the user has proper entitlements) and automatically selects a particular row of the Films grid by accessing `https://localhost/masteringextjs/#films/3`. When the user accesses this link, we can instruct the application to open the **Films** tab and select the row of the film that has the ID **3**.

To enable routes in our application, we are going to use the `Root` Controller that was created by Sencha Cmd automatically when we created the application.

Default token

We are going to start by enabling a default token. When our application starts, it is going to redirect to the `#home` hash token. To do so, we are going to add the following code to the `Application.js` file:

```
defaultToken : 'home',
```

Then, inside the `Root` Controller, we will listen to this hash and redirect to the `onHome` method, as follows:

```
routes : {
    'home'  : 'onHome'
},
```

Inside the `onHome` method, we want to activate the first tab (**Home**) of the `Main Panel`. Use the following code to do this:

```
onHome : function() {
    var mainPanel = this.getMainPanel(); //#1
    if (mainPanel){
        mainPanel.setActiveTab(0);
    }
},
```

We are using a `getMain` method (#1), which refers to a `ref` of the Controller. We need to declare it as well. We are going to declare `ref` configuration inside the `init` method:

```
init: function() {
    this.addRef([{
        ref: 'mainPanel',
        selector: 'mainpanel'
    }]);
    this.callParent();
}
```

Loading a Controller programmatically

At the beginning of this book, you learned that the Controllers are loaded when the application is loaded (MVC). As our application has a **Login** screen, we do not want to enable the routes when the application is loaded. We only want to enable the routes after the user is logged in. The Root Controller is going to be loaded when the application loads, and we do not want that to happen.

Inside Application.js we are going to comment the Root Controller:

```
controllers: [
    //'Root',
    'Menu',
    'StaticData'
],
```

When the Main View is loaded, we want to initialize the Root Controller. So we are going to init the Root Controller inside the init method of main.MainController:

```
init: function() {
    Packt.app.createController('Root');
},
```

And this is how we create a Controller programmatically in Ext JS. The Router will be enabled only after the Main View is loaded. We could place all the routes inside MainController, but it would coexist with the existing code that we have in MainController already, and maintaining this code in the future could be a little difficult. This is also a design decision that we need to make: do we keep all the routes inside a single Controller or do we separate the code? Feel free to organize the code as you see fit. In big applications, it can be difficult to maintain many hash tokens organized in a single Controller.

With the code we have so far, when we render https://localhost/ masteringextjs application, it will be redirected automatically to https://localhost/masteringextjs/#home.

Handling routes

Inside the routes configuration of the Root Controller, we will handle the possible routes for our application. We will use the xtypes we created for our application. It is a good thing we kept track of them in the menu table in our database (className column)!

The following are the possible hash tokens we have in our application: user, actorsgrid, categoriesgrid, languagesgrid, citiesgrid, countriesgrid, films, and salesfilmcategory. We can define a method for each one of them as we developed for the home token. But what should be done when the user accesses any of these tokens open in the respective tab. So what we want to do is handle multiple tokens in a single method. This is the code we will add inside the routes configuration in the Root Controller:

```
'user|actorsgrid|categoriesgrid|languagesgrid|citiesgrid|countries
grid|films|salesfilmcategory': {
    before: 'onBeforeRoute',
    action: 'onRoute'
}
```

When we want to handle several tokens in the same method, we can use | to separate them. Note that in the preceding code, we are declaring two methods: onBeforeRoute and onRoute. We might want to check whether the user has entitlements to access the screen (after all, what is stopping a smart user trying to access a screen that the user does not have permission via routing?). So we can handle it in the following code (however, this is not necessarily the best way to secure an application):

```
onBeforeRoute: function(action){
    var hash = Ext.util.History.getToken(); //#1

    Ext.Ajax.request({
        url     : 'php/security/verifyEntitlement.php',
        params  : {
            module : hash
        },
        success : function(conn, response, options, eOpts) {

            var result =
            Packt.util.Util.decodeJSON(conn.responseText);

            if (result.success) {
                action.resume();    //#2
            } else {
                Packt.util.Util.showErrorMsg(result.msg);
                action.stop();      //#3
            }
        },
        failure : function(conn, response, options, eOpts) {
            Packt.util.Util.showErrorMsg(conn.responseText);
```

```
                action.stop();              //#4
            }
        });
    },
```

As we are using generic code here and we want to send to the `className` parameter the user is trying to access to the server, we can retrieve it using the code in line #1. The `before` action method only receives one parameter, which is the `action` parameter. Depending on the result, we can resume it (#2), which means the user has access to the screen—and the `onRoute` method will be executed next. Or, we can stop the action (#3 and #4), which means the `onRoute` method will not be executed next.

Let's take a look at the method `onRoute` method:

```
onRoute: function(){
    var me = this,
        hash = Ext.util.History.getToken(),
        main = me.getMain(); //#5

    me.locateMenuItem(main, hash); //#6
},
```

This method will call the `locateMenuItem` (#6) method passing the `mainmenu` reference (#5):

```
{
    ref: 'main',
    selector: '[xtype=mainmenu]'
}
```

Refactoring the Menu code

Let's take a look at the `locateMenuItem` code:

```
locateMenuItem: function(mainMenu, hash){
    var me = this,
        root, node;
    Ext.each(mainMenu.items.items, function(tree){
        if (tree.getXType() === 'menutree'){
            root = tree.getRootNode();
            node = root.findChild('className', hash);
            if (node){
                me.openTab(node); //#1
                return;
            }
        }
    });
},
```

The previously mentioned method is searching for a node in each menutree we created for the menu of the application that matches the hash of the route. If we find the node, we call the openTab method (#1):

```
openTab: function(record){
    var mainPanel = this.getMainPanel();

    var newTab = mainPanel.items.findBy(
        function (tab){
            return tab.title === record.get('text');
        });

    if (!newTab){
        newTab = mainPanel.add({
            xtype: record.get('className'),
            glyph: record.get('glyph') + '@FontAwesome',
            title: record.get('text'),
            closable: true
        });
    }

    mainPanel.setActiveTab(newTab);
},
```

If we take a look at the code of the onTreePanelItemClick method from the Menu Controller, we will note that it is exactly the same as the openTab method. Although we are handling routes at the end of this book, it is best if we start handling them when we start developing the application. So, if you are planning on using routes, make sure routes is part of the design, because it might require some code changes if you decide to implement it after the application is developed.

The onTreePanelItemClick method will have the following code now:

```
onTreePanelItemClick: function(view, record, item, index, event,
options){
    this.redirectTo(record.get('className'));
},
```

When the user clicks on the Node of the Tree of the menu we implemented, it is going to redirect to the hash of the className parameter of the Node, and the Root Controller will handle opening the tab.

Handling unmatched routes

If the user tries to access a route that is not defined in the application, we can execute some code as well. In the `Root` Controller, we can add the following code:

```
listen : {
    controller : {
        '*': {
            unmatchedroute: 'onUnmatchedRoute'
        }
    }
},
```

And we can display an error message to the user, as follows:

```
onUnmatchedRoute : function(hash) {
    Packt.util.Util.showErrorMsg('Hash does not exist!');
}
```

Handling parameters

Now let's develop more complex route handling. For the **Films** screen, let's say we want the user to be able to select a row from the Films grid using a hash token, as demonstrated in the following screenshot:

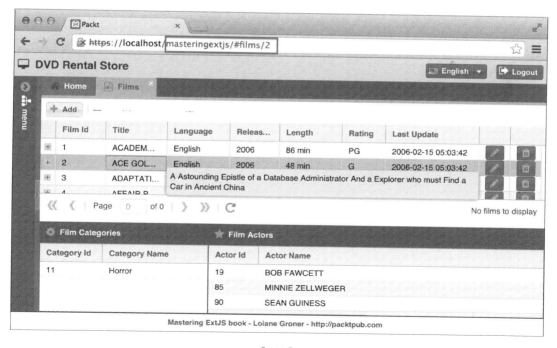

We can define the following route:

```
'films/:id' : {
    action: 'onFilmSelect',
    before: 'onBeforeFilmSelect',
    conditions : {
        ':id' : '([0-9]+)'
    }
}
```

This means the user can try to access a URL with the format `https://localhost/masteringextjs/#films/2`. If the user tries to access `https://localhost/masteringextjs/#films/ace`, it is not valid because of the condition of the `id` parameter—it needs to be a numeric value. This means we can also define regular expressions to validate the parameters of hash tokens.

Before we execute `onFilmSelect`, we want to do a few things:

```
onBeforeFilmSelect: function(id, action){

    var me = this,
        main = me.getMain();

    this.locateMenuItem(this.getMain(),'films'); //#1

    var record =
    this.getFilmsGrid().getStore().findRecord('film_id', id);
    if(record) {
        action.resume();
    }
    else {
        action.stop();
    }
},
```

We need to open the **Films** screen (#1) and check whether the record the user wants to select exists in the Store. If the result is positive, continue the execution and if not, stop it.

The reference for `filmsGrid` is given here:

```
{
    ref: 'filmsGrid',
    selector: '[xtype=films-grid]'
}
```

And finally, the reference for the `onFilmSelect` method is given here:

```
onFilmSelect: function(id){
    this.getFilmsGrid().fireEvent('selectfilm', id);
}
```

We are going to fire the `selectfilm` event of `films-grid`, as shown in the following code; this requires some new code inside the `FilmsGrid` class:

```
listeners: {
    itemclick: 'onItemClick',
    selectfilm: 'onFilmSelect'
}
```

We are going to handle the listeners in the `FilmsController` class, as shown in the following code:

```
onFilmSelect: function(id){
    var me = this,
        grid = me.lookupReference('filmsGrid'),
        store = me.getStore('films'),
        record = store.findRecord( 'film_id', id );

    if (record){
        grid.getSelectionModel().select(record);
    }
},
```

What we are doing in the preceding code is finding the record by `film_id` given and selecting it in `FilmsGrid`.

When the user clicks on a row of the grid, the `onItemClick` method will be fired:

```
onItemClick: function( view, record, item, index, e, eOpts ) {
    this.redirectTo('films/' + record.get('film_id'));
}
```

We are simply going to redirect the request to the `Route` Controller so that it can handle the selection with the code we developed in this topic.

> As mentioned before, routing can become very complex in some applications, so the best thing is to start handling them from the very beginning of development. For more details, please check out Sencha guides and documentation about routing.

Using the responsive design plugin

Another new capability introduced in Ext JS 5 is the option to develop responsive applications. Mobile devices are part of our lives. We basically have a computer in our pockets. It is very common nowadays to have tablet or mobile compatible as an item listed in a user requirements document. Fortunately, Ext JS 5 provides good support and allows us to achieve this requirement without too much effort.

Ext JS 5 introduces the responsive plugin and mixin. The plugin can be used in any component, and the mixin can be used in any other class. This plugin responds dynamically to changes in screen size and orientation by controlling `responsiveConfig`.

For example, let's do a quick example in our project. If the width of the screen is less than 768 pixels and the screen is in `tall` mode, we are going to hide the application menu and display a new button that is going to render the menu as displayed in the following screenshot:

In the `Packt.view.main.Main` class, we are going to add the responsive plugin to the `west` region. The code is presented as follows:

```
{
    xtype: 'mainmenu',
    region: 'west',
    plugins: 'responsive',
    responsiveConfig: {
        'width < 768 && tall': {
            visible: false
        },
        'width >= 768': {
            visible: true
        }
    }
}
```

Inside `responsiveConfig`, we can add some conditions and set the component's configuration accordingly. We can change the layout, render a different component, and do whatever is needed in the application. With only the preceding code, if we execute the application and decrease the browser's width, we will see the menu will be hidden automatically when the criteria are met. It is really nice!

In `Packt.view.main.Header`, we are going to add a new component as well, as follows:

```
{
    xtype: 'tbfill'
},{
    xtype: 'responsive-mainmenu'
},{
    xtype: 'translation'
},
```

The code for this component is presented as follows:

```
Ext.define('Packt.view.main.ResponsiveMenuButton', {
    extend: 'Ext.button.Split',
    xtype: 'responsive-mainmenu',

    requires: [
        'Packt.view.main.MainModel'
    ],
```

```
        text: 'Menu',

        plugins: 'responsive',
        responsiveConfig: {
            'width < 768 && tall': {
                visible: true
            },
            'width >= 768': {
                visible: false
            }
        },

        menu: {
            xtype: 'menu',
            items: [{
                xtype: 'mainmenu'
            }]
        }
    });
```

We are reusing the menu we developed at the beginning of this book. Of course, we could develop a UX that is more user friendly, but we are just focusing on the functionality here for a quick test.

Google Chrome has a really nice feature if we need to work with responsive design. It is the capability of emulating the project in different devices to see how they are going to look. In Google Developer Tools, click on the mobile device icon as shown in the following screenshot and start the adventure:

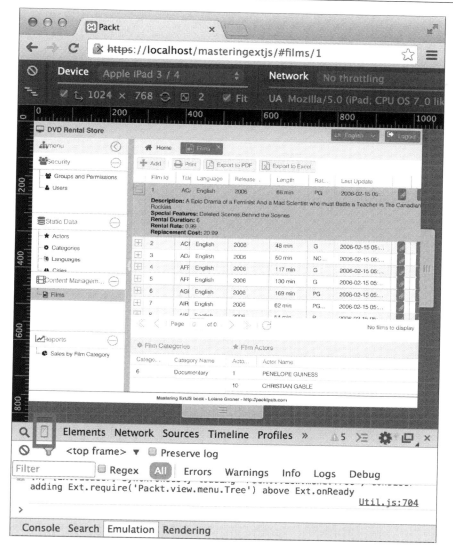

For more information about Ext JS 5 and responsive design, please read `http://www.sencha.com/blog/designing-responsive-applications-with-ext-js` and check the source code of this example `http://goo.gl/odce6j`. Firefox also has a mobile view in its developer toolbar. Go to **Tools** | **Web Developer** | **Responsive Design View**.

Enabling touch support

In this section, we will quickly discuss responsive design. Since it is not the primary topic of this book, we will implement a very simple example that will give us an idea of what we need to do if we need to develop a responsive application with Ext JS. And speaking of responsive design, we know Ext JS is great to develop desktop applications (that will be executed from a desktop computer or a laptop), but mobiles have now become a very integral part of our lives. We will figure out the means to run the same application running on a desktop and also on a mobile device. We will also discuss how to enable touch support in our application as well.

The major difference between running an application on a desktop and a mobile device is the events, among other details. On a desktop, when the user clicks on a button, we listen to the `click` event. On a touch mobile device, there is no `click` event; there is the `tap` event, because we are touching the screen and not working with a mouse.

Another detail is the size of the components. The Ext JS classic theme is really nice, but small for touch screens. Throughout this book, we have been using the `Neptune` theme, which is the default theme set to the application when we created it with Sencha Cmd. The `Neptune` theme has larger components than the `classic` theme but still is not good enough to be used on touch devices. Let's experiment! If you have a touch device, try executing the application we developed throughout this book on it. If you do not have a touch device, you need not worry; you can do this experiment using the Google Chrome emulator mentioned in the preceding topic.

The following screenshot exemplifies the application being executed on an iPad mini:

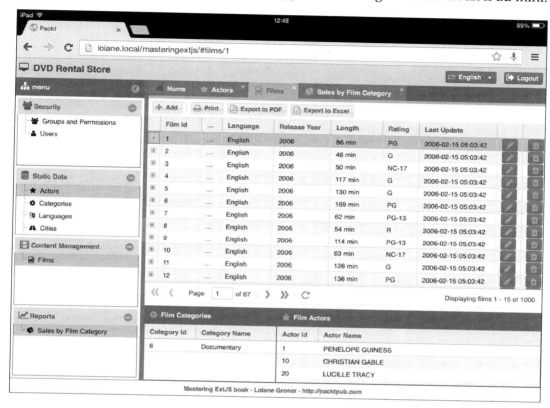

If we try to use the application as is, we will be able to use most of its capabilities. Because we are using a desktop theme, with small icons, it will not work 100% in a mobile device. For example, the RowExpander + button doesn't work very well because the + icon is very small for a mobile device.

Ext JS 5 introduces new themes that were designed specially for touch devices. There is a special version of the Neptune theme and also a special version of the Crisp theme (also introduced in Ext JS 5). We can add the touch support to our application by changing the theme in the app.js file:

```
"theme": "ext-theme-neptune-touch", //or "ext-theme-crisp-touch"
```

With `sencha app watch` being executed in a terminal, try changing the theme to one of the previously mentioned options. Don't forget to clean the browser's cache to make sure you will get the new version of the CSS file next time you refresh the application. Now let's try the application again, as follows:

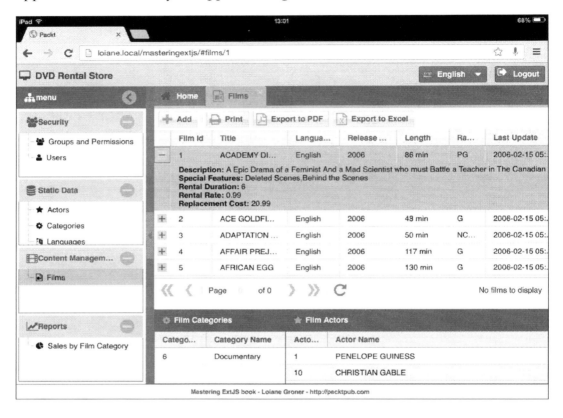

Note how there is more space between the components now. This is to make sure we can tap (touch) the components.

We don't have a touch-optimized application. To make it 100 percent, we can review any size that we set (for example, column width) and use some responsive design techniques to have the application looking great in mobile devices!

 For more information, please visit `http://goo.gl/VnT7bT`.

From Ext JS to mobile

What if the product you are developing requires a special app implement, especially for touch devices? We are not talking about the techniques we implemented in the previous topic; we are talking about a mobile app for the same product. For example, Facebook has a version for desktop, but it also has an app for mobile devices. It might be what you need as well.

We would like to introduce Sencha Touch, the cousin of Ext JS! Sencha Touch was the first HTML5 mobile framework on the market. And there's more good news: you do not need to rewrite all of your code to have the same application also available to mobile devices.

Sencha Touch and Ext JS share the same API. The data package, such as models, stores and the core of the framework, is the same. Sencha Touch also uses MVC. The Controller and View (components) work in a way that is very similar to that of Ext JS Controller and View. Of course, the biggest difference is in the views since a web component is different from a mobile component. However, Sencha Touch also offers forms and lists, and we can find even grid components customized for mobile devices. The charts are also shared between the frameworks.

The following diagram shows the analysis of how much code we can reuse after using Sencha Touch:

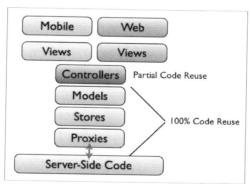

The amount of code we can reuse is huge! And we also have two ways of implementing it: the first one is to have a mobile app, where the user will access a URL pointing to a Sencha Touch deploy (Sencha Touch and server-side code at the same domain). And the second option is to have the Sencha Touch code running on the user's device (Sencha Touch offers native packaging to iOS and Android, but we can also have native Blackberry 10 and Windows Phone 8 native apps with Sencha Touch) and the server-side code running on a server on the Web. In this case, we can use CORS (http://enable-cors.org/) to make the Ajax communication between the app and the server-side code.

To learn more about Sencha Touch, please go to `http://www.sencha.com/products/touch/`.

On mobile, it is also possible to access the hardware features such as contacts, camera, geolocation, and more. We can use an open source framework called **Apache Cordova** (or **Phonegap**, which is a Apache Cordova implementation). Sencha Cmd also has commands that support the integration with Cordova. The following links provide more information about this topic:

- `http://docs.sencha.com/touch/2.4/tutorials/cordova_camera.html`
- `http://cordova.apache.org/`
- `http://phonegap.com/`
- `http://vimeo.com/76568053`

Debugging Ext JS applications

The art of debugging is as important as the art of programming. We usually write code that we think is going to work as soon as we execute it, but this is not true sometimes. We write the code, then we get an exception or JavaScript error, and then we need to dive into the code again to see where we went wrong. It's part of being a developer and it is also part of life!

Throughout this book, you learned that debugging is important, especially when we were learning an easier way to figure out the correct **Component Query** selector. When developing applications with Ext JS, it is mandatory to use a debug tool. This is so because it is not only for debugging, but you will also be able to learn more about the framework, and it is a great learning exercise.

A few things we always need to remind ourselves of while creating Ext JS applications: case-sensitive matters—the `LoginScreen` class is different from `Loginscreen`. Be careful with reserved words (`http://mattsnider.com/reserved-words-in-javascript/`)—you cannot use them as namespaces, names of classes and packages, or as variable names. Check the spelling; this is very important—sometimes when we are typing, we can type an extra character (*fat finger* syndrome).

If you have programmed in JavaScript for almost 10 years now, you will know that before, our only friend was the dear `alert` prompt. We used to put several alerts on the code, execute it, and then see which alert was not executed so that we could find where the error was. Now we have our dear friend `console`. Abuse the use of console for `log`, `warn`, and `error`!

We also have great tools to debug! The two most important are Google Developer Tools and Firebug for Firefox! Learn to use at least one of them (they are very similar).

For example, let's use Google Developer Tools. It comes with a few tabs; on the **Network** tab, we can see the files that were loaded as follows:

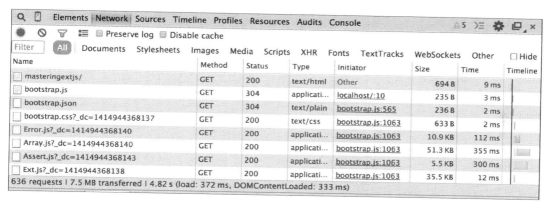

And speaking of files that are being loaded or not, this is a very huge deal! Simple mistakes, such as the name of the class (using MVC), path of CSS, and JS on the `index.html` file, can be verified using the **Console** or the **Network** tab. This tab is also very important as in some chapters we verified the parameters that were being sent to the server. Even though it might be the first time we are working with an Ext JS component, and we do not know how to handle the data that will be sent to the server, we can take a look at the parameters of the request in the **Network** tab, and then it is easier to read the correct parameters in the server. The same applies when we receive any information from the server, for example, check whether the JSON is coming as per Ext JS expectations.

On the **Elements** tab, we can see details; the HTML code that was generated by the Ext JS code and also the CSS that is being applied to the components. This is very useful when we want to apply some custom CSS and debug why the style was not applied.

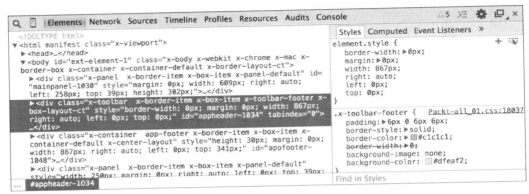

When we move the mouse over, the portion related to that HTML is highlighted on the screen. We also have the **CSS** and **Script** tabs. We can change the CSS and script in real time and see the changes applied in real time! This is simply amazing! So, it is very important to learn how to use a debug tool.

In the **Sources** tab, we can take the source code that was loaded in the form of the project's structure. This tab is very important for us because it allows us to use the debugging capabilities of the browser to debug our code. The debugging technique is very similar to what is used with server-side languages; we add a breakpoint, execute the code, and then watch and inspect variable values and see what happens in every line of the source code, as follows:

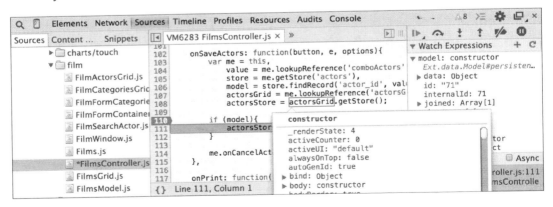

To learn more about Firebug, please visit `http://getfirebug.com/`. And to learn more about Google Developer Tools, please visit: `https://developers.google.com/chrome-developer-tools/` and `https://developer.chrome.com/extensions/tut_debugging`.

And, of course, there are the special add-ons we talked about in *Chapter 7, Static Data Management*: Sencha add-on for Chrome and Illumination for developers for Firebug.

Mastering one debugging tool is important as mastering the art of programming in Ext JS. After all, we don't know if we will have the opportunity to work on a project from scratch or we will need to maintain other developers' code. In this case, knowing how to debug is a must-have skill! Choose your favorite weapon and have fun coding and debugging!

Testing Ext JS applications

Testing is a very important part when developing applications or providing maintenance. When we do not write tests, we need to verify each use case manually, and if we change anything on the code, we will need to perform all the testing manually again. The same happens when we need to maintain the code; developers usually test only what has been changed, but the correct thing to do would be regression tests to see whether the change did not break anything else. So spending some time writing tests can be a win at the end. You will spend a little bit more time writing code, but then you will be able to run all the tests with a single click and then verify what is broken and what is still working.

We are also very used to performing unit tests on the server-side code. Java, PHP, Ruby, C# communities offer a lot of options to perform unit tests on the server-side code, and sometimes, we can forget to test the frontend code (in this case Ext JS). But do not worry; there are a few tools we can use to include Ext JS on the tests as well.

One tool that is very popular for JavaScript testing in general is **Jasmine** (`http://jasmine.github.io/`). Jasmine is a testing tool that is used for **Behavior-Driven Development (BDD)** — (`http://en.wikipedia.org/wiki/Behavior-driven_development`). In Ext JS documentation, you can find two guides explaining how to test Ext JS applications with Jasmine: `http://docs.sencha.com/extjs/4.2.0/#!/guide/testing` and `http://docs.sencha.com/extjs/4.2.0/#!/guide/testing_controllers`. Although the guides were written for Ext JS 4.x, they can also be applied to Ext JS 5.

There is also a testing framework designed specially for a Sencha application called **Siesta** (http://www.bryntum.com/products/siesta/). Siesta can also be used to test JavaScript code in general, but the cool side of Siesta is that it provides a special API so that we can test Ext JS applications, including tests on user interface components. Siesta comes with some great examples that can be used to start writing our own test cases.

Helpful tools

In this topic, we will present some tools that can help developers a lot while implementing Ext JS applications. You can find all the links of the tools mentioned here at the end of this topic.

The first tool is **JSLint**. JSLint is a tool that can help you to find JavaScript errors and can also help you to clean your code.

The second tool is **YSlow**. YSlow analyzes web pages and tells you why they're slow based on the rules for high performance websites. YSlow is a Firefox add-on integrated with the popular Firebug web development tool.

Ext JS is a JavaScript framework, and JavaScript performance is a topic that is a concern for a lot of companies. The minimum the user needs to load on the browser, the better. That is why it is very important to make a production build using Sencha Cmd and not simply deploy all the application files on production.

Sencha Cmd is also going to minify the Ext JS CSS file to a smaller CSS, and we can also include only the CSS for the components that we are going to really use (just in case we create a custom theme). It is also important to create any application custom CSS inside the sass/etc or sass/var folders so that the CSS can also be added to the main CSS file generated by Sencha Cmd.

CSS Sprites is another very important topic. Font icons such as Font Awesome are really nice, but sometimes that is a need to use image icons. In this case, we can create a CSS Sprite, which involves creating a single image with all the icons. And on the CSS, we simply have a single image and pass a background-position property of the icon we want to display, like this:

```
.icon-message {
  background-image: url('mySprite.png');
  background-position: -10px -10px;
}
```

```
.icon-envolope {
  background-image: url('mySprite.png');
  background-position: -15px -15px;
}
```

There are a few tools that can also help us to create CSS Sprites, such as **SpritePad,** **SpriteMe,** and **Compass Sprite Generator.**

Here are all the links for the tools mentioned in this section:

- **JSLint:** `http://www.jslint.com/`
- **YSlow:** `http://developer.yahoo.com/yslow/`
- **SpritePad:** `http://wearekiss.com/spritepad`
- **SpriteMe:** `http://www.spriteme.org/`
- **Compass Sprite Generator:** `http://compass-style.org/help/tutorials/spriting/`

Always remember that Ext JS is JavaScript, so we need to care about performance as well. With all these little tips posted on this topic, an Ext JS application can improve its performance as well.

And last but not least, there are two tools from Sencha: **Sencha Architect** and **Sencha Eclipse Plugin.** Sencha Architect is a visual designer tool that is very similar to Visual Studio: you drag and drop, and you can see how the application looks, and the entire configuration that you need to do is done using the **Config** panel. Only methods, functions, and templates are free to enter whatever code you like. The good thing about Sencha Architect is that it helps to follow all the best practices and the code is very well organized. You can also develop all the Ext JS code using Sencha Architect, and on the server side, you can continue using the IDE you like the most (Eclipse, Aptana, Visual Studio, and others).

And Sencha Eclipse Plugin is a plugin for the Eclipse IDE that has the autocomplete feature enabled. Both Sencha Architect and Sencha Eclipse Plugin are paid tools. But you can download a trial version for testing at `http://www.sencha.com/products/complete/` or `http://www.sencha.com/products/architect/`.

Another great IDE to develop Sencha applications is **WebStorm** (or **IntelliJ IDEA**). WebStorm also has the autocomplete feature (if we set it up), support for Sass and Compass (used by Ext JS for theming), and JSLint to validate the JavaScript code, among other features. It is also a paid tool, but you can download a trial version for testing at `https://www.jetbrains.com/webstorm/`. The source of this book was written with IntelliJ IDEA.

Third-party components and plugins

Although Ext JS provides great components, we usually will also want to develop our own components or maybe use other developers' components. The Ext JS community is great regarding this subject. A lot of developers share their own components, extensions, and plugins with the community. There are two main places you can find them:

- **Sencha Market**: https://market.sencha.com/
- **Sencha Forum**: http://www.sencha.com/forum/forumdisplay.php?82-Ext-User-Extensions-and-Plugins

Summary

In this chapter, you learned how to enable routing, and you also quickly overviewed responsible design and touch support for Ext JS applications. You learned about the importance of knowing how to debug an Ext JS application and about some tools that can help us with this task. You also learned that performance is really important and that we can do a lot more to improve the performance of our Ext JS application with the help of some free tools. We also listed where to find great plugins, extensions, and new components that we can use in our projects.

In the next chapter, we will customize the theme for our application, and we will perform the production build.

11
Preparing for Production and Themes

We completed our application in the preceding chapter. Now, it is time to create a nice theme to put a personal touch on the application and also prepare to deploy it on production. After all, we have been working on the development environment, and when we want to go live, we cannot simply deploy all the files; we need to do some preparation first. So, in this chapter, we will cover:

- Creating custom themes
- Packaging the application for production

Before we start

The main tool we are going to use in this chapter is Sencha Cmd. With Sencha Cmd, we will be able to create custom themes and make the production build. We always need to make sure the Sencha Cmd version we are using is compatible with the Ext JS version we are using. If you downloaded the preceding version of Ext JS from the Sencha website, please also get the latest Sencha Cmd (it will be compatible).

So far, this is what we have developed throughout this book:

All the code we created is inside `app`, `index.html`, `php`, `resources` (custom image icon, font, and custom locale files), and `sass` (custom application CSS). The other folders and files were created by Sencha Cmd, as you learned in *Chapter 2, Getting Started*.

Creating a new theme

The first task we will perform in this chapter is to create a new theme for our project. To do so, we will use Sencha Cmd and the terminal application of the operating system.

Sencha Cmd now has the capability to generate the complete file structure we need to create a brand new theme.

So, let's create a new theme step by step. First, with the terminal open, change the directory to the project's root folder. Then, we will use the following command:

```
sencha generate theme masteringextjs-theme
```

The output for the preceding command is as follows:

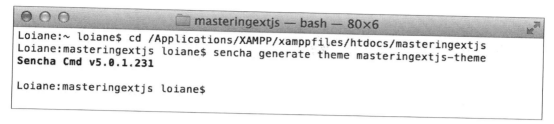

Here, `masteringextjs-theme` is the name of our theme. This command will create a new directory with the name of our theme inside the `packages` folder, as follows:

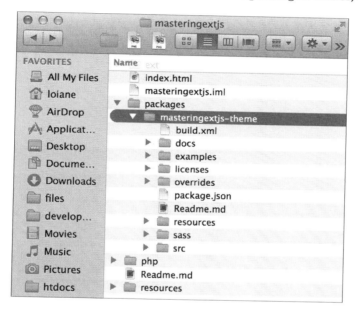

The `package.json` file contains some configurations of the theme used by Sencha Cmd, such as theme name, version, and dependencies.

The `sass` directory contains all the Sass files of our theme. Inside this directory, we will find three more main directories:

- `var`: This contains Sass variables.
- `src`: This contains Sass rules and mixins. These rules and mixins use variables declared on files inside the `sass/var` directory.
- `etc`: This contains additional utility functions and mixins.

All the files that we create must match the classpath of the component we are styling. For example, if we want to style the button component, we need to create the styles inside the file `sass/var/button/Button.scss`; if want to style the Component Panel, we need to create styles inside the file `sass/var/panel.scss`.

The `resources` folder contains images and other static resources that will be used by our theme.

The `overrides` folder contains all the JavaScript overrides to components that might be required for theming these components.

> Spend some time exploring the contents of the following directories that we can find inside the `packages` folder to get more familiar with this way of organizing the Sass files: `ext-theme-classic`, `ext-theme-gray`, and `ext-theme-neptune`.

By default, any theme that we create uses `ext-theme-classic` as a base (the classic Ext JS blue theme). We are going to change to the Neptune theme that we have been using until now. To change the theme base, open the `package.json` file and locate the `extend` property. Change its value from `ext-theme-classic` to `ext-theme-neptune`. The content of `package.json` will be something like this:

```json
{
    "name": "masteringextjs-theme",
    "type": "theme",
    "creator": "anonymous",
    "summary": "Short summary",
    "detailedDescription": "Long description of package",
    "version": "1.0.0",
    "compatVersion": "1.0.0",
    "format": "1",
    "slicer": {
        "js": [
            {
                "path": "${package.dir}/sass/example/custom.js",
                "isWidgetManifest": true
            }
        ]
    },
    "output": "${package.dir}/build",
    "local": true,
    "requires": [],
    "extend": "ext-theme-neptune"
}
```

We can use any Ext JS theme as the base theme of our custom theme. These are the possible options:

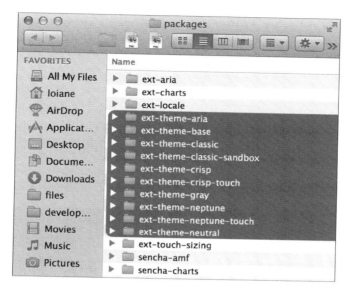

We can use any theme package from Ext JS. We can find these packages inside `ext/packages`.

 You can try the Theme Viewer example from the Ext JS example pages to try each theme.

After the theme structure is created, and we have changed the base theme, let's build it. To build it, we are going to use the terminal and Sencha Cmd again. Change the directory to `packages/masteringextjs-theme` and type the following command:

```
sencha package build
```

The result will be somewhat like the following screenshot:

```
● ○ ○                  🗀 masteringextjs-theme — bash — 101×34
Loiane:masteringextjs loiane$ cd packages/masteringextjs-theme
Loiane:masteringextjs-theme loiane$ sencha package build
Sencha Cmd v5.0.1.231
[INF] Processing Build Descriptor : default
[INF] Concatenating output to file /Applications/XAMPP/xamppfiles/htdocs/masteringextjs/packages/mast
eringextjs-theme/build/masteringextjs-theme-debug.js
[INF] Compressing data with YuiJavascriptCompressor
[INF] Concatenating output to file /Applications/XAMPP/xamppfiles/htdocs/masteringextjs/packages/mast
eringextjs-theme/build/masteringextjs-theme.js
[INF] writing sass content to /Applications/XAMPP/xamppfiles/htdocs/masteringextjs/packages/mastering
extjs-theme/build//masteringextjs-theme-all-rtl-debug.scss
[INF] writing sass content to /Applications/XAMPP/xamppfiles/htdocs/masteringextjs/packages/mastering
extjs-theme/build//config.rb
[INF] writing sass content to /Applications/XAMPP/xamppfiles/htdocs/masteringextjs/packages/mastering
extjs-theme/build//masteringextjs-theme-all-debug.scss
[INF] executing compass using system installed ruby runtime
    create resources/masteringextjs-theme-all-debug.css
    create resources/masteringextjs-theme-all-rtl-debug.css
[INF] writing sass content to /Applications/XAMPP/xamppfiles/htdocs/masteringextjs/build/temp/masteri
ngextjs-theme/slicer-temp/masteringextjs-theme-all-rtl-debug.scss.tmp
[INF] writing sass content to /Applications/XAMPP/xamppfiles/htdocs/masteringextjs/build/temp/masteri
ngextjs-theme/slicer-temp/config.rb
[INF] executing compass using system installed ruby runtime
    create masteringextjs-theme-all-rtl-debug.css
[INF] Writing content to /Applications/XAMPP/xamppfiles/htdocs/masteringextjs/packages/masteringextjs
-theme/sass/example/bootstrap.json
[INF] Writing content to /Applications/XAMPP/xamppfiles/htdocs/masteringextjs/packages/masteringextjs
-theme/sass/example/bootstrap.js
[INF] Capturing theme image
[INF] Capture complete
[INF] Slicing images...
[INF] Slicing complete - generated 320 images

Loiane:masteringextjs-theme loiane$ ▊
```

The result of this command will be the creation of the `build` directory inside the `packages/masteringextjs-theme` folder, as follows:

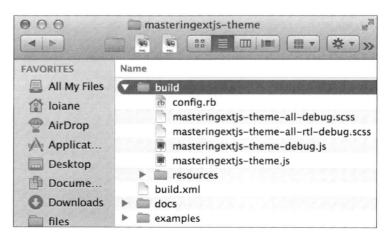

Inside this `build` folder, we can find the `resources` folder, and inside the resources folder we can find a file named `masteringextjs-theme-all.css`, which contains all the styles for all the components we styled on our theme (which is none so far, but we will get there). Even though we created a complete theme (styled all components), it is not 100 percent certain that we will use all the components in our application. Sencha Cmd has the ability to filter and create a CSS file with only the components we are going to use in our project. For this reason, we do not need to include `masteringextjs-theme-all.css` manually in our application.

 A `masteringextjs-theme.pkg` file will also be created inside `build/ masteringextjs-theme`. We can use this file to distribute the theme package to other developers. For more information, please read `http://docs.sencha.com/cmd/5.x/cmd_packages/cmd_packages.html`.

So let's set up our project so that it can use our theme. Inside `app.json`, locate the theme entry and change it to:

```
"theme": "masteringextjs-theme",
```

With `sencha app watch` being executed in a terminal, we will be able to see that `Packt-all.css` will be overwritten. When we refresh the application, there will be no changes because we have not started to customize our theme yet.

For the next steps, it is very important to keep `sencha app watch` executed while we make the changes. This way we will be able to see the modifications by simply refreshing the browser.

Changing the base color

Let's start customizing the theme right now! Let's go back to the `packages/masteringextjs-theme` folder. Here's how we customize the theme:

1. Inside the `sass/var` folder, create a new file named `Component.scss`. Let's add the following content to it:

   ```
   $base-color: #317040 !default;
   ```

2. In the preceding code, we are declaring a Sass variable named `$base-color` with a greenish value. This will change the base color of the theme from blue to green. Let's apply the changes on our theme and see the changes.

3. Open the browser and we will have something like the following screenshot:

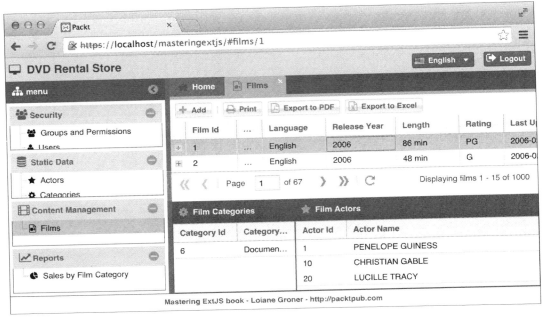

With a single line, we have a complete new theme! We can continue to add more styles to our custom theme and customize each and every component.

Customizing components

Let's make some changes in our theme. Inside Component.scss, add the following code:

```
$neutral-color: #8DF98B !default;
```

The output will be the following:

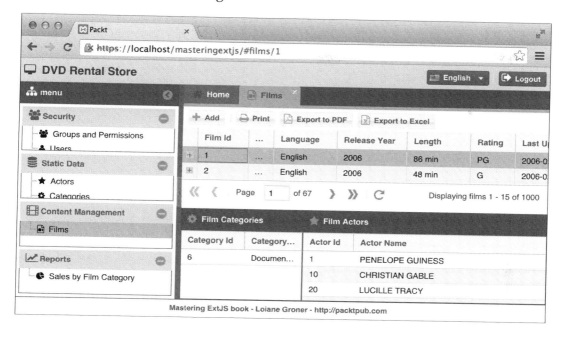

Note how the button background, the Grid Column header, and the Panel header inside the accordion menu have changed.

Let's go ahead and create some other files so that we can add more custom styles, as follows:

1.   Create the following files and folders:

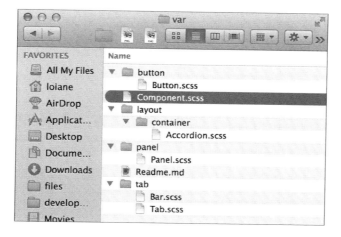

2. Inside `Accordion.scss`, we will add the following code:

    ```
    $accordion-header-color: #336600 !default;
    ```

    This will change the color of the header title of the panels inside the accordion menu.

3. Inside `Panel.scss`, we will add the following code:

    ```
    $panel-light-header-color: #336600 !default;
    ```

    This color will be used to create a different shade of green for the Panel component.

4. Inside `Bar.scss`, we will add the following code:

    ```
    $tabbar-background-gradient: 'bevel' !default;
    ```

    This will change the gradient of the tab panel bar. Possible values can be found at `http://goo.gl/fapTBA`.

5. Inside `Tab.scss`, we will add the following code:

    ```
    $tab-base-color-active: #E6F5EB !default;
    $tab-base-color-focus-over: #339933 !default;
    $tab-base-color-focus-active: #B2E0C2 !default;
    ```

    This will change the tab color to different shades of green.

    So far, this is the output we have:

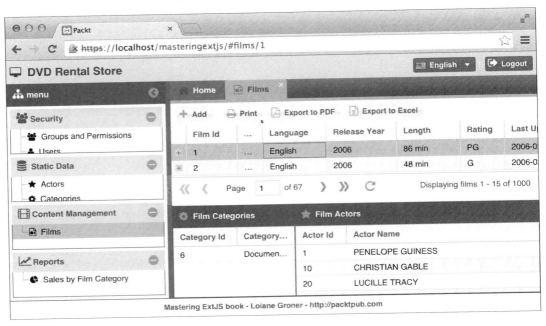

Try comparing it to the previous output screenshot.

6. Inside `Button.scss`, we will add the following code:

```scss
$packt-background-color: #669999 !default;
$packt-mate-gradient: 'matte' !default;
$packt-light-color: #339933 !default;
$packt-dark-color: #006600 !default;

$button-default-base-color: $packt-background-color;
$button-default-base-color-over: $packt-dark-color;
$button-default-base-color-pressed: $packt-dark-color;
$button-default-base-color-disabled: mix(#000, $packt-dark-color, 8%);
$button-default-border-color: $packt-dark-color !default;

$button-small-font-weight: bold !default;
$button-medium-font-weight: bold !default;
$button-large-font-weight: bold !default;

$button-default-color: #fff !default;

$button-default-glyph-color: $button-default-color;

$button-small-border-radius: 1px !default;
$button-medium-border-radius: 1px !default;
$button-large-border-radius: 1px !default;

$button-default-background-gradient: $packt-mate-gradient;
$button-default-background-gradient-disabled: $packt-mate-gradient;
$button-default-background-gradient-over: $packt-mate-gradient;
$button-default-background-gradient-pressed: $packt-mate-gradient;

$button-toolbar-border-color: $packt-background-color;

$button-toolbar-background-color: $packt-light-color;
$button-toolbar-background-color-over: $packt-dark-color;
$button-toolbar-background-color-pressed: $packt-dark-color;
$button-toolbar-background-color-disabled: mix(#000, $packt-dark-color, 8%);

$button-toolbar-color: #fff !default;
```

```
$button-toolbar-background-gradient: $packt-mate-gradient;
$button-toolbar-background-gradient-disabled: $packt-mate-
gradient;
$button-toolbar-background-gradient-focus: $packt-mate-
gradient;
$button-toolbar-background-gradient-over: $packt-mate-
gradient;
$button-toolbar-background-gradient-pressed: $packt-mate-
gradient;

$button-default-glyph-color: #fff !default;
```

This will be the output for our new custom buttons:

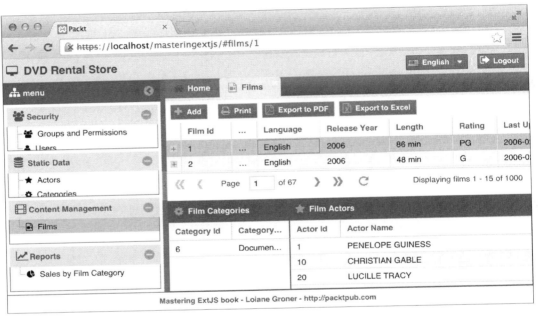

The buttons (normal ones and the ones placed inside a toolbar) look very different now.

Some useful tips while creating new themes

There is no recipe or detailed tutorial on how to create a completely customized theme in Ext JS. Usually, the names of the Sass variables used by Ext JS are self-explanatory. For example, `$button-default-glyph-color` is the color used to render the glyphs for buttons.

The following are some tips that could prove useful in the process of creating Ext JS themes:

- Try learning Sass and Compass. Sass and Compass have mixins and useful functions to work with colors, among other functionalities (`http://sass-lang.com/documentation/file.SASS_REFERENCE.html`).

- Take a look at the variables and the current values used by the theme you are using as the base theme. You can find its source code at `ext/packages/ext-theme-neptune/sass/var`.

- Experiment! The best way to learn something new is to practice it. A good approach can be to copy the original file (for example, `Button.scss`) from the directory listed previously, start changing the variable values, and see what happens!

- While experimenting, try using different colors (with contrast, such as red, yellow, black, blue, or any other color of your preference) so you can see exactly what is being changed in the theme!

- Consult the documentation. Each class in Ext JS has a section of the Sass variables used, with a description and possible values. Make sure to make the most of it:

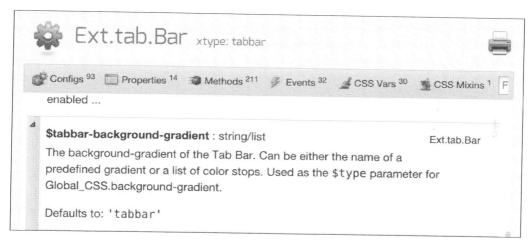

Creating custom UIs

Ext JS also supports UIs, which are special themes that can be applied to specific components. For example, let's say that for the buttons **Print, Export to PDF** and **Export to Excel**, we want to apply a different theme. We can create a UI.

1. The first step is checking the documentation for what UIs, known as **CSS Mixins**, are available:

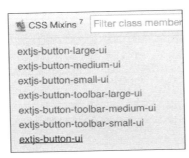

2. Then, check all the variables needed to create this mixin. We can declare the custom variables inside the `masteringextjs-theme/sass/var/button/Button.scss` file we created earlier, as follows:

```
$button-packt-custom-color: #336600 !default;
$packt-custom-base-color: #C2E0D1 !default;

$button-packt-custom-small-border-radius: $button-small-
border-radius;
$button-packt-custom-small-border-width: 1px;

$button-packt-custom-base-color: $packt-custom-base-color;
$button-packt-custom-base-color-over: $packt-dark-color;
$button-packt-custom-base-color-focus: $packt-dark-color;
$button-packt-custom-base-color-pressed: $packt-dark-color;
$button-packt-custom-base-color-disabled: lighten($button-packt-
custom-base-color, 40%);

$button-packt-custom-small-border-radius: 0px;
$button-packt-custom-small-border-width: 1px;

$button-packt-custom-border-color: darken($button-packt-
custom-base-color, 20%);
$button-packt-custom-border-color-over:$button-packt-
custom-border-color;
```

```scss
$button-packt-custom-border-color-focus:$button-packt-
custom-border-color;
$button-packt-custom-border-color-pressed:$button-packt-
custom-border-color-over;
$button-packt-custom-border-color-disabled:lighten($button-
packt-custom-border-color, 40%);

$button-packt-custom-small-padding: 2px;
$button-packt-custom-small-text-padding: 4px;

$button-packt-custom-background-color:$button-packt-custom-
base-color;
$button-packt-custom-background-color-over:$button-packt-
custom-border-color;
$button-packt-custom-background-color-focus:$button-packt-
custom-background-color;
$button-packt-custom-background-color-pressed:$button-
packt-custom-base-color-pressed;
$button-packt-custom-background-color-disabled:$button-
packt-custom-base-color-disabled;

$button-packt-custom-background-gradient: 'mate';
$button-packt-custom-background-gradient-over: 'mate';
$button-packt-custom-background-gradient-focus: 'mate';
$button-packt-custom-background-gradient-pressed: 'mate-reverse';
$button-packt-custom-background-gradient-disabled: 'mate';

$packt-custom-font-size: 12px;
$packt-custom-font-family: helvetica , arial , verdana ,
sans-serif;

$button-packt-custom-color-over: #fff !default;
$button-packt-custom-color-focus: $button-packt-custom-
color-over;
$button-packt-custom-color-pressed: $button-packt-custom-
color-over;
$button-packt-custom-color-disabled: $button-packt-custom-
color-over;

$button-packt-custom-small-font-size: $packt-custom-font-
size;
$button-packt-custom-small-font-size-over: $packt-custom-
font-size;
$button-packt-custom-small-font-size-focus: $packt-custom-
font-size;
```

```scss
$button-packt-custom-small-font-size-pressed: $packt-
custom-font-size;
$button-packt-custom-small-font-size-disabled: $packt-
custom-font-size;

$button-packt-custom-small-font-weight: $button-small-font-
weight;
$button-packt-custom-small-font-weight-over: $button-small-
font-weight;
$button-packt-custom-small-font-weight-focus: $button-
small-font-weight;
$button-packt-custom-small-font-weight-pressed: $button-
small-font-weight;
$button-packt-custom-small-font-weight-disabled: $button-
small-font-weight;

$button-packt-custom-small-font-family: $packt-custom-font-
family;
$button-packt-custom-small-font-family-over: $packt-custom-
font-family;
$button-packt-custom-small-font-family-focus: $packt-
custom-font-family;
$button-packt-custom-small-font-family-pressed: $packt-
custom-font-family;
$button-packt-custom-small-font-family-disabled: $packt-
custom-font-family;

$button-packt-custom-small-icon-size: 16px;
$button-packt-custom-glyph-color: $button-packt-custom-
color;
$button-packt-custom-glyph-opacity: .5;
$button-packt-custom-small-arrow-width: 12px;
$button-packt-custom-small-arrow-height: 12px;
$button-packt-custom-small-split-width: 14px;
$button-packt-custom-small-split-height: 14px;
```

3. Then, we are going to create a new file masteringextjs-theme/sass/src/
button/Button.scss with our custom UI:

```scss
@include extjs-button-ui(
  $ui: 'custom-btn-small',

  $border-radius: $button-packt-custom-small-border-radius,
  $border-width: $button-packt-custom-small-border-width,

  $border-color: $button-packt-custom-border-color,
  $border-color-over: $button-packt-custom-border-color-
over,
```

```
    $border-color-focus: $button-packt-custom-border-color-
focus,
    $border-color-pressed: $button-packt-custom-border-color-
pressed,
    $border-color-disabled: $button-packt-custom-border-
color-disabled,

    $padding: $button-packt-custom-small-padding,
    $text-padding: $button-packt-custom-small-text-padding,

    $background-color: $button-packt-custom-background-color,
    $background-color-over: $button-packt-custom-background-
color-over,
    $background-color-focus: $button-packt-custom-background-
color-focus,
    $background-color-pressed: $button-packt-custom-
background-color-pressed,
    $background-color-disabled: $button-packt-custom-
background-color-disabled,

    $background-gradient: $button-packt-custom-background-
gradient,
    $background-gradient-over: $button-packt-custom-
background-gradient-over,
    $background-gradient-focus: $button-packt-custom-
background-gradient-focus,
    $background-gradient-pressed: $button-packt-custom-
background-gradient-pressed,
    $background-gradient-disabled: $button-packt-custom-
background-gradient-disabled,

    $color: $button-packt-custom-color,
    $color-over: $button-packt-custom-color-over,
    $color-focus: $button-packt-custom-color-focus,
    $color-pressed: $button-packt-custom-color-pressed,
    $color-disabled: $button-packt-custom-color-disabled,

    $font-size: $button-packt-custom-small-font-size,
    $font-size-over: $button-packt-custom-small-font-size-
over,
    $font-size-focus: $button-packt-custom-small-font-size-
focus,
    $font-size-pressed: $button-packt-custom-small-font-size-
pressed,
    $font-size-disabled: $button-packt-custom-small-font-
size-disabled,
```

```
    $font-weight: $button-packt-custom-small-font-weight,
    $font-weight-over: $button-packt-custom-small-font-
weight-over,
    $font-weight-focus: $button-packt-custom-small-font-
weight-focus,
    $font-weight-pressed: $button-packt-custom-small-font-
weight-pressed,
    $font-weight-disabled: $button-packt-custom-small-font-
weight-disabled,

    $font-family: $button-packt-custom-small-font-family,
    $font-family-over: $button-packt-custom-small-font-
family-over,
    $font-family-focus: $button-packt-custom-small-font-
family-focus,
    $font-family-pressed: $button-packt-custom-small-font-
family-pressed,
    $font-family-disabled: $button-packt-custom-small-font-
family-disabled,

    $icon-size: $button-packt-custom-small-icon-size,
    $glyph-color: $button-packt-custom-glyph-color,
    $arrow-width: $button-packt-custom-small-arrow-width,
    $arrow-height: $button-packt-custom-small-arrow-height,
    $split-width: $button-packt-custom-small-split-width,
    $split-height: $button-packt-custom-small-split-height,
    $opacity-disabled: $button-opacity-disabled,
    $inner-opacity-disabled: $button-inner-opacity-disabled
);
```

Note that we are assigning our custom variables to the mixin variables needed to create this UI. As the button has three sizes in Ext JS, for now, we are going to declare the custom UI only for the small button, but it can be done for the other sizes as well.

Applying the UI

In our code, we are going to create a new file app/view/base/CustomButton.js with the following content:

```
Ext.define('Packt.view.base.CustomButton', {
    extend: 'Ext.button.Button',
    xtype: 'custom-btn',

    ui: 'custom-btn'
});
```

Then, we are going to replace the `xtype` class of the buttons to which we want to apply this UI (creating a super class is easier than applying the `ui` configuration to each component, but the choice of doing it or not is up to you). We are going to replace the `xtype` configuration for the **Print**, **Export to PDF** and **Export to Excel** buttons as shown by the following code (`Films.js` file):

```
xtype: 'custom-btn',
text: 'Print',
```

If we try to execute our application again, this will be the output:

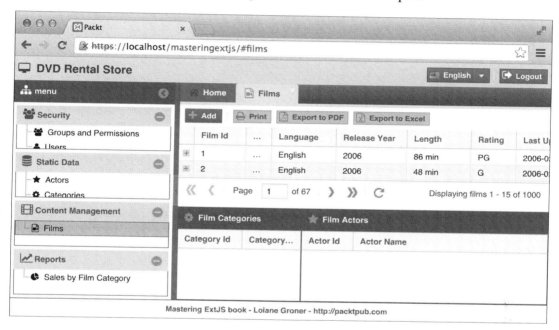

Note that the **Print** and **Export** buttons look different from the **Add** button.

We can create as many UIs as we need and for any component that supports it. It is also possible to create UIs that are not part of a theme, meaning we can create it inside the `masteringextjs/sass` folder following the same structure we followed in this topic.

Now, all you have to do is free the designer who exists inside yourself!

Packaging the application for production

Our theme is created, so now the only thing left is to make the production build and deploy the code on the production web server. Again, we will use Sencha Cmd to do it for us.

1. To do a production build, we need to have a terminal opened. We also need to change the directory to the application's root directory and type the following command:

   ```
   sencha app build
   ```

   Here's how the command looks on the terminal:

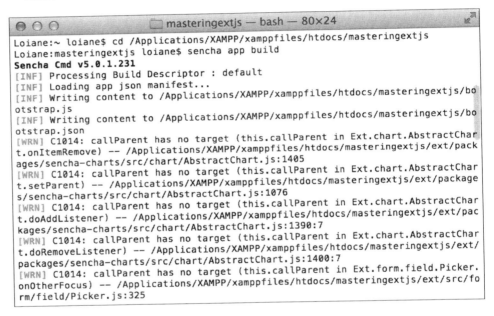

```
● ● ○              📁 masteringextjs — bash — 80×24
Loiane:~ loiane$ cd /Applications/XAMPP/xamppfiles/htdocs/masteringextjs
Loiane:masteringextjs loiane$ sencha app build
Sencha Cmd v5.0.1.231
[INF] Processing Build Descriptor : default
[INF] Loading app json manifest...
[INF] Writing content to /Applications/XAMPP/xamppfiles/htdocs/masteringextjs/bo
otstrap.js
[INF] Writing content to /Applications/XAMPP/xamppfiles/htdocs/masteringextjs/bo
otstrap.json
[WRN] C1014: callParent has no target (this.callParent in Ext.chart.AbstractChar
t.onItemRemove) -- /Applications/XAMPP/xamppfiles/htdocs/masteringextjs/ext/pack
ages/sencha-charts/src/chart/AbstractChart.js:1405
[WRN] C1014: callParent has no target (this.callParent in Ext.chart.AbstractChar
t.setParent) -- /Applications/XAMPP/xamppfiles/htdocs/masteringextjs/ext/package
s/sencha-charts/src/chart/AbstractChart.js:1076
[WRN] C1014: callParent has no target (this.callParent in Ext.chart.AbstractChar
t.doAddListener) -- /Applications/XAMPP/xamppfiles/htdocs/masteringextjs/ext/pac
kages/sencha-charts/src/chart/AbstractChart.js:1390:7
[WRN] C1014: callParent has no target (this.callParent in Ext.chart.AbstractChar
t.doRemoveListener) -- /Applications/XAMPP/xamppfiles/htdocs/masteringextjs/ext/
packages/sencha-charts/src/chart/AbstractChart.js:1400:7
[WRN] C1014: callParent has no target (this.callParent in Ext.form.field.Picker.
onOtherFocus) -- /Applications/XAMPP/xamppfiles/htdocs/masteringextjs/ext/src/fo
rm/field/Picker.js:325
```

2. Once the command execution is completed, it will create a new directory called `build/production/NameofTheApp`. As our application namespace is `Packt`, it creates the directory `build/production/Packt`, as follows:

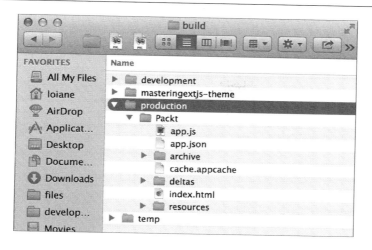

What this command does is get all the code we developed (inside the `app` folder) plus the Ext JS code we really need to run the application and put it inside the `all-classes.js` file. Then, using **YUI Compressor**, Sencha Cmd will minimize the code and obfuscate the JavaScript code; this way, we will have a very small JavaScript file that the user will need to load. Also, Sencha Cmd will evaluate all the components our application is using, filter the CSS that is not needed, and put it inside the `resources/Packt-all.css` file. All our custom images (icon images) will also be copied from the development environment to the `production` folder (inside the `resources` folder as well).

3. The next step now is to make sure that the production build is working as expected. To access the development environment we use `http://localhost/masteringextjs`. To test the production build, we need to access `http://localhost/masteringextjs/build/production/Packt`. When we test it, we will see that it is not working as we really expect. We will get some errors.

4. Next, we need to copy the php folders to the production folder as well, as shown in the following screenshot:

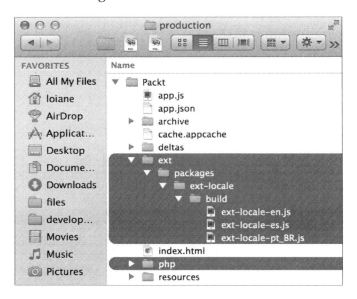

5. We should also copy ext/packages/ext-locale/build and the locale files we are going to use.

And now, we can test the application again. It should work as expected.

Compiling ext-locale

Here's a quick note about the ext-locale package: if you are using only one locale, you can add the ext-locale package in requires of app.json and a new entry "locale" : "es" with the code of the locale you want to use. Ext JS will compile the required files.

If you are using multiple locales, there are two options: doing like we did (manually copying the files) or making a production build for each locale. You can see an example of how to do it by exploring app.json and the source code of the **EXT JS Kitchen Sink** example (http://dev.sencha.com/ext/5.0.1/examples/kitchensink/).

What to deploy in production

Always remember that we have the `app` folder and all the code developed as our development environment. And inside the `production` folder, we have all the code that should be deployed in production.

So, let's say we want to deploy this application right now. Simply transfer all the content from `masteringextjs/build/production/Packt` to the desired folder on your web server, as follows:

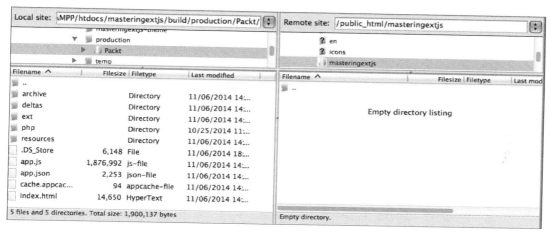

Happy production code!

Benefits

What are the benefits of the production build? Can we just deploy the development code? We can deploy the development code as is in production, but it is not recommended. With the production build, we boost the performance while loading the files, but the file is minimized, which makes the code harder to read as well.

For example, let's do the following testing: open the application on the browser, log in, and open the **Actors** screen from the static data module.

Using the development code, we will have the following result from Chrome Developer Tools (or Firebug):

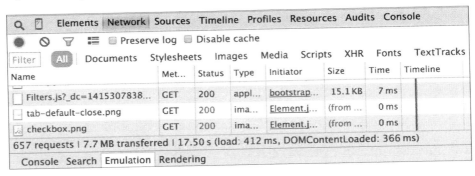

The application made **657 requests**, resulting in **7.7 MB** of data transferred to the user, and it took **17.50 s** to complete it. This is a lot, and talking about **7.7 MB** to be transferred to the user is unacceptable!

Now let's see the results using the production build:

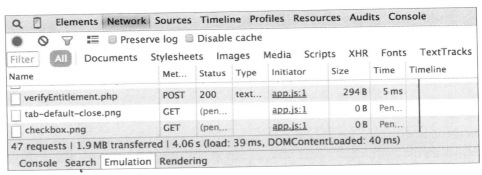

The application made **47 requests** and **1.9 MB transferred**. The most important change is the size of the data transferred: from **7.7 MB** to **1.9 MB**! This is a great improvement although **1.9 MB** is still a large amount of data to be transferred. The files will be cached, and this number will decrease even more.

Another thing to notice is the files that are being loaded. In the development environment, we can see each Ext JS class being loaded by the browser:

Q 🗋 Elements | Network | Sources Timeline Profiles Resources Audits Console

● ◎ ▽ ≔ ☐ Preserve log ☐ Disable cache

Filter **All** Documents Stylesheets Images Media Scripts XHR Fonts TextTracks

Name	Met...	Status	Type	Initiator	Size	Time	Timeline
☐ Countries.js?_dc=1415308...	GET	200	appl...	bootstrap...	492 B	3.14 s	
☐ Cities.js?_dc=14153082129...	GET	200	appl...	bootstrap...	485 B	3.14 s	
☐ StaticData.js?_dc=1415308...	GET	200	appl...	bootstrap...	4.6 KB	3.15 s	

At the end of it, it is going to be more than 400 JavaScript files being loaded just to render the **Login** screen.

If we try the production build, we will have the following:

Q 🗋 Elements | Network | Sources Timeline Profiles Resources Audits Console

● ◎ ▽ ≔ ☐ Preserve log ☐ Disable cache

Filter **All** Documents Stylesheets Images Media Scripts XHR Fonts TextTracks

Name	Met...	Status	Type	Initiator	Size	Time	Timeline
☐ app.json	GET	200	text...		(from ...	0 ms	
☐ Packt–all.css?_dc=1415308...	GET	200	text...		390 B	67 ms	
☐ app.js?_dc=1415308124264	GET	200	appl...		1.8 MB	185 ...	

Only one JavaScript file is being loaded with the application's source code and the required Ext JS SDK code (`app.js`).

So, for performance purposes, always deploy the production build. Use the development code only for development purposes.

If the application starts to grow, the amount of data that will be transferred to the browser will be greater than 2 MB, which is not good. You can create separate small applications and combine them as in a portal application. This way, the user will be able to download only the application files to the portion of the application that is going to be used at that moment and will not need to download all the application's source at once. This link contains a good discussion about the topic: `http://goo.gl/az8uVT`.

Summary

In this chapter, we learned how to create a new theme, and we also learned how to create custom component UIs. You learned why it is important to make a production build and how to do it, including the difference between the files from the development environment to the production environment.

I hope you have enjoyed this book! Now, let the creativity flow to create really awesome Ext JS apps!

Index

E

F

session data, saving manually 295, 296
session, working with 293, 294
film table
  description field 277
  film_id field 277
  language_id field 277
  length field 278
  original_language_id field 277
  rating field 278
  release_year field 277
  rental_duration field 277
  rental_rate field 278
  replacement_cost field 278
  special_features field 278
  title field 277
Firebug
  URL 23
Firefox
  URL 23
Font Awesome
  adding, to Login screen 68, 69
  URL 68
footer, main screen
  creating 105, 106
  modular CSS 106, 107

G

Glyph icons 68
Google Chrome
  URL 23
Google Developer Tools
  URL 343
GridPanel
  about 11, 12
  content, printing with GridPrinter
      plugin 302, 303
  exporting, to Excel 298-301
  exporting, to PDF 297-300
GridPrinter plugin
  about 302
  URL 302
  used, for printing GridPanel
      content 302, 303
group name
  displaying, in Grid 199, 200

H

header, main screen
  creating 107-110
  Font Awesome icon color,
      customizing 110, 111
  Header CSS, creating 110
HTML5 API
  using 301
HTML5 input types
  URL 60
HTML5 local storage
  about 126, 127
  URL 126

I

IDE 20
iFrame 299
Illuminations for Developers
  about 244
  URL 245
Init method 129
initViewModel method 130
installation, Ext JS
  about 15
  prerequisites 15, 16
IntelliJ IDEA 345
interactions, Sencha charts
  Crosshair 306
  CrossZoom 306
  Item Highlight 306
  Item Info 306
  Pan/Zoom 306
  Rotate 306
Inventory 248
iText
  URL 301

J

Jasmine
  URL 343
Java environment variables
  URL 23
Java JDK
  URL 23

Thank you for buying
Mastering Ext JS
Second Edition

About Packt Publishing

Packt, pronounced 'packed', published its first book, *Mastering phpMyAdmin for Effective MySQL Management*, in April 2004, and subsequently continued to specialize in publishing highly focused books on specific technologies and solutions.

Our books and publications share the experiences of your fellow IT professionals in adapting and customizing today's systems, applications, and frameworks. Our solution-based books give you the knowledge and power to customize the software and technologies you're using to get the job done. Packt books are more specific and less general than the IT books you have seen in the past. Our unique business model allows us to bring you more focused information, giving you more of what you need to know, and less of what you don't.

Packt is a modern yet unique publishing company that focuses on producing quality, cutting-edge books for communities of developers, administrators, and newbies alike. For more information, please visit our website at www.packtpub.com.

Writing for Packt

We welcome all inquiries from people who are interested in authoring. Book proposals should be sent to author@packtpub.com. If your book idea is still at an early stage and you would like to discuss it first before writing a formal book proposal, then please contact us; one of our commissioning editors will get in touch with you.

We're not just looking for published authors; if you have strong technical skills but no writing experience, our experienced editors can help you develop a writing career, or simply get some additional reward for your expertise.

Ext JS 4 Plugin and Extension Development

ISBN: 978-1-78216-372-5   Paperback: 116 pages

A hands-on development of several Ext JS plugins and extensions

1. Easy-to-follow examples on ExtJS plugins and extensions.

2. Step-by-step instructions on developing ExtJS plugins and extensions.

3. Provides a walkthrough of several useful ExtJS libraries and communities.

Enterprise Application Development with Ext JS and Spring

ISBN: 978-1-78328-545-7   Paperback: 446 pages

Develop and deploy a high-performance Java web application using Ext JS and Spring

1. Embark on the exciting journey through the entire enterprise web application development lifecycle.

2. Leverage key Spring Framework concepts to deliver comprehensive and concise Java code.

3. Build a real world Ext JS web application that interacts with dynamic database driven data.

Please check **www.PacktPub.com** for information on our titles

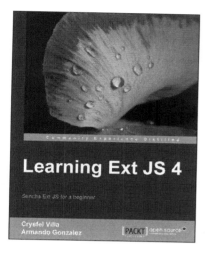

Learning Ext JS 4

ISBN: 978-1-84951-684-6   Paperback: 434 pages

Sencha Ext JS for a biginner

1. Learn the basics and create your first classes.

2. Handle data and understand the way it works, create powerful widgets and new components.

3. Dig into the new architecture defined by Sencha and work on real world projects.

Ext JS Data-driven Application Design

ISBN: 978-1-78216-544-6   Paperback: 162 pages

A step-by-step guide to building a user-friendly database in Ext JS using data from an existing database

1. Discover how to layout the application structure with MVC and Sencha Cmd.

2. Learn to use Ext Direct during the application build process.

3. Understand how to set up the history support in the browser.

Please check **www.PacktPub.com** for information on our titles

Printed in Great Britain
by Amazon